I am a seeker of truth. Very 1
me as "*When The Golden E* 1
a pre-published copy of it, I a
dramatic impact on my life. e
to allow me to be a portal between our phys .s
and to be allowed to enter and experience the spiritual reality and to
allow enlightened beings to enter my world and experience my journey.
Sharing the realities of both worlds has been a great desire of mine.

Susan is a true blessing of this reality. She has been given the mystical
gift of being a portal between realities. I welcome the existence of
DreamMyst into my world. After reading *the book*, I honestly believe
DreamMyst is sharing great wisdom and knowledge with all seekers of
Truth. I have read this fabulous book several times. Every reading of
this masterpiece has enlightened my world and lifted my soul. "*When
The Golden Egg Cracks*" is destined to become a classic resource for
enlightenment and joy.

Hugs and Blessings, **Brian Standly**

I believe people will get more out of "*When The Golden Egg Cracks*" than
watching Doomsday Preppers on National Geographic!

Shelley Lynn

I first stumbled across the "ASK DREAMMYST SHOW" in June 2011,
and from the moment, I heard it, it changed my life. I decided to research
the information given, only to find that everything DreamMyst had said
and predicted either had come true, or was manifesting.

I've always felt that the American people have been left in the dark
about how our country is run, and that is why I recommend "*When The
Golden Egg Cracks*" to EVERY AMERICAN across this nation as A
MUST-HAVE for those ready to face the challenges of the coming years.
You'll find tips on everything from learning how to grow your own food,
to natural health cures, to learning how to put together a bug-out bag.
And, MOST IMPORTANTLY, how to stay out of the emotion of fear and
move into a place of love and peace. Blessings, and remember, the future
belongs to those who prepare today!

Rachel Burnett

I feel such gratitude for speaking to DreamMyst in my lifetime.
DreamMyst is an energy being full of such love and light...and her
words are so so powerful. On one side of the coin, her predictions are
unfolding now within a matter of weeks/months and should not/cannot
be missed. On the other side of the coin, her kind words encourage unity
and love. Everyone on the planet should be asking, "Who is DreamMyst"
and finding the answer in "When The Golden Egg Cracks".

Thanks, **Tracey Gordon**

Considering the tragic problems of planet Earth and inhabitants today, I welcome the voice(s) of sanity and solution offered by Susan Norgren. The illuminated beings who come through her begin where most of us have left off . . . guiding our thinking and feeling into loftier levels of psychological, philosophical, and metaphysical understanding . . . until, lo and behold, we begin to realize that maybe our planet is, after all, bearable and reasonable... even delightful! Our individual problems are also treated until we find them likewise transformed and resolved during such magical moments.

Personally, I have witnessed and benefitted from sessions with various trance mediums since 1967, and I can testify that not all "channels" (as they now are dubbed in the "New Age") are of consistently elevated stature. The beings of light who communicate with us through Susan not only provide the answers for which we are searching, but also are themselves engagingly empathetic, humorous, and entertaining. We have our cake and eat it too . . . a delectable treat indeed.

David Cottis, Fresno, CA

I had the privilege of co-hosting the "Ask DreamMyst Radio Show" with DreamMyst, who is a Universal Light Being channeled through Susan Norgren with the assistance of her husband, Rob Norgren. Dream is enlightened and knows what is ahead for the Earth. I was able to ask tough questions about what our future will look like, how it will affect people, and what we can do to prepare. In the past year, we aired shows about the economy, the American way of life, about what jobs will be essential in the future, and what energies we can align with so that we are not resisting the changes, but embracing them. I inquired about topics that make us question the government. I challenged a great deal of the misunderstood information on the internet, bringing it face-to-face with DreamMyst.

Our show followed DreamMyst's intent, which was always about how to prepare and not to scare. We wanted to know how to create awareness so that when the earth changes, we aren't spinning our wheels trying to survive, but are generating ways to create a better life.

In essence, she was giving us the tools to be leaders in our own communities. While people who like to stay in the dark shy away from her information, I invite you to step into your role as a leader. We are all here to share the future in a more conscious and collaborative way, in community, with grace and ease. This book will be a light for us, and because we listened, when our world changes, we can be the candles for others. We have our ducks in a row, food to eat, and supplies to keep us comfortable. I am in gratitude for my time with DreamMyst, Susan, and Rob...all of whom have shined a light on my own life and provided me the tools to explore new possibilities and become a leader.

Peace & Blessings, **Alexandra Teklak**

When The Golden Egg Cracks

Survive and Thrive
During Economic and Natural Disasters

SUSAN NORGREN

BALBOA.
PRESS
A DIVISION OF HAY HOUSE

ISBN: 978-1-4525-5440-2 (hc)
ISBN: 978-1-4525-5438-9 (sc)
ISBN: 978-1-4525-5439-6 (e)

Library of Congress Control Number: 2012911723

Balboa Press books may be ordered through booksellers or by contacting:

Balboa Press
A Division of Hay House
1663 Liberty Drive
Bloomington, IN 47403
www.balboapress.com
1-(877) 407-4847

Because of the dynamic nature of the Internet, any web addresses or links contained in this book may have changed since publication and may no longer be valid. The views expressed in this work are solely those of the author and do not necessarily reflect the views of the publisher, and the publisher hereby disclaims any responsibility for them.

The author of this book does not dispense medical advice or prescribe the use of any technique as a form of treatment for physical, emotional, or medical problems without the advice of a physician, either directly or indirectly. The intent of the author is only to offer information of a general nature to help you in your quest for emotional and spiritual well-being. In the event you use any of the information in this book for yourself, which is your constitutional right, the author and the publisher assume no responsibility for your actions.

Any people depicted in stock imagery provided by Thinkstock are models, and such images are being used for illustrative purposes only.
Certain stock imagery © Thinkstock.

Printed in the United States of America

Balboa Press rev. date: 12/12/2012

Table of Contents

Also by Susan Norgren

Living Intuitively: A Comprehensive Guide to All Things Psychic. Susan's workbook for intuitive development is a touching account that reveals how her psychic gifts often created obstacles for her because she didn't understand how to use them effectively. Susan teaches step-by-step how to improve psychic and intuitive skills and how to use them effectively for personal development. Her frankness reveals her honesty outright—her honesty as a storyteller, and her honesty as a true psychic. Living Intuitively leads the reader to make a secret discovery . . . *an improved life hangs in the wisdom of ages.* Everyone has access to the wisdom because Living Intuitively is a comprehensive workbook that has many options for all types of believers and learners. It is interesting, funny, touching, and every once in a while, a little bit odd.

Lost Pallies: The Afterlife Has Found its Voice and Now It Won't Stop Talking. Lost Pallies is a compilation story of the paranormal from various individuals. Susan shares ghost sightings, hauntings and other mystical happenings as well as detailing after-death communications through personal stories.

❧ "It's me DreamMyst! Susan Norgren, *who is my human friend, and I, dedicate this book to you. We honor and salute you. You are the inspiration and the fruitful vision that changes your planet for the better. Be that butterfly that flutters by and share these messages with the one person in the world you care most about so they, too, can thrive, prosper, and manifest pure waves of Big Energy, bringing transformations for humankind. Please do not wait to do it. Act right now. Every day counts. Dwell in joy, peace and abundance."❧*

≈∾ "ONE LITTLE THING IMPACTS
EVERYTHING ELSE" ≈∾

≈∾ *DreamMyst* ≈∾

᭥᭥ "DreamMyst is a Universal Light Being who borrows a human body to communicate. She has an astonishing message for all people. DreamMyst uses the body of psychic, medium and trance channel, Susan Norgren. Through Susan, Dream has predicted a world of change for which humanity is unprepared. Her information includes suggestions that will assist people who want to live in harmony and comfort amid the chaos that is on the horizon for all. Being a wise, playful, loving, kind Universal Light Being, DreamMyst dwells beyond the farthest star in our Universe." ᭥᭥

"When The Golden Egg Cracks" is gripping, mesmerizing and provocatively informative. DreamMyst offers incredible assistance that will help individuals and society thrive during upcoming life-altering changes. Her wisdom covers topics such as social unrest, financial collapse, food shortages and riots, natural disasters, nuclear radiation—the collapse of life, as humanity has become accustomed.

When Ordinary Meets Extraordinary

This book was written because America needs help, Big Time. There is mutiny on the horizon. No one on the planet will be exempt. DreamMyst, a magical being, has stopped by for coffee a few times. She has shared a message that she wants me to extend. Since she can't speak without my voice, she speaks through me. She predicts coming changes for America, and they aren't pretty. If you really think about the impact of the coming events, DreamMyst's version is downplayed. Even though the economy will crash, the government will go bad, tremendous earth damages will occur, martial law will reign, power will be out long-term, and many deaths will occur, DreamMyst offers hope.

Dream's hope is in the form of a comprehensive survival manual. When she was sharing the survival information, I was in awe of her wisdom and foresight. How does she know all? How did she think of everything? Once you read it for yourself, you will see what I mean. I am not a woman who keeps abreast of politics or social issues. Heck, I barely watch TV. Yet, here is this book with all these political details and answers to questions I didn't even know to ask, with my name on it. Wow! I'm amazed at what has been born.

There is no way to explain a universal light being, an energy essence that communicates with us from another reality. Would the source of this information jeopardize the credibility of the messages given? In order not to explain where or how I got this information, I thought about sharing the material and claiming to be the author. It would have been so much easier that way.

No one needed to know that I would never have attempted to write something of this magnitude or this controversial, for that matter. I knew the information contained in this book needed to be available for others. The real author, DreamMyst, would not have minded either way.

How did a personality who has no body or physical eyes write a book? We recorded and transcribed the sessions, keeping Dream's personality, knowledge and expressions that are unique to her. During her visits, she shares wisdom and enters the mind and consciousness of all who speak or listen to her. Lives have changed for the better, and many have experienced dramatic changes in their lives, swearing they feel her energy of love surrounding them. Others say they have dreams of DreamMyst, and this, too, is not surprising. She is a capsule for the wisdom of the ages.

While I serve as the medium for DreamMyst to communicate her messages, my husband Rob plays an extremely crucial role in this process. DreamMyst has a lot to share with humanity, but the only way she can do this is to use my voice and physical body. Rob guides me into a deep trance or altered state of consciousness. I have to thank DreamMyst for caring and sharing, and picking me. I have to thank you for reading, too. You'll be glad you did. Well, I have got some packing to do, so I better get ready. But, first I wanted to introduce you to DreamMyst.

Thriving together,

Susan Norgren

ॐ "Hi Every Buddy! I am DreamMyst, an enlightened being that comes from a different place in time and space. You could say I am as old as time. We may not be able to see each other but I exist, just as you exist. Where I am, time does not exist; so, I need to adjust my energies when I come see Susan. Sometimes it isn't easy for Universal Light Beings and people like Susan to connect. In your world, there are not many people who will accept our messages in this way from the spiritual realms."

"Only human beings in their uniqueness have emotions. We do have personalities. Some of us keep our eyes closed all the time. Some barely speak, and other beings, such as me, will sound young or fun. It depends on the personality of the being. Many of us come for a reason, such as helping humans in their time of need, and often will be seen during your human times of extreme stress or social upheaval. We come through you, but are not from you. Although we are with you, we do not belong to you. We give you love, but not thoughts. We have our own thoughts, and you have yours. We love you because all of us, you included, come from a place of unconditional love and will go back when your physical time on Earth is complete. You continue to be that which you are, nonphysical energy. There is no pause in consciousness. It is up to humankind either to benefit from these messages or not. Thank you my beautiful beings of light for allowing me to share with you my love and insights." ॐ

Acknowledgements

This is to acknowledge in joy and love your contribution to this book. Thankfulness and gratitude are offered because so many took the actions to help. Without Susan's parents Johnnie L. Noland and Darla Crawford, DreamMyst a Universal Light Being would not have found her voice via Susan Norgren.

ﾊﾞ DreamMyst

"Those who have taken responsibility and said 'I will do this,' they are the light-bringers. They hold the light so others can see. Because of what you have done, this book has been created. The words in this book, the radio show, and your words help people understand, so humans can prepare. This book exists because of you. I rejoice and embrace the 'All-ness' of you."

"To Rob Norgren, twin flame and divine complement to Susan, It took us thirty years to renew the love relationship carried over from before time. Your love, belief, acceptance and protection of Susan transcends all else. This is a natural thing for you two souls, who have chosen to come through many lifetimes, to help during this time."

"Levi Wadleigh and Desiree Miracle, your names together mean 'long awaited and desired beloved messenger of God,' the love between you and your mother, Susan, endures beyond this and any future lifetime. You are soul flames conjoined with your mother and your sister Theresa Parker-Pierce."

"Sandy, you are the loving protector of the friend you know as Susan, and for this, we are grateful. Know we will never put Susan at risk. Thank you for listening to the words of the little squirt, DreamMyst."

"Stacey Powers, you have been with Susan from the beginning of her first trance channeling experiences. Your support and belief is worth more than its weight in gold. Plus, you are the first friend, besides Rob and Susan, I met!"

"Jo Ann Tidwell, the love and support you have given these many years are treasured."

"Erika Mecklem Parsons, your belief and love for Susan, Rob and me, DreamMyst, reaches beyond all barriers. It is with affection and joy we greet you once again!"

"Thank you to Shawn Troeger for your friendship and support of Susan."

"Shelley Spaulding, the musical rhapsody of your kind, loving heart is the inspiration you bring to the world. We thank you for your actions of support. You are loved."

"Marcia, the physical actions toward empowering and validating Susan as a deep trance channel, and your commitment to documenting my messages of humanity's survival are infinite."

"Sheri, you know how to use the many human written words that transform lives."

"Pierre Lengauer, thank you for creating the beautiful cover of our book."

"Alexandra Teklak, your extraverted bundle of energy and free spirit created the vitality and perfect balance for our *Ask DreamMyst* show."

"Rebecca, we thank you for your enthusiastic dedication, and your months of transcribing, editing and re-editing. Your actions were essential to bring together all aspects of our book."

"Dany Pellerin your attune-ness to spirit and energy inspired Susan to finish writing, which was the most important part!"

"Brian Standly, I am happy you enjoy the DreamMyst energy of your dragon. Thank you for the passion you share with your writing."

"Tracy Ann Gordon, thank you for opening your mind, heart and soul to the greater awareness of 'what is.' Your insights have been invaluable. The show transcriptions and editing the first rough edit of the book brought reality—inspired thoughts to assist humans in their earthly journey."

"To the beautiful Miss Rachel Burnett for transcribing radio shows and sharing the messages. As a scraped knee kisser, you shift and raise the vibrations of the universe. Within your arms, you hold to you the future of humanity."

"Joanie Morgan, your abilities for organizing and connecting people is a focal point for others. Thank you for speaking of me. Every time you do, someone listens."

"Hi to all the people who listen to the Ask DreamMyst show and many, other unnamed friends. Your questions influence your world and environment in ways you do not realize. You are the ones who will recreate a new civilization. Without your questions there would not have been a book by the name of "When The Golden Egg Cracks". It is with love and appreciation I watch as you shape the future."

Robin Noland, Johnnie and Shannon Noland, Jimmie Noland, Jammie Matherly, Jimmie Noland Jr., Christal, Sabrina, Linda Noland, Narissa Ramnarain, Ella Wadleigh, Jerad Miracle, Talon Parker, Tim Rios, Stephanie Dean, Robert Norgren, Marc, Elia and Carl Norgren Diane Tuck, Kimberley Simon, Jose Mascarenhas, Eneida De Pina Mascarenhas, Jim Reimann from Florida, Kelly Gable, Gina Kelly, Mike Palmer, Glory Anne Perez, Wesley, David, Jose, Tammy Gill, Rebecca, Erik Wilson, Jerry Walczak, Leonor, Rochelle, Dave Bartlett, Debby Bucklin, Mary, Anne/Allaure, Cerise, Dawnielle, Nathalie, Shakiyla Carter, Martin, Bibiana, Jennifer Rundall, Julian Sundby, Gina Kim from Korea, Ivor, Nermina, Patty, Anand-Sara,Chris, Catherine Chandler, Darlene M. Santos Balch Chavez, Summer Russell, Vince Lucchesi, Nila DuBose, Frederik Lapre, Rudy Kraan, Barbara, Tony De Andrade from South Africa, Nancy, Debra, Amanda, Molly, Tricia, Marissa, Carol, Tricia, Lisa, Brooke, Sylvia, Elizabeth, Robert, Lars (Larry) Wredberg, Cristina Longo, Isabella from Spain, James Couter, Richie in the UK, Annique Savage, Renee Hodgden, Janet Moore, Bonnie Easterling Pridgen, Richard Wright, Brack, Susan Powell, Carol, Debbie Gladen, Eva, Sue Lewis, Hayat Donna Bain, Shawn Johnson, Laura Moore, Susan Jordan, Cheryl Krueger, Jesie Newsome, and Rachel Erixton.

With profound love,

DreamMyst ⅏

Chapter 1

Government ...
For the People? By the People?

Freedoms Surrendered Never Come Back

ଛ୶ Once upon a time there was a man who decided to become the president of the United States of America. He worked hard to achieve this goal. He learned how to play dirty, make false promises, and give bribes. Many considered him an ambitious person with a mission to accomplish.

Eventually he was elected and was loved, admired, and adored by millions. His illustrious position puffed his self-esteem to the point he thought he could do no wrong. He forgot he worked for the American people. He did not want America to be a world power, and he knew that if he spent all of America's money, the economy would plummet. Then he could take away the people's freedoms and civil liberties.

One day, he made one too many bad decisions, and suddenly the people realized the American Dream was a big Ponzi scheme. No longer did the people adore the president. They hated him and wanted him dead. Fearing for his life, the president desperately created another flawed solution, making things worse. The angry crowd outside his doorstep continued to grow ... young college students, middle-aged people, parents with children and careers, and finally, older adults who owned businesses and homes. Like angry bees, the buzzing people swarmed together, seething in anger. A revolution began ... a revolution of "We the People."

The president, afraid for his life, turned the country into a military state. The military now had the burden of deciding whose orders to follow. As Americans with family and loved ones they did not want to turn against, their decision was for the people. Mainstream America got the power back. Americans unified to uphold the Tenth Amendment, which reserves all rights not specifically granted to the federal government to be held by the people. The president found a safe bunker to hide in, and a new government was born. America survived this transition. The way was lit for those who realized knowledge is power.

To care for and provide for future generations, it is important to see clearly what is happening with the United States government and the economy. The government is eroding and siphoning off as many of your freedoms as they possibly can. Do not allow your government to take away your Internet or any of your Second Amendment rights.

శ•ఆ

How did a spiritual being without a physical body write a book? DreamMyst communicates through Susan Norgren. Susan is an authentic Deep Trance Channel. She has the rare ability to go into a deep trance that allows spiritual beings, like DreamMyst, to use her voice to speak with humans. Recorded sessions with DreamMyst captured her loving personality, expressive language, and permitted her intelligent discussions to be transcribed. This is DreamMyst's book.

DreamMyst is a spiritual being who offers wisdom and insights. This book is a collection of her responses to questions asked about the present and future. The answers offer guidance to all of humanity. DreamMyst warns us about cataclysmic coming events. Anyone who chooses may use this book for preparation to thrive and prosper during, and after, the rapidly approaching period in which our golden egg, our world, cracks.

DreamMyst has always existed. Her universal knowledge spans eternity, from before the Big Bang that created earth, throughout all the ages, to our present lifetime, and the future. DreamMyst knows the future.

DreamMyst explains: "My existence is timeless. Knowing the future is knowing what the past has held." History repeats itself. I see reality from an altered perspective that is not from a human, earthly existence. Asking me a question allows me to open to the energy of the question that is asked, and the ability to give insights. The questions open the door, lifts the curtain or the veil, for me to see what is occurring in your world. The questions are so important; they allow me to respond to you in a way that helps humans today."

Susan completed extensive research on facts and important survival information.

☙❧ This symbol signifies DreamMyst's dialogue. ☙❧

For ease of clarity, DM represents DreamMyst
in the question and answer section.

Barack Obama

Q: Where was Barack Obama born?

DM: He was born in the same country as his father.

Q: His father was born in Kenya. Are there people in Kenya who know the truth—that Barack Obama was born in Kenya? Why hasn't anyone come forward to speak the truth about Barack Obama's birth?

DM: They do not want to be killed. Also, there are people who were paid money. Why do you think it took him so long to show a birth certificate? It took time to make agreements, and there were bribes. It no longer matters where he was born. What matters is how much longer you choose to allow him to take away what America has always stood for. This is what the New World Order (NWO) is counting on. When they take over, they want Americans to be downtrodden and ready to accept what they offer. President Obama talks with a smile that is not really a smile.

Q: Is there a chance if Obama is not elected, he will call an emergency to remain president? How big of a chance is there of him doing this?

DM: He may declare an emergency. About an 80% chance.

Q: Doesn't Obama know what he is doing to the country?

DM: As he sees it, he is moving you not into the NWO but into his world order.

Q: Well, won't the NWO execute him for that?

DM: No, he will remain. Look at how he has been campaigning. He is not trying to do fuzzy-wuzzy feel-goods for the American people. Look at the difference in how he is campaigning. It is very different. This time he is saying, "This is what I am going to do, I *am* doing this." His signing of so many executive orders erodes your liberties and freedom as Americans. In many ways, your president is considered by some to be the Antichrist. However, he is only the puppet for those who will put into effect the New World Order. Before this happens, he will do his best to create an anticolonial, socialist government. He will control TV, radio, and the Internet.

He makes America weaker in any way he can. Having more American military overseas in different parts of the world creates instability within your United States, and your police will become more like the military.

Your President Obama believes in anticolonialism. He is not concerned with your United States of America. He focuses on removing the world power from America and disbursing it to make it a balanced world power. He is not for Americans. He does not cultivate; he tears apart the United States and allows other countries throughout your world to benefit as he weakens your country by sending the military overseas. The instability within your United States places the police in a position of military power.

Even the poorest in America are better off than people in other parts of the world. Obama wants countries besides the United States to have access to growth and power. He believes the United States became rich by occupying, looting, and invading poor countries. This is how the United States became the biggest world power. Because he believes this is unfair, if there is a cost, he will put it on the United States to pay. He wants everybody to have a little piece of the pie, with Americans having the least amount of pie.

Q: How close are they to actually having homeland security in charge of the Internet?

DM: Only a matter of time. The president has to make the people think there is a need. He is already doing it. It will be after the election, probably within three to six months.

Q: Well, he did sign an executive order (EO) not too long ago that states that many of the routers and many of the servers on the Web have to now be set aside for the government and military and cannot be used by the average people in the world.

DM: See, he is taking actions regardless of whether 'they are illegal or not. In this case, Congress backs him.

Q: This is a bill to control the Web, charge you for e-mails, all that kind of stuff, in the future. Charge you just like the post office.

DM: The Internet is your last free resource in the United States jurisdiction. To control it, there will be a pretend threat that takes down parts of the Internet. This will be the government's creation to get the people angry and ready to accept Internet protection. The president will then set this in place with his EO that takes away your Internet freedoms. He will set up the rules for the Internet in the way he wants them to be.

৵৵৵

Tyranny is on the horizon and a globalist president is at the helm. Global governance is the treasonous foothold; and, like a pimple coming to a head, 2012 has experienced massive changes within the government, leading to the removal of constitutional rights.

The rights and freedoms guaranteed to all American people have been stolen under the ruse of national security. With the signing of the Patriot Act on October 26, 2001, and it's reauthorization by Congress on May 26, 2011, government power over Americans increased. The Patriot Act is used against Americans, and the government is preparing for martial law and civil war. As far as the government is concerned, Americans are now terrorists.

There seems to be little discussion or scrutiny by Americans or the mainstream media of Obama's signing of numerous executive orders. The signing of the disaster preparedness EO on March 16, 2012 gives the office of the president complete control over all the resources in the United States in times of war or emergency. The president now controls and allocates food, transportation, energy, and water resources in the name of national security and national defense.

On July 6, 2012 president signed "'Assignment of National Security and Emergency Preparedness Communications Functions,'" Executive Order 13618, to seize the Internet and control *all* forms of communication infrastructure, both public and private, in the United States. The reason given was that, come hurricanes, earthquakes, or nuclear war, the US government must have the ability to communicate at all times and under all circumstances, in order to carry out its most critical and time sensitive missions using the government's existing emergency communication preparations. It is reasonable for the government to plan for all kinds of emergencies—wars, meteor strikes, and rebellions—and have them in place.

However, President Obama claims the authority to order all communication infrastructures to be seized under federal control. With this new order, the right to kill you without due process is claimed by a president who is accelerating unrestrained executive power.

America has moved from an open society to a closed society. I wonder if the Obama administration realizes that his new slogan, "Forward," echoes the European Marxists' march of history? Why aren't Americans sounding the alarm at the actions taken by the Obama White House against this new paradigm shift of government control?

Life-changing government controls are listed below, including a list of emergency powers and martial law EOs. In addition, there are EOs that force Americans to submit to international regulations to integrate the United States, Canada, and Mexico into a North American Union, which abolishes the US Constitution.

Power of Executive Order

Government Control

EO 10990 allows the government to take over all mode transportation and control of highways and seaports.

EO 10995 allows the government to seize and control the communication media.

EO 10997 allows the government to take over all electrical power, gas, petroleum, fuels, and minerals.

EO 10998 allows the government to take over all food resources and farms.

EO 11000 allows the government to mobilize civilians into work brigades under government supervision.

EO 11001 allows the government to take over all health, education, and welfare functions.

EO 11002 designates the postmaster general to operate a national registration of all persons.

EO 11003 allows the government to take over all airports and aircraft, including commercial aircraft.

EO11004 allows the Housing and Finance Authority to relocate and establish new locations for populations.

EO 11005 allows the government to take over railroads, inland waterways, and public storage facilities.

EO 11049 assigns emergency preparedness function to federal departments and agencies, consolidating twenty-one operative executive orders issued over a fifteen-year period.

EO 11051 specifies the responsibility of the Office of Emergency Planning and gives authorization to put all executive orders into effect in times of increased international tensions and economic or financial crisis.

EO 11310 grants authority to the Department of Justice to enforce the plans set out in executive orders, to institute industrial support, to establish judicial and legislative liaison, to control all aliens, to operate penal and correctional institutions, and to advise and assist the president.

EO 11921 allows the Federal Emergency Preparedness Agency to develop plans to establish control over the mechanisms of production and distribution of energy sources, wages, salaries, credit, and the flow of money in US financial institutions in any undefined national emergency. It also provides that when the president declares a state of emergency, Congress cannot review the action for six months.

With over nine hundred EO orders signed by President Obama and his fondness of producing new EOs, it makes one wonder why he has not signed an executive order to abolish the Supreme Court and Congress.

Act of War

ה–הGet ready for a false-flag attack. President Obama does not walk his talk. Pay attention to his actions, not his words! His actions show you where he wants America to go.

An act of war with Iran has been brewing since before 2011. President Obama needs a war; it will look good in many ways for him. This is a way to get Americans to think Iran is at fault. This is not the case. The New World Order (banks) wants to invade the rich oil lands.

Q: How can we possibly go to war when we do not have enough money to support our own country?

DM: You have money going to the military. There is a lot of money in the United States for the military and weapons of war.

ה–ה

President Barack Obama's strategy is to ignore the Constitution's rules on lawmaking with his policy changes. Most EOs are the signing of executive-branch policy by the president. The exceptions to this are when the president claims authority not granted by the law or the Constitution.

One of these executive signings against the American people occurred in December 2011, when President Barack Obama signed the National Defense Authorization Act (NDAA).[1] Another was ""Authorizing The Implementation Of Certain Sanctions Set Forth In The Iran Threat Reduction And Syria Human Rights Act Of 2012 And Additional Sanctions With Respect To Iran"" EO on October 9, 2012.

To remove and alter our constitutional rights, the definition of "terrorist" was broadened to include freethinking American citizens. They can be detained without charge and held indefinitely under House Resolution (HR) 347, the National Defense Authorization Act. We have active Federal Emergency Management Agency (FEMA) camps, martial law, government farmland seizure, and mass disregard of First Amendment rights.

Next will be Internet seizure with increased surveillance of e-mail, GPS, PlayStation, phone calls, and text messages. This isn't science fiction or a conspiracy theory; it is the reality of living in America in 2012. Police departments currently use phone tracking without a search warrant.

This is only a small part of how the government is controlling and investigating individuals on social network sites, with personal information stored by the US government.

The Fourth Amendment of the Constitution states we have the right to privacy—free from Big Brother looking over our shoulders, tracking and watching everything we do. The list of privacy invasion via cell phones, Internet tracking, and chipping student ID badges looms even larger with a one billion dollar face-recognition system scheduled to go nationwide by 2014.

Back in 2005–2006, the FBI outlined the Next Generation Identification (NGI) project to the Justice Department. The new system overhauls the FBI's fingerprint database.[2] Law enforcement will have a better way to keep track of citizens by matching palm prints and all other criminal data with mug shots of faces in a

---

1   The Media's Blackout Of The National Defense Authorization Act Is Shameful http://www.businessinsider.com/the-medias-blackout-of-the-national-defense-authorization-act-is-shameful-2011-12#ixzz1fMUpcL2t

2   Face Recognition http://www.fbi.gov/about-us/cjis/fingerprints_biometrics/iafis/iafis

crowd, which can be taken even if the person isn't looking at the camera. This data can be compared with the FBI's photographic database to identify suspects. The FBI has collaborated with issuers of state drivers' licenses for photo comparison. Trials begin in mid-January of 2013, in unidentified locales in Michigan, Washington, Florida, and North Carolina, before it will be offered to other justice professionals across the country in 2014. The NGI uses biometric information such as iris scans and voice identification. The database will accumulate and archive information on every man, woman, and child in America.

Any database of personal identity information will have inaccuracies. What about abuses perpetuated against American civil rights, including swapping information with other government agencies? The role of the local police will not be to protect the people but rather to act as spies for the federal government as they collect information for a massive surveillance system. Will the federal government subject innocent Americans, not guilty of any crimes, to unwarranted surveillance? NGI's privacy statement as to whether civilian photos will be added is unclear. What is needed is a separate nongovernmental agency to oversee these technologies, guarding against the issue of an invasion of Americans' privacy.

Director of the FBI J. Edgar Hoover is quoted in an article from Elks Magazine in 1956, "The individual is handicapped by coming face-to-face with a conspiracy so monstrous he cannot believe it exists. The American mind simply has not come to a realization of the evil, which has been introduced into our midst. It rejects even the assumption that human creatures could espouse a philosophy which must ultimately destroy all that is good and decent." Was Hoover concerned about the plans to end our nation's sovereignty with the implementation of the New World Order and one world government? We will never know. Today his words should bring a shiver of apprehension to every American.

Technology is advanced; in 2012 and 2013, cities like New York City are using spy equipment to watch every move of the people.

Our nation's existence depends on stopping all intrusive data collection and spying technologies. The federal government will use all information against the people of the United States.

Osama Bin Laden

☙⚛ The United States says it killed the terrorist. Osama bin Laden claims the title. This is why he was protected for many years from being caught. You could say that bin Laden was paid to keep quiet about his death when he was paid by the government for the 9/11 attack.

The president, in claiming the honor for Osama bin Laden's death, benefits in the eyes of the public. The American public thinks, "The terrorist is dead. That's a good thing. Now the economy is going to be better." The government had to "catch him" because the president decided to take the next step to start a new war. This is why the lie was created about killing bin Laden.

The US Navy Seal team did not kill Osama bin Laden on May 1, 2011. Bin Laden was not the person killed. The Seals killed a patsy—someone they could say was bin Laden. This is why the person was shot in the face, and why the navy put the body in the ocean. This is also why they did not show pictures, so there could be no identification of the body. Osama bin Laden died in the mountains hooked up to medical devices. Washington has not proved a DNA match that the man killed was in fact bin Laden.

This is the same kind of ploy used September 11, 2001. The false attack on 9/11 was used as a reason to begin a war. Your government brought in and paid terrorists to bring down the Twin Towers and to bomb the Pentagon. The government could then go to war and set in place the antiterrorism acts (Patriot Act, Homeland Security). Your government has an agenda, and its motivations are greed and power.

Washington made sure the people important to the government stayed home from work by phoning people at home and telling them not to go to work on 9/11. Many Americans blame Osama bin Laden for the destruction and deaths on 9/11. Bin Laden was paid by the United States to fly the planes into the buildings and take the fall for 9/11. Your government hired and paid him to take these actions.

The planes on impact burned inside the buildings. Then the bombs began to explode, with firemen running out of the buildings yelling, "There are bombs going off!" Washington paid a different company or person to detonate explosions, and specifically set up the buildings to go down in a certain way. Then the US government paid a private crew to carry away the rubble. The rubble was loaded on boats and hauled offshore by a salvage company. Why?

A plane did not go into the Pentagon on 9/11 because it would not have penetrated a bunker wall. The only thing that could have done this was a bunker-penetrating cruise missile. During this time, the United States was the only country that manufactured cruise missiles. Did someone sell the technology or the cruise missile itself to foreign interests?

The United States is shopping for a war. Expect threats of terrorist acts to increase in the United States, and know your government is behind most of them.

Later there will be war. The invasion will happen about the same time the economy totally crashes. Your country is divided. Band together; you can win to begin a new government.

War with Iran

❧❧ The United States of America will be going to war with Iran after November 2012. Washington sold bunker bombs to Israel in the first half of 2011. Before this time, the United States would not sell smart bunker bombs to Israel. War will kill the economy.

An Israel-United States alliance means that either party will involve the other country when one goes to war. The president is going shopping for a war.

The government has its own secret armies, so it does not have to worry about the laws. The federal government pays Afghan and Iraqi warlords and their troops as undercover "military contractors," which is another name for mercenaries. When they are paid, they turn over a good part of it to al-Qaeda or the Taliban for ammunition and weapons. The people in Iraq and

Afghanistan know about this. When a warlord troop murders someone, Americans get the blame. Washington is paying for the bullets that are killing Americans.

The United States government made up stories of threat to unite Americans and justify getting into the Libyan war. It allowed the government to place the military in strategic places.

War creates economic chaos and destroys the American dollar. Expect higher taxes and more pretend money to be printed. Expect gas prices to soar.

U S Government Tracking Devices

Identity location devices for students in public schools will become required throughout the United States within the next two to three years. It will become unsafe to take your children to public schools because government location identification will become mandatory just as vaccinations are now. These will become standard unless Americans protest government demands regulating what you must do. Establishing the tracking devices in Texas is an experiment now, before the federal government requires them by law for all students.

If children wear or carry a tracking device, people who could hurt them can follow them. It is not good that the US government will require this dangerous system. The tracking devices invade the privacy of each individual. In the not-too-distant future, babies will have a chip imbedded when they are born. The government will use the tracking device to collect data. The US government should focus on using money for providing the best education by financing schools so they can buy the supplies they need.

Beginning in 2012, a San Antonio, Texas, school district is forcing students to wear radio-frequency identification (RFID) badges in order to track their locations, just as you are tracked every time you use the Internet to e-mail, make a purchase, or have a little fun on your social media page with your smartphone or tablet.

RFID has been available for more than fifty years. This electronic device consists of a small chip and an antenna. Stores are beginning to use them. In Walmart, tags were inserted in packages of lipstick, allowing researchers seven hundred and fifty miles away to watch consumers as they shop. For the price of about ten cents apiece, Gillette bought 500 million RFID tags to put on the items they sell. Even after you leave the store, RFID devices are still active. Using RFID technology, it would be easy for a thief with a scanner to know what is in your bag or to pull up the information of what is in your home before he robs it.

Soon passports will have these tracking devices for border crossings and at the airport. Scanners could track the location of every passport, broadcasting your location as you get out of your car, go into the restroom, and get on the plane.

Drones

Cities have drones flying overhead, and there is evidence that radio signals both to and from the drones allow them to be hijacked. The drones can be stolen in the air and reprogrammed midflight. What a danger this might become! Within ten years, the air force will fly drones the size of mosquitoes or golf balls over America on any given day.[3]

US Census Bureau

Maybe you are of the mind-set that this is not something that will happen in your United States of America? During World War II, Japanese American citizens were taken to concentrations camps. The US Census Bureau keeps track of everybody. Now your government has the Internet and all of the technology to use to spy on Americans. Maybe history is repeating itself![4]

---

3   Drone use in the U.S. raises privacy concerns http://www.cbsnews.com/8301-505263_162-57409759/drone-use-in-the-u.s-raises-privacy-concerns/

4   Census Bureau website http://www.census.gov/population/race/about/faq.html

It is a violation of your Fifth Amendment right to be forced to give the US Census Bureau any of your information. The bureau says that by law they cannot reveal your information to the federal government. What they do not tell you is they can suspend these rules at the request of any federal official who drops sentences such as, "In the interests of national security ..." The US Census Bureau has given out personal information in the past, and if history is repeating itself, as DreamMyst suggests, they will use it against you as well.

Months before Japan's so-called sneak attack on Pearl Harbor on December 7, 1941, President Franklin D. Roosevelt, at the Atlantic Charter conference, mentioned to Churchill that he was secretly looking for a way to get into the war. To do this, he secretly sent cruisers and destroyers to invade Japanese home waters and cut off Japan's oil supply, machine tools, machinery, and supplies of metal. After numerous warnings, the Japanese attacked.

Roosevelt decided it was in the government's best interest to round up one hundred thousand Japanese and put them together in what he called "war relocation camps." This action was in violation of the US Constitution, so he sidestepped Congress and issued Executive Order 9066, which said that military commanders were granted the "administrative right" to declare entire states to be "exclusion zones" from which people of Japanese ancestry were excluded. The internment camps were then placed outside of the exclusion zones, and the Japanese were forced to evacuate in obedience to the executive order.

Back in 1942, there was no Internet from which to get information, so the War Department paid the Census Bureau for the locations of the Japanese. The Census Bureau released racial profile details about individual Japanese Americans, giving block-by-block data for neighborhoods in California, Arizona, Wyoming, Colorado, Utah, Idaho, and Arkansas to the War Department.

In 1942, there was no FEMA. Instead, United States Government prepared war relocation camps, but the relocation centers were concentrations camps. One day, without warning, Japanese Americans were held under gunpoint, taken from their homes, businesses, and farms, and moved to the camps. No charges were filed and there was never a trial. But these innocent Japanese Americans remained in detention until the end of the war. Some were detained until 1946.[5]

Gun Control

~~ The gun control bill does not allow your children to inherit Great-Grandpa's gun. This is not about hunting. Your Second Amendment says you have the right to bear arms. This bill cripples Americans who choose to give up their guns; they cannot protect themselves. If people sell their guns, the bad people, including your government, will have guns to use against you. The criminals will always have the AK-47. If the gun control bill becomes a law, it works against law-abiding American citizens.

Expect conspiracy theories that your government starts in regards to shootings. The government will track gun sales and will make it difficult to buy ammunition or guns over the Internet. The United Nations wants to have complete control so they can run the United States as the New World Order. Expect a new EO from President Obama that shreds the American people of their right to bear arms.

~~

The stage is being set for one world economic system, bringing closer the reality of a North American Union. Is it any wonder the Department of Homeland Security (DHS) creates and implements terrorist acts to instill fear among the people and divide the nation?

DHS was created after 9/11 to prevent future acts of terrorism in the United States. DHS has expanded its power with the newly authorized Federal Restricted Buildings and Grounds Improvement Act, HR 347. Protesters who disrupt a national special security event will be charged with a federal crime. The government can now go after any American blogger or freethinker and assassinate Americans on their own soil, or those who resist relocation to FEMA camps for safety.

---

5   Census Bureau website http://www.census.gov/population/race/about/faq.html

Over the past few months, DHS has bought 450 million hollow-point bullets, and ordered 650–750 million rounds of various types of ammunition, in addition to weapons and riot gear. The time when rubber bullets were used to subdue the masses is over. Hollow points are not used for target practice. They are designed to shatter and kill. This is why they are illegal for use in war. The federal government has decided to use them on Americans, just as DreamMyst has stated.

Homeland Security's goal is to take American lives if necessary. DHS has bought more ammunition than there are people in the entire United States. The next constitutional right to be destroyed will be the Second Amendment, which is the right to bear arms. Take away the guns of the American people, and the people do not have a way to protect themselves.

The Justice Department has assigned the Bureau of Alcohol, Tobacco, Firearms, and Explosives (ATF) the authority to seize property involved in controlled-substance cases. In other words, the ATF will take your firearms and other property, using any pretext. It can be done without due process because it is your seized property that is put on trial, so there is no constitutional right involved. Civil punishment is exceptionally lucrative for law enforcement agencies.[6]

As the president and federal government, swollen with power, spiral toward a systematic takeover of liberty, and replace freedoms with soft martial law during a time of peace. Militarization of police in America will become normal. Police weapon drones are armed with beanbag guns and Tasers. Predator drone spy planes fly over the land of America.

American eyes will soon become familiar with military checkpoints. Americans will encounter the National Guard on the streets as these young men and women direct traffic and maintain order. Even they will not realize they are performing civilian training exercises for the state. They will simply be following orders. They are not here to enforce martial law, enforce vaccinations, or relocation to FEMA camps ... at least not yet.

---

6   Authorization To Seize Property Involved in Drug Offenses for Administrative Forfeiture (2012R-9P) www.federalregister.gov

As DreamMyst says, expect President Obama to replace the Internet Cybersecurity Act of 2012 with an executive order that strips more freedoms and rights from the people possibly weeks after his reelection. Homeland Security will decide what and who is a threat. They are tracking everything, every single person.

Homeland Security is authorized to enforce cybersecurity standards for the private sector. Recently, soldiers who came back from Afghanistan and Iraq were placed directly under the authority of Homeland Security. DHS has permission to control the people of America. The majority of the military personnel do not realize the responsibility this entails. They are in the military to perform a job. If that means killing people, they will do it. Eventually, the military will come back and stand for the people rather than the government.

Liberty Dies Slowly

≈⤙ The same American government that took away your freedom and liberty controls the economy. The Federal Reserve directs the money supply. Then there is the global economy that has resulted in a decline in real estate, stocks, and the US dollar. The government's approach is to feed the people, giving them federal and state services so they do not have the desire to take care of themselves. People do not think about or realize how complacent they have become.

≈⤙

It seems a pattern of targeting right-wing extremists—normal, ordinary Americans who speak out against the government—is emerging. Labeled as socially dangerous, these Americans are now faced with the prospect of forced protective custody. Today a socially dangerous person can be arrested without being accused of a crime. But what exactly does a person of this nature do? Does he hurt or kill other people? Does he break the law? Or is he a little too patriotic for the government's taste because he speaks out about his political views about martial law, owning firearms, and survivalism? The government targets this type of person. If the Founding Fathers were alive, they would be considered socially dangerous, right-wing extremists too.

Are people socially dangerous for using their First Amendment right of free speech? Within the past few years, that certainly appears to be the case. Federal officials and local police have visited three honorably discharged veterans and two innocent civilians, all gun owners, within the last two years. All five of the individuals were arrested without being charged with a crime, handcuffed, and abducted. Each of these men was taken to a mental health institution for protective imprisonment because of their nonconformist political views and belief in preparing and surviving any possible threat to life. This lifestyle choice is known as "Prepping."

When a Marine combat veteran publicly expressed doubts and posted comments on his Facebook page about the government, the FBI and Secret Service violated his constitutional right to freedom of speech. Descending like locusts on his home, they arrested him without giving him Miranda rights. A few hours later, they took him to a mental facility three hundred miles away from his family and friends. The victim of this crime against Americans was not a criminal suspect or a suicide risk. His story ended well: the detention was invalid.

> » You might be a terrorist if you save silver and gold.

> » You might be a terrorist if you want to bear arms.

> » You might be a terrorist if you pay with cash.

> » You might be a terrorist if you believe in conspiracy theories involving grave threat to national sovereignty and/or personal liberty.

> » You might be a terrorist if you want those elected to preserve your rights and freedoms.

> » You might be a terrorist if you don't believe in centralized federal authority.

> » You might be a terrorist if you love individual liberty.

DreamMyst says it is time to prepare to defend ourselves. Civil unrest is smoldering, ready to explode in the next eighteen months when history, as it so often does, repeats itself. Catastrophic changes are occurring within our government to downsize the influence of the United States. America will no longer be the land of the free.

American Freedoms and the Government

༜The loss of freedom does not equal safety! Do not be fooled when your president pats you on the head, saying, "Don't worry your little head about all these matters." Believe the opposite of what the White House tells you. Do not for one moment believe the government is "for" the people. Know that your media is feeding you information the government wants you to hear, and will divert your attention to a different topic in the news to distract you.

༜

Q: Why is it okay for the CIA to pay for and receive illegal drugs? What right does the government have to sell guns to a cartel when its antigun policies penalize you from defending your life?

DM: The actions of the president reflect on all of those below him. The effects channel outward like tentacles. They filter down to all the other, smaller facilities and groups that act as your president behaves. Because they are following these orders, they're filled with power, saying it's good to do this because we can, because it's the law. You will find more and more that your police and sheriff's departments, as well as the marshals and whoever else has authority, will not be very friendly as they become powerful.

Q: DreamMyst, what information can help Americans understand the corruption of the US government?

DM: When the economy crashes and when earth changes happen, your government is not going to feed you, clothe you, or take care of your medical needs. They will be busy taking care of themselves and will be in a place of safety—such as a bunker.

The government does not want you to know about anything that is happening, such as the coming solar flares or the economic collapse. If you know what is coming, you will panic. They don't want you to panic. They want you ignorant.

Your media—newspapers and television news—are paid by the government not to report information. Your best way to get information is through another source, maybe from a different country. Washington is paying the news reporters to report, or not report, what it wants. Your government has bought the news outlets. The government does not want you to know anything that can help you to save your life. It does not care about you. It does not care about your children. Those in power only care about themselves and their survival. I am talking about the politicians, the president, and those people who rule the country—their safety. They hope when they come out of this untouched, they will put into place what they started: the New World Order.

❧❦

All governments lie, cheat, and steal. America's brilliant founders and revolutionary forefathers were not exempt. More than 230 years ago, they opened a government-owned central bank, initiated a bond scam, and made the unconstitutional Louisiana Purchase. They defaulted on their debt to France, which led to an unconstitutional war with France.

When will the government tell the truth and defend the freedoms of the people? Never. The government does what it forbids the American people to do, breaking its own laws to accomplish what it desires.

On November 11, 2011 (11–11–11), the federal government hijacked every radio, television, and broadcast station across the United States. With a flip of the switch, they controlled the power of mass communication. Later in 2012, the government controlled the Internet from 11:00 p.m. to 3:00 a.m. for an emergency preparedness drill, shutting down credit card servers on September 7 and 14. The president's National Preparedness Month 2012 proclamation, is an ulterior move to start a war, control the Internet, or both.

The Bilderberg Group and the New World Order

❧❦ The larger the government, the sooner the fall of civilization. Political power and governmental power corrupt judgment and morals.

Did you know the ruling elite have secret meetings? The name of the group is the Bilderberg Group.[7] President Obama went to this

---

7   The True Story of the Bilderberg Group" and What They May Be Planning Now http://www.globalresearch.ca/the-true-story-of-the-bilderberg-group-and-what-they-may-be-planning-now/

group in 2008 for their acceptance of him as president. Hillary Clinton was there at the same time. The group meets in America, Canada, the Netherlands, and other places in Europe. It meets to affect national governments and economies from behind the scenes, preparing your nation for the New World Order. Eventually there will be a handful of people who rule America.

The group wants to have a world company (government), a single global marketplace, one world (central) bank with one global currency, and NATO as the one world army.

This group of the elite has begun to keep track of people through DNA sampling. Bill Gates, founder and chairman of Microsoft, is involved in researching this in the United States; it will be used for population control. In order to program and control the human mind, all children are being brainwashed in school by controlling their education.

The Bilderberg Group's globalist agenda is to have no democracy and no middle class, only rulers and servants, with all wealth and power going to the rulers. The UN will become the world government, imposing a UN tax on "world citizens." Americans need to take care of what is yours so that the New World Order does not take over your world.

The elite rule the country the way they want to. It is not good. If you have this kind of leadership, you can call it one world order, one world government, one world financial banking institution, or one world legal system. It is dangerous. It is like nothing Americans are used to. It will be very similar to third-world countries because the ruling elite will put the power, money, and decisions about human life into the hands of a few people who are powerful or have the most money.

The New World Order is a way of bringing all of the finances, money, and people together as one: one world financial institution, one world policy for the people. People will work hard and be poor. There will not be entrepreneurship or the freedom that existed in the old America. Everybody will work for the government. It does not mean there will be much money. When the government tells you where to live, you will have to do what it says. The government will tell you how to raise your children. Parents will not be able to raise their children in the way they would desire. Your children will be encouraged to tell on you. Unless you are one of the few wealthy people, you will not be able to send your children to the schools you want. You will have to send them to the school your government decides.

In the new world government, you won't be able to elect a president. Maybe you will be able to go through the motions as you do now, but the outcome will remain the same. The ruling government will put into place the person it wants to rule.

The United Nations created this. There are not many countries who are not a part of this, but there are a few who are not. China is not a part of the NWO because they want to be the power of the world. China has aligned with Iran because both countries do not want to be a part of the New World Order.

Countries have different laws, correct? What happens when you have a global government with the same laws internationally? There will be a global police force, global tax, and global court. All these things will be mandated and become homogenized. That is why it is necessary for your government to have brainwashed people instead of human beings, who think and take action to create change.

Get rid of the people who want to control your world. Senators, Hillary Clinton, and the United Nations are helping to create a New World Order. The world banking system is in effect now. It is the banks and those who fund the banks who decide where and when wars begin and which states to help in times of disaster.

The one world government is not something to be proud to have. It is about the control of the planet and of human beings worldwide. It is about controlling your money and finances. A global monetary crisis is occurring not only in the United States of America, but everywhere.

Bilderberg Group is an organized cabal of powerful people who secretly rule the world.

Probably the earliest reference to the "new world order" is a concept from Baha'i scripture in the early nineteenth century. It appears again after World War I as an expression of Western political thought. President Roosevelt in 1933 ordered the all-seeing eye placed on all new dollar bills, along with the motto *Novus Ordo Seclorum*, which is Latin for "A New Order of the Ages."

In 1990, for the first time in history, the leaders of both superpowers were using the same phrase—"new world order"—during their public speeches. Soviet leader Mikhail Gorbachev on April 11, 1990, mentioned the term "new world order" at the conference of the World Media Association in the Kremlin when he said "We are only at the beginning of the process of shaping a new world order." President Bush Jr. told a news conference on August 30, 1990, "I think we do have a chance at a new world order."

The Rothschilds

"Let me issue and control a nation's money and I care not who writes the laws." —Mayer Amschel Rothschild, 1790

ॐ The Rothschilds own the world, and the United Nations wants your president to do exactly what he is doing because it fits the UN agenda. He is the pawn of the UN and is setting up the takeover of America. If he is re-elected, then shortly after your economy will crash. The American military will have the illusion of control. Then they will be phased out and the mercenaries will take over.

The Rothschilds have paid huge amounts of money in many places for their name to be kept quiet. They are not Americans, although the Rothschilds are in America and all over the world. They control the banks and politicians. If they want a war to start, it will be so.

Over in England they have a name: "The House of Rothschild." There are many lines in that family. They spread out like tentacles, and they boss everybody around. They carry the power. They rule the world. The Rothschilds' businesses are everywhere.

There exists a hidden, shadow government that rules America and most of the world. The founders of this shadow government are the Rothschilds. As the world's wealthiest family, they have families placed in every country, operating banks. The Rothschilds' bloodline, or, as DreamMyst so aptly states, their tentacles, extend to the Rockefellers (through a female bloodline) in the United States. The royal families of Europe, Astors, Bundys, Collins, DuPonts, Freemans, Kennedys, Morgans, Oppenheimers, Rockefellers, Sassoons, Schiffs, Tafts, and Van Duyns have all intermarried with the Rothschilds, extending their bloodline throughout the world.

As we have gathered from DreamMyst, the House of Rothschild is an international banking firm worth over five hundred trillion dollars. Since they own and control the banks, they also own the governments, and have for hundreds of years. The United States has not been immune. Congress passed a bill permitting a Rothschild central bank, known as the Second Bank of the United States, in 1816, which included a twenty-year charter.

Andrew Jackson

President Andrew Jackson removed the government deposits from the Second Bank of the United States and placed them in the banks of democratic bankers in 1833. The Rothschilds squeezed the money supply, causing a depression. President Jackson, who knew what they were doing, stated, "You are a den of thieves, vipers, and I intend to rout you out, and by the Eternal God, I will rout you out." He claimed the Rothschilds were responsible for the January 30, 1835, assassination attempt on his life, and went on to banish the Rothschilds' Second Bank of the United States in 1836.

Abraham Lincoln

The Rothschilds created the Civil War to divide and weaken the United States many years before the actual war became a reality. They did not want a strong, confident, and self-providing republic because then they would not have control of the country. During the war, history shows the Rothschilds financed both sides of the war. Lincoln got the better of the Rothschilds when he drew up interest-free United States notes (money). By April 1862, Lincoln's debt-free money had been printed and distributed. In, 1865, President Abraham Lincoln made a statement to Congress, "I have two great enemies, the Southern Army in front of me, and the financial institutions in the rear. Of the two, the one in my rear is my greatest foe." Later this same year, Lincoln was assassinated.

James Garfield

In 1881, our one-hundred-day president, James A. Garfield, was an expert on fiscal matters. When he appointed an unpopular collector of customs in New York, two senators from New York—Roscoe Conkling and Thomas Platt—resigned their seats. Two weeks before he was assassinated, Garfield openly stated, "Whoever controls the volume of money in our country is absolute master of all industry and commerce ... and when you realize that the entire system is very easily controlled, one way or another, by a few powerful men at the top, you will not have to be told how periods of inflation and depression originate."

John F. Kennedy

In order to eliminate the Rothschilds' Federal Reserve Bank, President John F. Kennedy signed Executive Order 11110 on June 4, 1963. The US government now had the power to issue currency. Less than six months later, on November 22, 1963, Kennedy was assassinated in part because of the issue of the Federal Reserve. President Lyndon Baines Johnson flew from Dallas to Washington the day JFK was assassinated. Johnson rescinded Executive Order 11110 on November 22, 1963.

Four presidents used their power and foresight to print American money for the American people. Unfortunately, this was not to be, and the Rothschilds, as DreamMyst says, rule the world.

In 1862, a Rothschild agent in America, John D. Rockefeller, formed an oil business called Standard Oil, which eventually took over all of its competition. On January 1, 1875, Rothschild money continued to finance John D. Rockefeller's Standard Oil Company, Andrew Carnegie's steel empire, and Edward R. Harriman's railroad empire.

Eventually, the Rothschilds gained control of every aspect of the American government, as you will see from the short list below.

Federal Reserve Bank

During a speech in 1907 New York, Jacob Schiff warned, "Unless we have a central bank with adequate control of credit resources, this country is going to undergo the most severe and far-reaching money panic in its history." A few months after this speech, in October 1907, the Rothschilds brought in their agents, J. P. Morgan, Kuhn, Loeb and Company, creating a Rothschild currency crisis.

The panic of 1907 was an orchestrated ploy to show how much the American people needed a Rothschild central bank. The Rothschilds got their bank in 1914, placing control of United States finances with the Federal Reserve system and Wall Street.

On December 23, 1913, Congressman Charles Lindbergh spoke an absolute truth following the enactment of the Federal Reserve Act. "The Act establishes the most gigantic trust on earth. When the president [Wilson] signs this bill, the invisible government of the monetary power will be legalized. The greatest crime of the ages is perpetrated by this banking and currency bill."

Since its origin in 1914, the Federal Reserve, with its misleading name, has had no reserves and is about as federal as Federal Express. Twelve banking families, including the Rothschilds, privately own it. Company employees are not in the civil service. It pays for its own postage. The physical property it occupies is held under private deeds. It is subject to local taxes, and generates unnecessary national debt.

The Federal Reserve manipulates the economy and enlists the government to enforce its demands. It has never published accounts.

Efforts to audit the Federal Reserve have met with failure. Finally, on September 1, 2012, for the first time in almost a hundred years, an authorization for the first Government Accountability Office (GAO) audit of the Federal Reserve was passed due to Ron Paul and Alan Grayson.

There are only four or five nations in the world left without a Rothschild-controlled central bank. The long arm of the Rothschilds reaches unusually far, indeed.

Internal Revenue Service

The Internal Revenue Service is a private corporation established by the Rothschilds in 1933.

Q: People are saying that the IRS is no longer a US government agency, that it's actually now an agency of the International Monetary Fund (IMF), an organization that is part of the UN. Is this true?

DM: Yes, it is, but it is still your IRS. It's all part of corporate America.

Ministry of Justice

Rothschilds founded the American Bar Association in 1870 in Indiana. All bar association members are lawyers. Lawyers make up 100 percent of the judiciary and 71 percent of the state, local, and federal legislatures, placing two branches of our government under their control.

Media

In the late eighteen hundreds, the Rothschilds bought Reuters and thereby gained control of twenty-five of the greatest newspapers in the United States. Congressman Oscar Callaway informed Congress in March 1915, that "The J. P. Morgan interests, the steel, shipbuilding, and powder interest, and their subsidiary organizations, got twelve men high up in the newspaper world and employed them to select the most influential newspapers in the United States and a sufficient number of them to control the policy of the daily press."

Today, the Rothschilds are seldom reported in the media. They control NBC, CBS, and ABC. In 1991, at the Bilderberg Conference in Germany, billionaire David Rockefeller (a Rothschild) made the following statement: "We are grateful to *The Washington Post*, *The New York Times*, *Time* magazine, and other great publications whose directors have attended our meetings and respected their promises of discretion for almost forty years. It would have been impossible for us to develop our plan for the world if we had been subjected to the lights of publicity during those years. But the world is now more sophisticated and prepared to march towards a world government. The supernational sovereignty of an intellectual elite and world bankers is surely preferable to the national auto determination practiced in past centuries."

China (Insights from 2009–2012)

༈༈ China will take the opportunity to invade should the United States become weakened. This is another reason to move away from big cities and seaports. China would welcome partners if Russia, North Korea, or another country joined it. The US military will fight, but that doesn't mean they will win. The act to win America will be when the United States is most vulnerable. The decision to invade will be after China finds out America is going to default on the deficit loans. China is partnered with other countries so they will try to bring America down by the economy and will also try to invade physically. This is when the United States will be at its weakest. Once the economic bubble bursts, government will be no more. There will be total global economic collapse. That's when China will come in and take over.

China will start by shooting nuclear weapons high up in the atmosphere. The electromagnetic pulse (EMP) will take out the electricity if there is still electricity when China attacks. Then Chinese military will arrive by sea and air. They live now within your United States and will begin to prepare.

In the past, the United States has fought all wars outside of America, with the exceptions of the Civil War and the American Revolution. This war will be fought in the United States of America. It will take every bit of strength, with all people persevering and taking actions now, to prevent the Chinese from successfully ruling America. The war can be prevented or its outcome changed. Fill the vacant military bases with soldiers and weapons to protect the country. All of you working together as a team can change your world. From 2011, you have about two years before there is a massive crash in your economic system. The crash could last anywhere from two to ten years. Banks will be recreated, and the youth will recreate the government.

That's why it's very important to keep your military strong and not scattered. As long as the Chinese perceive America still has a strong military, they will not take those actions.

In order to have enough service personnel, the US government will draft men into the military in 2014. The government has updated the law allowing men between the ages of eighteen and forty-two to be drafted. More military in other countries will make America weaker. Along with the economic depression and the lack of electricity from either an EMP or a super solar flare, China will do its best to attack America and physically invade. As long as America keeps a strong military force, China will not be able to invade, but China will if it can.

Americans need to help themselves. Stop sending money out of the country. Shut your doors. Shut down all of the importing and exporting of goods. Take the money and put it into the United States of America.

There is hope. The first president after Obama will have to do a lot of cleaning up. Then there will be another president. He will be the one who will bring the United States back together as a whole, to the degree it can be brought back.

It is important for the military to stay a military power. You will have a short period of reorganization after the economic depression and the possible loss of electricity. The New World Order is coming. I hope your United States of America fights back, because the New World Order is going to take over as much of the world as possible in a new way and style. It has already begun, which is why President Obama is in the position he is in. He is a tool, a puppet president, to be used by others who are even more corrupt. Hillary Clinton is included in as well as the other presidential candidate, Romney. Puppets do the bidding of others to get what they want.

DreamMyst says China will attack in the future. This determination is based on the energy of events that are happening now. The threat of attack from China is an excellent lesson in how Americans can determine a future outcome. She advises that China will not invade if our military is not scattered around the world as it is now. Barack Obama and most presidential candidates have a plan to continue stationing troops around the world. Who Americans choose for their president will be a determining factor in deciding if war with China comes to the United States.

There are three possible scenarios with China:

1. The United States military establishes a strong presence in America; therefore, China never invades.

2. American military remains scattered around the world, yet the small American military force and citizens band together, fight hard, and win against China's invasion.

3. American military remains scattered around the world. The small American military and citizens do not band together. China wins America.

China's attack will happen after the United States defaults on its loans. America will be experiencing an economic depression.

The Crushing of Freedom

Only government institutions can legally force their will against innocent people.

࠵ It looked good for the National Defense Authorization Act (NDAA) to pass because it has important elements that will help your military. The president demanded more changes. He is just as bad as those who voted to eliminate the Constitution and your rights. One thing is certain: the option to use NDAA against you is why this bill was created in the first place. It affects Americans by taking away your amendment rights and freedoms. No one has freedom unless you are willing to do what you need to do to protect it. Your government is saying, "Either do what we want you to do, or we are going to make your life very, very difficult." Unite for your lives, for your children, and for your country.

NDAA turns your country away from freedom. The government held a meeting late at night so it could do its sneaky tricks. This didn't just happen. The government could not have the Patriot Act until they had you all trained. So they fed you lies and untruths. This is the United States government and what it is doing to strip Americans of their rights and freedoms.

Washington gives you lies. The media is paid to keep quiet. Not too many people know about NDAA or how these changes can harm you. Many younger people don't have an idea of how important the Constitution and its amendments work in their lives.

Your United States of America is special; it is the only country that has a Bill of Rights. What those rights says is that because you are here on Earth, you have God-given rights. Many hundred years ago your forefathers set into action a way to protect you. Your forefathers did this for a good reason.

Your government, your legislature, they say, "Well, the American people don't really need this one freedom. We'll make changes to it." The US government does not want anything to mess up its plans, which are to take away your rights as American citizens. Soon you won't have any constitutional rights because Congress and the president will have changed or erased them from your Bill of Rights.

How did the United States government get away with it? For the last thirty or forty years, it has been feeding you a spoonful of sugar with medicine in it, and the medicine it has been giving you is poison. That poison was to prepare you for today, so it could get the act into the Senate, get the act passed, and take away your rights.

Americans think their government is going to protect them. The President set up your Patriot Act and created the war on terror. The war on terror is not anything other than a tactic in case of real terrorism. Never was it meant to be used on Americans. The only reason the Patriot Act was crafted was for people from other countries who came to create terror in the United States. Your government creates terror and has paid so-called terrorists to create terrorist acts like Osama bin Laden attacking the Twin Towers and the Pentagon. Then another branch of your government has the honor of busting the terrorist. The Government has rescued all of you from a terrorist act that wasn't a terrorist act. It keeps you afraid. They want you to fear, and then they rescue you because they are here to help America fend off terrorists.

In 2012, the Senate decided to eliminate your Bill of Rights. You will not be able to claim the Fourth Amendment, because the Patriot Act states the police can take you away without due process if they so choose. Your government has full power. You now live in a police state. Soon the police will act as if they are the military. They will take over your property and food, live in your house, and send you away. That is not good.

Many think—and you may be one of them—"Well, the Bill of Rights doesn't benefit me very much." The reason the Bill of Rights was put into place was to protect Americans from being hurt and taken advantage of by the government. Your government is creating a terrorist act against you, and it will treat you as a terrorist. It will take you away without due process, without even saying you are a terrorist. You might ask, "Why is it doing this?" The US government is taking away your rights to gain control, to bring in the one world power. It is doing this to control the masses. It is not the Chinese, Russians, Democrats, or Republicans who are the enemy—it is political power.

Did you know your United States is going to be sliced up like a piece of pie? It will be divided up into many areas, and each of the ten top senators will control a piece of your United States. These ten people are the ones who will decide who they want to have for president.

You will have to fight to reinstate the Bill of Rights. The problem, though, is that the NDAA is now a law. This law affects everyone. It will not matter if you live a good life, work hard, or never do anything wrong toward the government. The government and the banks want complete control.

The Rothschilds are the ones who fund economic turmoil. They are the ones who fund recessions and depressions in all different countries, not just the United States. The Rothschilds are the ones paying your government to set up the New World Order.

Right now, you do what your government says to do, regardless of whether you want to or not. This began, as I said, many years ago. Then you had 9/11. Your government created a terrorist act. The government did so to bring in the Patriot Act, the war on terror, and the 2012 National Defense Authorization Act. The next step is setting up martial law and putting it into effect.

The more humans are informed, the more knowledge they have to make choices. Knowledge is power. So share the knowledge and execute what you know. Gather in the federal buildings and all those places people go, and get names on legal petitions. The part that is difficult for people to believe is that your government is setting all this up. It wants you to think the government protects you, when the reality is the government will herd you into relocation camps. Of course, it wants you to believe it is doing this for your protection. But that's a big fat fib! It's not good! It's your choice: you can be free, or you can be slaves to your government.

FEMA

The Federal Emergency Management Agency (FEMA) is not the Red Cross, everybody. FEMA is not your friend. There are many FEMA camps. The government started converting them before 9/11. Years later, when the camps became public knowledge, the government said these places were here to protect you from the bad guys. The government is saying, "Government wears the white hats, and government is going to take care of you." The reality is that government is the bad guys and wears the black hats.

Some of these camps are huge, some smaller. There's over a thousand camps, and they are all over the United States. Many of the military bases have been shut down and can be easily converted to camps. Many have barbed-wire fencing and guard towers in place. Other large areas, such as schools and sport stadiums, can be converted. Now if that fenced-in area happens to be close to railroad tracks, then how convenient to use the train to transport people to the camps.

The police and military will herd you into the train cars and take you away from what you know, take you away from your home, and take you to these camps. What are they going to do when they put people into these camps? FEMA camps will not be anything you will enjoy. Did you know you will be working in concentration camps, like prisoners? You will not be paid. You'll just be working.

The red list is for people who have what the government wants: money and control. Activists will be on the red list. Important people the government does not like are put on this list. Notice I am not saying terrorists from another country are on the list. These are Americans. People in the red camps will die immediately. They will be executed.

The blue camps are for brainwashing. The blue lists are for those people who are listening to and influenced by the activists on the red list. They will be brainwashed.

The yellow camps are for regular people reacting to a state of emergency or martial law. The government will say, "You can come to the camp and the government will help you." Instead it will poison you with germ warfare and the use of drug-resistant "superbugs." The government will use what Bill Gates and John Holdren, your science czar of the United States of America, wants—population control.

How will the government do this? It is going to eliminate the people who decide they need food, and help those it considers dispensable. They will kill with poison in the water and a manufactured superbug virus.

Big cities will be most affected because big cities have lots and lots of people in them. Imagine what could happen if your economy crashes. There won't be food in the grocery store and there won't be water. Many will die during this period.

Do *not* get caught in a riot. If a gathering turns ugly, do your best to get away from it. If you are in the wrong place at the time FEMA is herding people, do your best to blend in and move away from that FEMA camp line! If you have to, find someplace to stay, even if it is under the street. Find a place to hide until it is safe to leave. If you can, leave the big cities. The military will focus on the populated areas. They will not worry about the smaller rural towns. They will be too busy.

To avoid relocating to FEMA camps, get prepared, get your food ready as quickly as you can, and make or buy a water filter to clean dirty water. This way you can stay in your home and have what you need to survive. People will die or go into FEMA camps. If there is not enough food and water, even the FEMA camps will not have enough food.

The next chapter will be martial law and civil war, followed by the overthrow of the government. When your government is brought back, it will establish a limited government, not an all-powerful dictatorship. Did you know the people elected a man named Hitler? The National Socialist Party (Nazis) used propaganda, and they made Hitler look very good to the people who wanted to live.

You have time to create a new government. You have the time to prosecute and eliminate those people who voted against your American rights. The divine expects you to take responsibility for *all* actions. You pay the consequences of your choices, both here on earth and on the other side. Take action. You are the ones who can create freedom for your children and your children's children. Your Bill of Rights and your Constitution are very much like having insurance. They are always there when you need them until the government supersedes them with something else.

Your government needs to go away. So make it go away. Elect those people who will not corrupt your new government. Have a good plan of action. Gather in groups. Work together. Join the masses and create change for your new world to stop the invasion of the New World Order. Get ready, Americans. If you don't take action, you're in for a long, difficult journey.

Civil War

৵৽ Americans will fight Americans and learn which countries are their real supporters. Violent acts will happen, especially in political areas and big cities. Think about how bullies and gangs act. State and local politicians stripped of power will be just as panicked and concerned as every normal person, and less prepared for the situation they find themselves in.

Be prepared with clean water and food. Your government will say terrorists will try to destroy or poison the water source. This is not true. Water is poisoned with the chemicals the US government allows to be added to the water and sprayed from the sky. Terrorists will not control the Internet; your government controls the Internet.

The turmoil you face in regard to your monetary system and political unrest shows that none of your politicians are trustworthy. The ones who would be good as your future president will not be elected. People with a sincere desire to create balance, change, and a new beginning will create the future. Those who are going to live in the new world will be concerned with bringing your world back to a place of prosperity.

৵৽

Sixty-one United States Senate members and the president of the United States abolished what they say are antiquated documents, the Constitution and the Bill of Rights. What the senators have not stated is that these documents are what preserve the freedoms of Americans.

While millions of Americans in 2011 were celebrating New Year's Eve, the president of the United States, with the stroke of a pen, signed the death warrant of America's Bill of Rights and Constitution by signing the National Defense Authorization Act (NDAA). The act included a provision allowing American citizens to be indefinitely detained in military custody without charge or trial. Peaceful protesters can now be arrested and held forever.

Say good-bye to freedom of speech, freedom to protect what is yours, and freedom from the military taking your food and shelter and locking you up without due process. Say hello to martial law, FEMA camps, chemical warfare, and genocide by the United States government.

The government has a plot to convince us there are terrorists on every corner and to build fear so we agree to hand over our rights for security. The United States government's new laws make it easy to establish martial law. The military, FBI, and CIA can take anyone away for merely disagreeing with them. They can seize your assets. The Bill of Rights guarantees our freedoms, until it is no more.

The American government is staffing empty FEMA camps in preparation to seize and control Americans. Using the war on terror as a fear tactic, the government convinced Americans that the Patriot Act was needed for their protection. In truth, it was a ploy to make it legal for police to listen to, record, spy upon, search, and arrest citizens without just cause.

This is an erosion of American rights and freedoms. Next to the US government and Barack Obama, the real threats to America are China, Russia, and North Korea. The American golden age can be restored if Americans take action now.

The only petition you want to sign are official recall or impeachment petitions circulated in your state to force a recall election in order to remove these treasonous senators from office. Online petitions are meaningless and accomplish nothing politically.

As DreamMyst predicted in 2010, the Stop Online Piracy Act, an Internet censorship bill, went into committee in Congress. President Obama promised to veto it. He did not, and on January 18, 2012, Americans protested and won the first round of the Internet censorship battle. On September 12, 2012, Obama drafted a cybersecurity executive order to be implemented at a moment's notice. The Obama administration pushed through an unconstitutional, police state, cybersecurity executive order. This will not happen until he finds a way to justify such an action to the American people. September 2012 is now National *Preparedness* Month. Want to bet that another red-flag event occurs during the month of September? The first one was 9/11. (This did indeed occur on September 11, 2012 in Libya, when CIA operators were told to "stand down" instead of assisting the ambassador's team. Four Americans including a United States ambassador were killed, in the Benghazi Attack.)[8]

Occupy Movement—a Revolution

On September 16, 2011, a small group gathered in New York City to protest corporate greed and banking corruption. The protests, referred to as Occupy Wall Street, quickly spread across the United States, and have now reached a global level. People are speaking up for their freedoms.

☙❧ The movement has begun, the movement of freeing yourself from the bondage of slavery. Let your government officials know you are not going to tolerate or accept certain behaviors. Even if everything changed overnight, your country would still be in tremendous debt.

Your government officials put you in this position. Every human being deserves to have a paycheck and not have the majority of it used up in taxes. You have the right and the obligation to stand up for the United States of America. This is the beginning of the revolution. It has begun.

The revolution of change will snowball. This will not be a quiet economic depression. Americans will not stay in their home and worry about feeding their families. This will be more of a vocal revolt about the weight put on the people. Just as when the civil rights movement began, it didn't end; it kept growing and evolving. Some people got hurt, but the movement grew, and the laws changed.

---

8   http://www.foxnews.com/politics/2012/10/26/cia-operators-were-denied-request-for-help-during-benghazi-attack-sources-say/#ixzz2CjGGEMMx.

It is good America is awakening now. This is beautiful. People are listening. They are waking up as if from a bad dream. Unfortunately, when they wake up, the bad dream will not go away. It has become a reality, and you cannot afford to passively watch or listen. It is time for every single adult American, old and young alike, to start a movement in the towns, in the cities, and begin uniting the people to bring back all that has been taken from you.

The billionaires and the banks decide who will be president. Really? Look at who you want to run your country, who can work with the country's circumstances. Eventually Americans will take back their United States of America. It will be the land of the free again, but it takes a brave people to take action. Get angry enough to say, "*No*, we are not doing this!" Use your passion. Focus your passion. A globalist New World Order means your children and grandchildren will live in a totalitarian world, a world without rights or freedoms.

Message to Protesters

 You are in your second wave, the second flow. The world will not forget what you have begun.

Focus your energies, change your government, and eliminate the Federal Reserve. These are the issues to change. A movement is action to create results that will make your life better. You are creating momentum. Your day will come, and what you have worked so diligently for will manifest itself because of your actions. Keep your focus on the desired outcomes. Find someone to represent you, and then submit that person as a possible candidate for the new government that you will create. Right now, you are in unchartered territory, but it won't stay unchartered for long. If you do not take these actions, the government will. Then it will not be to your liking. Stay strong, thrive, and prosper.

Message to American Police Officers

≈∽ It might be your mother, father, brother, or sister who is protesting. Even though you need to do your job, do it with dignity and respect for others. A peaceful protest can turn nasty, and yes, there is the threat of physical harm. This is why when you go after the bad guys. You experience the adrenaline rush during and after such an event. You are paid to put your life in danger. Some of you see the rightness of this movement. Be prepared to save Americans against your government. It will take all your training and skills when this time arrives.

Message to American Service Personnel and Veterans

≈∽ I would like to say if you are enlisted in the United States military, I honor you, and others do as well. Very much like firefighters and police officers, the military exists to protect and serve.

Your willingness to risk your life in a war that is contrived by your government, in a war that makes your government money, shows your devotion to the job you do. The fact that you have been brainwashed does not take away from your courage and bravery. You are barely making ends meet.

Your job is to keep your country safe. There will come a day when you will do this on American land. The military will side with the people after you recognize the lies and the brainwashing done to you by your government. You will be there to defend the people of America. You have the skills Americans need to survive. The path that leads to true freedom and liberation from tyranny is led by you.

When there is martial law, you will be paid to protect government officials like the president and politicians against the people of America. The military will side with the people, for the people. This will be the beginning of the new recovery and new government. You will defend the people of America in America. Live in beauty because you have always walked in courage.

Those of you who may be considering going into the military, I recommend reconsidering this choice. When the United States brings back the draft, many of you may do a difficult thing, which is to move to a different country. The government and politicians create war to fill their pockets. If you are in another country, you may not be able to come home for many years. ≫≪

Message to the American Media

≫≪ The owners of the media tell you what to write, and it is not the truth.

When you get sick and tired of having to state half-truths, look at better ways to serve your fellow Americans. Telling untruths, minimizing an issue, and misdirection are disservices to your readers. Ask yourself if this is why you decided to become a journalist. Look at why you wanted to be a journalist. It's not an easy job to stand for truth. Look at your truth and make your choices. Protect your freedom of speech, and do not use your position to manipulate the truth. It needs to be shared.

Q: How long will the economy disintegrate in America and around the world until everyone figures out that they are being lied to by the media?

DM: Unfortunately, this may not happen until after your economy collapses. Too many people do not know. They believe the media is telling them the whole truth and nothing but the truth! Even people with a large amount of school knowledge do not know about the media lying to them. They do not realize that knowledge is power, and think those of you who know about such things must be crazy. Later they will wish they had been as crazy as you!

Chapter 2

Economic Issues Weaken America's Foundation

≈≈ The Great Unraveling of Life as Humans Know It Has Begun. ≈≈

CONSTITUTION vs. Constitution

≈≈ Your beautiful, almost brand-new United States *for* America Constitution was designed for Americans. Over a hundred years ago, this was your Constitution until a new fraudulent constitution superseded the organic Constitution. The new corporation made a different United States *of* America—notice the change of words. That's the corporation.

One hundred and forty one years ago, the United States finances, much like your economy today, was challenging. The USA had just come out of a big war that almost bankrupted the country. The officials in your government were thinking, "How we can get money so we can pay the bills?"

It was not going to work if they said, "I would like to get some money. I'll pay you back. I promise." Congress needed to get a loan. Congress put towns together and had ten acres, but they still had to figure a way to turn that space into their own little country. They made up new laws and a new constitution and became the District of Columbia.

The only ones who could give them a loan were over in England. The English were not going to say, "Okay, I can shake your hand for all this money you want." What they did say was, "Let us help you set this up so we can give you a loan." The leaders of your country wanted this loan badly. One hundred and thirty-one years later, the bankers are still being paid. At that time, the House of Rothschild owned the banks in England. The Rothschilds wanted to control your country and the money. They had tried many times to take your beautiful, brand-new country and its beautiful Constitution hostage.

The land of America was the collateral. The new corporation said, "As the people of America work, they have to pay taxes to pay back the government. That's part of their privilege of being Americans; they get to be a part of our corporation." The people knew they were being taxed, but the corporation was presented in such a way that Americans thought they still had that very same beautiful Constitution and Bill of Rights. The corporation had enslaved the people of America by allowing them to think they were free and still sovereign. Americans really do *not* own their land. There is no such thing as private property for the "citizens" of America. This is but an illusion.

The United States of America is a corporation. In many places, it is illegal to collect rain that falls out of the sky onto your yard. The reason you cannot collect rainwater in a bucket is that your government owns the water rights and the land if it wants them. The term the government uses is "eminent domain." This means the government can steal the land away at any time and use it for what it desires.

If you're saving your water in a barrel, then your water bill isn't going to be as high. So there you have it! You pay state taxes and all the other fees, and this is why it is illegal to collect rainwater in many parts of your United States of America. It's an old law.

Your government owns the land that is America, and it can take your land from you with the laws. The government owns the land, so it can freely grab any part of your United States. President Nixon's environmental law was a way to keep the land pristine and to use it as collateral. The government can take a piece of wilderness, thousands of acres, all the beautiful areas in your United States, and say it is saving the land; you can only visit.

During the Vietnam War, in 1971, President Nixon did this to pay back a loan to a man named de Gaulle. De Gaulle wanted his money, and he wanted to be paid in gold. Nixon didn't want to give away all the gold in Fort Knox. Yes, they did have gold in Fort Knox in those days. Nixon thought he had a great idea to stop de Gaulle from taking all the gold, and it was great for the government. What is great for the government is not great for America. When Nixon took your silver dollars and said no more silver dollars, he took your dollar off the gold standard.

The government leader's job is to spend the money and let the Americans pay the taxes to pay off those loans. That's why you pay so much in taxes, and that's why in 2013 your taxes will rise.

The government owns your land. You pay rent on your land, which is yours. There are fewer and fewer people working, so they have to leave their homes. The government-controlled Freddie Mac and Fannie Mae are buying up large blocks of properties and offering them to investors. The investors are not in America. They are primarily in China. Freddie Mac and Fannie Mae say to the foreign investors, "Hey, they have all this property in America, and it's for sale. You can come and buy it." When the Chinese or any foreign investors come to buy the properties, they get a very special EB-5 visa. It gives incredible tax deductions and permanent residency. When people are hired to help with the business, those employees also get the same visa. The country that buys American land has to employ only ten U.S. citizens. Once the SEZ in Idaho is put in effect, SEZs may be set up in other areas of your United States and requires legislation at the national level.

Targeted Employment Areas and free trade zones will lead to large blocks of properties becoming Special Economic Zones (SEZs). China hopes to buy a SEZ in Idaho, which will become the arm of the Chinese Communist government. China, as I have stated, has never been your friend. They will bring in military and weapons and drop them from the sky onto their land. If you think about it, one of these properties is very close to the Boise airport. With SEZs the Chinese do not have to follow American rules or the US Constitution. It becomes their own zone, just like Washington, DC, has its own laws.

It is not like your land that is held in protection with the environmental law . The physical land is sold to a different country. They are taking away homes and people's property. Your government is taking homes Americans could not afford to live in any longer. Officials are saying how wonderful this is going to be for your state. Depending on how it's set up and used, it could be very dangerous.

A Chinese company in Texas now owns oil and gas in the United States. This is beginning to happen even more than it did in the past, because your economy is so bad that your government wants to get more money so it can spend more money. What I see is that Americans are doing this to America. The Chinese are not bad for doing this. It is good business for them.

There were not many land sales until 2008. Now many more people are buying land. Currently the government is physically selling property in California to investors. The policy is going to expire at the end of 2012 or in 2013. That's why there is such a big hurry to sell. The government will extend it.

Now you can see that the "constitution" is not the Constitution you have been led to believe. The altered constitution for the District of Columbia is an unconstitutional document. It is a forgery that supersedes the original, organic document.

☙❧

The research we did after the revelations from DreamMyst shows these insights are correct.

The Constitution was born on July 4, 1776. The United States with its carefully designed, brilliant Constitution and Bill of Rights limited the power of the government keeping the American people free of the tyranny of the government and was the champion of individual freedom and prosperity.[9]

Congress passed an unconstitutional document titled "An Act To Provide A Government for the District of Columbia" (Act of 1871), a ten-mile square parcel of land located between Maryland and Virginia.

---

9   The Most Successful Fraud in American History by Gary North http://www.lewrockwell.com/north/north445.html

Washington, DC, (the District of Columbia SEZ) is now the seat of the government of the "United States" (corporate America), removing the White House and our federal government from the constitutional United States. Citizens of the "United States of America" are presumed to reside in and operate from the District of Columbia. The new "constitution" supersedes the original Constitution.

The original United States Constitution was changed to "The Constitution of the United States of America." This act by Congress formed a "corporation" known as "the United States." The corporate constitution operates the economic capacity of "the United States" with foreign interests. The second fraudulent copy of the Constitution is the structure of the corporation and serves to benefit the corporation and *not* Americans. Congress had to create a new, reworded constitution because the original *does not* apply in Washington, DC. The original Constitution *can never* apply to Washington, DC. The "United States code" (remember, the term in quotation marks is the corporation, not the republic) Title 28 3002(15) (A) (B) (C) states that the "United States" is a corporation.

The new American republic is a corporation. The people do not have freedoms unless the corporation allows them to believe they do. This is why in 2012 under Obama's rule, our so-called liberties and freedoms are quickly eroding. Obama radically alters these freedoms using his authority as president every time he signs an executive order. Every president has done the same to some degree or another for 131 years.

The federal government owns the land and can use it as collateral or sell large chunks of American land to foreign countries. The corporation of the "United States" claims it as its own.

Your birth certificate says you are a sovereign. A social security number is a bank account number for the federal government. When you apply for a social security card, driver's license, or wedding license, you become a citizen by default of the United States of America.

For 131 years you have been led to think you had inalienable rights and sovereignty under the Constitution our forefathers drafted. The Constitution says the government derives its power from the people of the United States. Only the people under the original Constitution can be sovereign. The Constitution exists to serve and protect the people of the United States for America.

Americans struggling to live on low incomes are forced to rely, at least in part, on food stamps in order to make ends meet. Unemployment for October 2012 was 7.9%,[10] for many, unemployment checks have become a replacement income. The official US debt tally for November 11, 2012 is $16,278,932,378,520.93. Forty five million Americans have fallen into poverty levels with 3.5 million homeless, 18.5 million homes standing empty, with an all-time record number of foreclosures. Imagine for a moment what would happen if a national, outage of all federal entitlements came to a standstill. How would such a large percent of society receiving some sort of federal assistance react? With no paycheck or retirement pension benefits for federal workers, or social security checks, Medicare, and useless EBT cards, massive social unrest ushers in Martial Law.[11]

Major banks are working on a version of a living will in the event of an economic collapse. Many smaller banks have filed bankruptcy. Four hundred and twelve banks bankrupted in the four years from 2008 to 2011, compared to eleven banks in the five years from 2003 to 2007.

When you blow up a balloon, how big can it get before it pops? The economy in the United States is a balloon at its popping point. All it will take is for the euro to crash, and it easily can. China, Germany, and the euro keep America just under the popping point. Every time the United States prints money from thin air and the money devalues, China and the Eurozone deflate their currencies. If a country has a strong currency and desires to sell its products to the United States, it has to keep the value of its currency at the same level as the dollar so trading/buying in the United States continues. The value of the product needs to be at a price Americans can afford. Why do other countries do this? Because it is great business for them, but in truth it is bad business for America.

10   Analysis: Even at 7.9%, mostly good news for Obama http://www.usatoday.com/story/news/politics/2012/11/02/jobs-election-obama-romney-analysis/1675239/#

11   Food stamp system goes down, millions can't use cards http://www.myfoxorlando.com/story/20119120/food-stamp-system-down-millions-affected#ixzz2CkDkSiaR

We import most of our goods from other countries, even those things that say "Made in the USA." Those products have components made in other countries. An example of this would be our American car industry. America does not export even close to what we import. The trade deficit is so much against us. Before the 1970s, we exported much more than we imported; that is what made America strong. Other countries wanted American-made products, and only the rich were able to afford these products overseas. Americans used to have the best steel mills in the world and exported around the globe.

At one time America was the biggest manufacturing country in the world, with jobs to keep Americans working. Not so today. Corporate America sold the American people out. Americans used to have innovators and inventors who created new products that made jobs to produce the products sold. Then US companies began to outsource their work all over the world, giving technology to companies in other countries where the products were made.

Today you cannot buy an American TV, but not that long ago twenty-seven American television companies led the world in TV technologies. Koreans bought Zenith, the last American television company, to sell its patents.

In fact, the Chinese economy thirty years ago was worthless compared to the US economy. Now they have almost outdone us. Do you still wonder how this happened? We shipped thousands of our factories, millions of our jobs, and trillions of our dollars to other countries. Even small businesses in the United States cannot wait to get into bed with the Chinese. The reason? It is cheaper to do business in China than it is to order or have the parts made in the United States. So what do these countries do who now have made billions from American ingenuity? They loan the United States money to pay the bills, and rush to buy American land. I am sure they think we are very stupid for allowing them to do this.

The problem is *nothing* can save us from an economic crash, which will take the world's economy down as well. Until the crash, we will have either inflation, deflation, or both at the same time (hyperinflation). Disaster will ravage our economy. America would be better served to forgive mortgage debt and rebuild into a country that is sustainable once again. It can be done.

America was sustainable because our currency was backed by gold and because we taught our children to be critical thinkers. Until the Federal Reserve was established, America did not borrow more money than it could pay back. This is kind of like your checkbook. If your checkbook does not balance, do you write hot checks or deposit counterfeit money to balance your account? Won't doing so get you a federal prison sentence? Why is it the Federal Reserve Banks and our government are allowed to counterfeit, spending money they do not have? It will be many years before America can become king of the hill once more, but it never will if the Chinese keep buying American land.[12]

Nixon invented the Environmental Protection Agency, not to keep America beautiful or to help the environment. He set aside huge territories of American land with their vast natural resources to prove to the holders of foreign debt that US citizens were not drilling, mining, or otherwise developing those resources. Each president continues to take more of the land, claiming it as wetlands, a heritage river, or wilderness area, taking away the right of the people to use the land. It has nothing to do with conservation but everything to do with collateral. One of these days, Americans will wake up to find the land of the free and the home of the brave has a new property owner.

There are large quantities of distressed properties that the government is buying and selling to the highest bidder. The land is sold in blocks by mortgage companies owned by the government to investors in other countries.

China's super rich have created a phenomenon across the United States with an invasion of Chinese buying US properties. The most popular locations seem to be on the coasts, but other distressed properties are sought after as well. From 2003 to 2011, Rhodium, a global economic research firm, counted 236 private investment deals worth a total of $6.3 billion. Real estate is listed as the asset with the second-largest value for private Chinese investment in the United States.

Chinese investors paid $2.15 million cash for a restaurant complex on the Maumee River in Toledo, Ohio. Soon they put down another $3.8 million on sixty-nine acres of newly decontaminated land in

12   Why are the Chinese investing in Toledo? http://finance.fortune.cnn. com/2012/06/20/toledo-china-real-estate/

the city's marina district, promising to invest $200 million in a new residential-commercial development. Another Chinese firm spent $3 million for an aging hotel across a nearby bridge with a view of the minor league ballpark.[13]

In Texas, a Chinese company, CNOOC, is dealing with Chesapeake Energy. This is the largest purchase by anyone of an interest in US energy assets. Idaho has a Chinese national company interested in developing a 10,000–30,000 acre technology zone for industry, retail centers, and homes south of the Boise Airport.

In 1990, a loophole to get around immigration laws was created by the government. Known as EB-5, this loophole is a special green card that provides permanent US residency on the conditions that the foreign national invest one million dollars and create jobs for ten US citizens. Any employee the foreign national wants to bring over also receives EB-5 immigration status. Chinese state-owned companies receive massive tax breaks, encouraging immigration from China through the EB-5 program. The minimum investment in high-unemployment areas, such as East Toledo, is $500,000.

In addition, the government is talking about a Special Economic Zone (SEZ), which is "a geographical region that has economic and other laws that are more free-market-oriented than a country's typical or national laws. 'Nationwide' laws may be suspended inside a special economic zone."[14] What this means is that if SEZ zones were to pass legislature, the Chinese landowners would be able to create their own laws within the SEZ area. EB-5[15] visas can be issued in what are called "Targeted Employment Areas," and transfer of property title alone cannot create a legal "zone."

It is bad enough the government of the United States buys our land. To allow China to buy the rest and not follow the same rules as Americans is a nightmare for the United States. National security alarms should be sounding.

---

13   http://finance.fortune.cnn.com/2012/06/20/toledo-china-real-estate/ 11-19-2012

14   Wikipedia, "Special economic zone" http://en.wikipedia.org/wiki/Special_Economic_Zone. 11-19-2012

15   EB-5 visahttp://en.wikipedia.org/wiki/EB-5_visa

Economic Insights

❧ Your silver will continue to skyrocket. It has already begun rising and will continue to do so. Now, following up with the economy, if your government continues to put pretend dollars, like Monopoly money, into the economy, what will happen is that the economy and the recession will continue. The US government is playing a very dangerous game. All the money floating around only buys a little bit of time. Inflation is the high prices you are paying now, compared to what you were paying last month.

Some of this has to do with your food cost. Inflation is going to continue and get worse. This is taking the long, slow way. The short, quick, fast way would be if your economy crashes.

During the past four years, inflation has caused turkeys to be more expensive. In deflation, even with reduced prices, fewer turkeys are bought for dinner. With fewer turkeys, fewer people are needed to produce the turkeys for market. Turkey companies make less money, so they buy less turkey feed, and the farmers who grow corn and soy don't make very much money. Turkey companies will need fewer people to work, so turkey companies will decrease their workforce, cut back on pay and benefits, and give the remaining workers a heaver workload. People who lose their turkey jobs and cannot find work will default on their bills and won't be able to buy a turkey for their holidays. When large amounts of people fail on their mortgages, credit cards, and loans, banks go broke. People will lose banking jobs. One thing affects everything else. *No one* will have a turkey dinner—unless you are the turkey farmer who is not making any money, but still has too many turkeys he can't sell.

The dollars the Federal Reserve is printing make the depression worse. Depression/inflation is hyperinflation; this is when everything is extremely difficult to buy, but no one can afford to buy food anyway.

America is not based on making physical products but on technology. Americans today do not have the tools or the manufacturing companies to fall back on. Many people will not know how to survive.

Your United States has at least a few months. Germany paid money to the banks. Had the euro not been given to those banks, the United States in a few months would have had an economic crash. This has been postponed for a little longer.

Americans still have time to buy supplies, to work at their jobs, and to prepare for the changes that are coming. As I mentioned earlier, in about eighteen months the crash will already have occurred. It is in fact happening but may take three to eighteen months.

❦

Q: Can we expect inflation?

DM: Inflation will blow up like a balloon.

Q: How expensive will gasoline become in the future?

DM: Gasoline will go over five dollars per gallon and will continue to rise. The high price of gas could easily make buying food and necessities almost impossible to afford.

Q: Are there actions to prevent or minimize an economic collapse?

DM: No; now it is too late. Close the borders, bring the majority of overseas military home, and keep as much money and jobs in the United States as you can by supporting small businesses and not corporate businesses.

Q: Will the economy be bad all over the globe?

DM: The United States will have the weakest economy it has ever experienced, followed by England. And yes, it will be a global crash.

Q: Will Americans get help from other countries during the economic depression?

DM: All countries, not just the United States of America, will have struggles with loss of electricity, a poor economy, and food shortages.[16] Everyone globally is going to go through these challenges. The United States is the first link in the chain of countries that starts it all off. Some countries will last a little bit longer, but ultimately everyone has to take care of themselves, their countries, their communities, and their people.

Q: Will China continue to buy United States debt?

DM: Yes, and China will continues to buy US land. You could say that China owns the United States. The debt will not begin to decrease. The United States will default on the debt and the businesses it has bought.

Q: When people buy land or a home, they think they own the property. Does anyone in America still really own a house anymore with the different things the President has done with regard to the executive orders? And how is the small print stated on the deeds?

DM: Look at your paperwork. Look at the tiny writing on the papers, and you will see that you truly do not own your property. You do not own the land your house sits on. If your government wants your home and your land, it can take the property away. That is called eminent domain.

Q: The only things we really manufacture anymore are weaponry and things of destruction, right? What I have heard from different sources is we're even in the process of selling off a lot of that technology now.

DM: This again is America giving to other countries the technologies which helped to create America as a world power. When you give away the factories, the money from the sales of the product, and then sell the technology to a different country, America has less and is dependent on other countries for the products America could have made. America used to have many companies that made televisions. Today America orders its televisions from other countries.

---

16   GrainCorp Shares Rise on Archer Bid http://www.nytimes.com/2012/10/23/business/global/graincorp-shares-rise-on-archer-bid.html

Q: Right. I do not think there are any televisions made in this country anymore, and most of the companies that made TVs here sold out to other companies in other countries.

DM: That made money for the person who had the patent, but it didn't help the United States or the people who could have had those jobs.

Q: Obama prevented the United States from building a pipeline from north to south in our country. We could have had our own oil. Instead of that, he stopped work on this and gave billions to South American countries to drill for oil. Thse countries will own the oil companies on their lands. Why would he do that?

DM: Obama uses debt as a form of global redistribution. He takes away from Americans the ability to create an income. Expect an economic crash in three to eighteen months. How deeply the sideways slide will be depends on what your leaders choose to do. Do not let the state of your government or the economy brings you to your knees; let it bring you to your feet! Awaken the sleeping giant that is America.

Food Inflation

 Weather is changing drastically. There will be more rain, colder winters, and drought in the summer. This will cause growers throughout your land to produce fewer crops.

Food inflation will hit hard and grow worse in 2013 and 2014. Food prices will rise so high that people will only be able to dream of sugar plums dancing in their heads.

When the economy crashes, prices will skyrocket even more. Begin to save now; you will be glad you did. The days of cheap food are over. Prices will continue to increase. In fact, the dollar won't buy you what it used to for food or necessities, let alone for entertainment. The wheat supply will continue to shrink. Bread will cost twenty-three dollars a loaf in fifteen to twenty years.

George Soros, a billionaire financier, now owns the United States' third largest conglomerate in the food industry. He purchased sixteen-grain elevators at twelve locations in eastern Washington in late March 2011.

This works for a globalist government but does not work for the American people. When corporations control the majority of the food market, prices are set by corporate decisions and the manipulation of supply. This means that if prices for food are too low in the United States, the grain is sold in other countries, creating an artificial supply problem in the United States, which produces the grain.

In a world of inflation and lack of jobs, 18 percent of Americans are struggling to feed their families. As prices continue to soar, many of the poor will go hungry for days at a time because they cannot afford to put food on the table. The drought of 2012 may force Americans to cut back on meals in 2013 because the cost of groceries will be higher.

Wheat, corn, and soybean harvests are scorching in the fields. This is the worst drought since the Dust Bowl of the 1930s, with 80 percent of the land parched and dry. The growing cycle for these plants is ten to twelve months before they reach the supermarket. Expect pork and beef prices to go through the ceiling.

The severe drought of 2012 is going to cause huge food inflation price hikes over the next eighteen months. Global corn prices have surged 23 percent in July, worsened by the severe deterioration of maize crop prospects in the United States, due to the excessive heat and drought conditions during critical stages of crop development.[17] Americans are used to having a land of plenty, and in the past 52 percent of fruits and vegetables have ended up in the garbage. This will change when people cannot afford to buy food. Even if we have enough food to feed the world, how do you feed your family if you do not have the money to buy food?

---

17   http://www.upi.com/Business_News/2012/08/09/US-drought-sparks-global-food-price-hike/UPI-83841344535114/ 11-19-2012

GrainCorp Shares Rise on Archer Bid http://www.nytimes.com/2012/10/23/business/global/graincorp-shares-rise-on-archer-bid.html

Gold and Silver:

᭸᭶ Oooo, I like gold and silver! They are so pretty. It is a precious metal and will always increase in value. Then it will increase and increase and increase; gold will be worth so much money that nobody will be able to buy it. So what will happen? It will come back down over a period of years and then restabilize.

Junk silver is old silver coins. If you buy smaller silver coins, they are easier to put away and save. You can take them out and look at them once in a while. But if you buy great, big pieces of silver that feel really good in your hands, guess what? Those are harder to use. Save them for your future.

᭸᭶

Many economists are saying the United States will be back on the gold standard within the next five years. If the gold standard replaces the fiat in the very near future, America just might hobble toward becoming a stronger, economically solvent nation. Unfortunately, by the time this occurs, it will be too late to prevent the economic crash.[18]

Currently America is the superpower of the world. China is in the process of changing to a gold-backed currency, making their currency very solid and strong. China buys US debt to sell products to America. Chinese wealth stems from, the products Americans buy. The amount of debt China buys from America is small compared to the products they sell.

China is buying gold and trading US bonds issued to them for paying off American debt. Then China exchanges the US bonds for gold and gold certificates at a loss. If the Chinese continue, in a few short years, they will be the superpower. What will happen then?

A rude awakening is in store for Americans. George Soros sold his shares in JP Morgan and Citibank and put his money in gold. Only gold and precious metals will protect you from financial crisis.

18   George Soros Called Gold The 'Ultimate Bubble' Just Two Years Ago http://www.businessinsider.com/soros-gold-action-speaks-louder-than-trumpeted-bubble-words-2012-8

Our economic and governmental shifts give a rocky, unstable platform. It is only a matter of time before inflation leaps forward. When people dump their assets, like real estate, stocks, and treasury bonds, a domino effect will begin. Buy as much gold and silver as you can possibly afford every month, beginning today if you have not yet done so.

Gold has been a safe haven for countries across the globe. The United States holds only 10 percent of the world's total. You have at least ten years before the gold bubble peaks. Continue to buy gold, silver, and platinum; these metals will be more valuable than cash or real estate. Expect gold and silver prices to skyrocket at the end of 2012 when inflation hits the hardest.

Consider investments in gold and silver (not stocks) as your retirement plan to survive the economic crash. Years from now, when gold and silver revalue, when the economy restabilizes, you will use the gold to establish a new life and make the economy strong.

If you have to choose between investing in silver or food, then yes, invest in those things that will keep you alive. It will be necessary to stockpile one to two years of supplies and water-making tools for each member of your family. If you live away from the city, a two-year supply of these items will allow you to plant, harvest, and provide livestock like rabbits, goats, and chickens for reproduction and butchering.

Credit Cards

Prior to 1971, one man with an average job made enough money to support his family and have a savings account. The United States went off the gold standard in 1971. It now takes two people working and credit card spending to maintain the same lifestyle. Going off the gold standard has not only put the nation in debt but also put the average family in credit card debt as well.

Many credit cards are simply adjustable-rate loans. When interest rates rise, so will the rates on many of the cards. Economists say to pay these off as soon as possible. You can pay down loan and credit debt by seeking a lower interest rate. This makes a huge difference over time, and you can still put some silver away. This may save your credit. But if there is a downward spiral, stop paying on your credit cards. Priorities like food and shelter come first. Better might be to pay the minimum on your mortgage now, forget about your credit card debt, and buy as much silver and gold as you possibly can. DreamMyst says the crash could occur anywhere from three to eighteen months from now. Even she does not know when this calamity will hit. If it strikes in a couple of months, then paying off your cards will have been a waste of money.

DreamMyst says to pay them off if you can and then buy as much silver and gold with plastic as you can. When the balloon bursts, at least you have silver and or gold to use later. The more financially independent you become, the better you can protect yourself.

What will happen to your finances when the economy, stock market, housing prices, and government debt crash at the same time? America is headed for some extremely rocky times which have not been experienced since the Great Depression.

DreamMyst says it is possible for a future stock market crash to begin near the same date as the first Great Depression. A crash will not happen during an election year, which leaves 2013 looking very bleak. The 1929 stock market crash occurred on Thursday, October 24. In 1932, when the crash was completed, stocks had lost nearly 90 percent of their value.

The bursting of the credit and housing bubble will be the least of our concerns in the next few years as we experience massive deflation. Printing stimulus money needs to end, but that will not happen because it would cause the economy to crash now.

There will be a mortgage implosion within the next few years, due to the 401ks and IRAs coming due from retirement accounts. By law, people have to cash in six percent of their wealth in retirement. There has been a steady increase in people taking money out of retirement accounts to pay bills. The huge withdrawal of these monies by the baby boomers will cause a stock market crash any time during the years 2013–2016 as inflation continues to rise.

Record amounts of new debt and the increase of inflation occur when governments keep printing money. This forces all countries to print more money, creating a currency war. China will stop buying our debt.

Hyperinflation is inflation and deflation occurring at the same time. If you have your savings in stock and paper, those savings will become worthless. The United States will experience hyperinflation like in 1779, when George Washington wrote, "A wagon-load[19] of money will scarcely purchase a wagon-load of provisions."

Americans who are vigilant and prepared will be ready for economic hardship when the money from local, state, and federal governments is nothing more than a tarnished memory. The average American standard of living will revert to the way it was in the late thirties and early forties.

In June 2010, DreamMyst informed us the United States government has the largest debt in world history and the worst economic since the Great Depression. There will be great economic changes, including falling tax revenue, because of pension promises coming due. Food prices will increase, and the value of the dollar will continue to decrease. Soup or food lines will be necessary to feed the people within the thirty-six to forty-eight months.

At the end of 2013, the United States economy spins into a period of deflation. Follow the bouncing ball as the stock market spirals downward, then picks up for a bit and appears to do well, and then drops lower, with a financial crash very possible after taxes rise again after January 1, 2013. Due to issues of approaching financial crisis such as the ending of the Bush tax cuts, American households will experience increased tax hits.

The wealthy are hit first. Then the United States government will target the middle-class. Finally, seniors living off their investment income will be hit the hardest. Even with all the tax increases, it will not be enough to solve the debt crisis.

---

19   http://www.history.org/foundation/journal/summer07/counterfeit.cfm 11-19-2012

In 2013, the Dow Jones Industrial Average will drop into the 9000s, the same as in 2008 and early 2009. Unemployment increases. People will spend less money, and the economy will go deeper into a financial abyss. In 2013, you can expect 10 to 30 percent higher inflation with rising interest rates, higher taxes, and more US debt lurking in the shadows.

Investing

৯৵ Get out of the stock market. If you can afford it, platinum is worth collecting and may become a new kind of money. If you have platinum jewelry, put it in your stash of precious metals, as it is an overlooked investment.

Diversify your investments—10 percent in a bank account for paying bills, 20 percent in food, 20 percent in gold, silver, or junk silver, and 50 percent in land for food production. Buy livestock and seeds. Buy your property away from the cities. Invest in water, food, and nonfood items like bars of soap, Toothpaste, floss, and toilet tissue for home storage.

Stocks

৯৵ All of the economies throughout the world flow into each other. If countries backed by the euro crash, then in the United States, a great big bubble of pretend money will pop and stocks will become dead, nonexistent, and useless. Unfortunately, if the companies who issued the stock you owned rebuild, they will change the name of the business, and the stock you had will not be worth the paper it is printed on.

For those who want to take investment action now, it might be a good idea to look into buying storage units to rent. Millions of people who will lose their homes will need to put their things in storage. Later the storage units can become living units. This investment will make some money now. Buy or create RV parks. RV parks have everything you need for a comfortable living environment. People need to have a place to live while they still have money. If you're in a safe area with water, you have the beginnings of a community.

Gold and silver coins are first investment choices. If you have a retirement fund like an IRA or a 401k, you might be able to take out some of the money you have invested. Some IRAs and 401ks will let you take money out without a penalty for buying a house for the first time, or if you get a disability check, go to school, or are almost ready to retire. You will still have to pay taxes on a withdrawal because the taxman hasn't gone away! Borrow money from your retirement accounts and buy gold and silver coins.

If people wait to take action, there will not be much in their retirement funds when your stock market begins to crash. It won't crash to the bottom, but it's going to creep down pretty low.

There is still the possibility of a solar flare or an EMP that will take down the electricity. With no electricity or Internet, the economy will crash and hits bottom. Without electricity, banks will close.

∽∾

Imagine watching helplessly as stocks plummet and the value of government bonds and life insurance are destroyed. Pensions will become unstable, and the money you have worked so carefully to save will shrink to nothing. There will be no warning of when it will occur. Write down three to five things you can do now to provide security and prosperity for your family.

Make provision for at least one year of food and water for your family. Keep your fuel tank full and cash equal to your monthly paycheck in reserve.

Real Estate

∽∾ The people who have money to invest know how to make a lot of money during a depression. There will not be better loans. Hmmm, whoever is making the money has the control, correct? Freddie, Fannie, and HUD are all government controlled. Banks will not make it easier for Americans to get a loan or to refinance their homes. It will become harder and harder to sell your home or get a loan. Refinance if you are able to refinance your house.

Pay the minimum amount if you have a fixed mortgage rate; it is less of a liability. If it is less of a liability, you may have more money to buy silver, gold, food, and other necessities. There will be fewer people able to buy homes in the next year because of the stock market and economic changes.

Buy property in a rural area. If you plan to buy a safe home, it is a good idea to look into what you will need and how much it will cost before loans are entirely too difficult to get. If you can afford it, buy a survival home now, but no later than the summer of 2014. It's getting more and more difficult, but there are still ways to buy real estate.

ॐ≫

Through Fannie Mae and Freddie Mac, the United States government owns or guarantees half of the outstanding residential mortgages in America. Within the next three to five years, your home's value will drop by 25 percent or more.

In the face of looming real estate mortgage foreclosure, there is a law from the Great Depression that allows you to walk away from your mortgage and the loan loss on the property. Simply put the key in the mailbox and walk away. Under this law, banks do not have the legal power to recover the outstanding balance

Life Insurance

If you have whole life insurance, it is a good idea to take out a lump sum payment and buy water, food, and gold. Insurance companies will fold, and those that manage to survive will have huge losses due to investment in long-term bonds, stocks, and commercial real estate when inflation increases to ten percent.

Student Loans

The government is offering information on its student loans disability discharge program. Go to studentloans.gov and click on the "Loan Discharge" link to see if you qualify for a total and permanent disability (TPD) discharge.

Banks

≈◠≼ You won't be very happy when you find out your bank went on holiday! Pay attention to the euro. In regard to the monetary system, after the economic collapse, the United States will not carry the standard currency. Countries that have the most gold will have the position of power. Will a new, physical money system be created? Yes, and it will happen globally. People around the world will set up new monetary systems that will work for them in each country, which is good.

≈◠≼

During the years 2008 to 2011, four hundred and twelve banks went bankrupt, compared to eleven banks during the five-year period from 2003 to 2007. In 2012 alone, thirty-nine banks have failed.

All nations aligned with a fiat paper standard are susceptible to economic ruin. Countries with a trade surplus and genuine manufacturing capacity are a better investment. The Swiss franc may be a more stable fiat currency.

Open your own bank for protection from the collapse of the dollar. Yes, it is legal to own your own bank, take out loans, and pay the loans back to your personal bank. If you do not own your own bank, keep some of your money in bills until the economy crashes, but do not keep it in the bank. You will not have your money or your safe deposit box available to you when the banks crash. Safe deposit boxes are not a safe place to store your silver and gold coins. If you do have valuables in a bank safe deposit box, remove them and store them in your home or an outside hiding place that is easy to gain access to in an emergency.

During a bank collapse, no one will be performing bank transactions based upon the laws. Banks will close their doors, and anything inside will remain inaccessible for an indefinite period. A banking holiday may mean you can kiss your safe deposit box contents good-bye. The FDIC does not insure contents of safe deposit boxes, so if the bank is looted by rioting mobs, you lose.

A failed bank insured by the FDIC will have arrangements made for another institution to take over and conduct business. If there is no buyer for the failed institution, the FDIC will arrange, within a few days, for you to remove the contents in your box. When banks collapse, they are not obligated to return your valuables.

Where to Live During the Economic Depression

ॐॐ The United States is going through big, big changes. At this point, the biggest problem is the economy, but there are also earth changes. Other countries are going through changes as well. The United States is modern but does not have the resources or knowledge to live a simpler lifestyle. That will be hard for Americans to do. For a while, Americans may be behind, but they will come out front again.

Some countries may not be affected very much at all, other than financially. If you move to any country, Switzerland is the best for more than economic reasons. Switzerland has more of the values and beliefs in freedom like the United States. There are mountain peaks high enough so people can be safe.

ॐॐ

Q: Will we return to being a country with factories and manufacturing? Is the industrial age ending in the United States?

DM: It has pretty much ended, but equipment and buildings will still be there. America does not manufacture very many of its own products. This can be changed, but it will take focus and determination among your people to move beyond survival, to work as a community that can prosper and grow.

Q: Are there proactive steps that can be beneficial before the government creates a worse economy?

DM: No. Prepare now to survive. Buy water, food, gold, and silver.

Chapter 3

Difficulties Mount as Events Unfold

෨෨ Once upon a time and many lifetimes ago, when the universes came into being, there were all these planets just floating around, minding their own business. One big, busy planet was roughhousing around, showing off its big energy. All at once it was going so fast it couldn't stop. It banged really hard into another planet, and then another and another. Boy! There was a Big Bang so big that all the planets bumped into a new solar system. (In 2010, DreamMyst was asked by a curious seven-year-old to describe how the earth was created. This was her explanation of the Big Bang.)

෨෨

Relaxing on the porch, listening as the thunder bellows and rolls, as streaks of lightning flash across the sky, the cloud behind the rainbow illuminates its colors radiantly. I am in awe of the powerful wonders of my world. Even the front-yard tree is special and amazing as it offers shade from the summer heat and sun. She is home for the hummingbirds with wings rapidly beating as they flit back and forth to the feeder, drinking the sweet nectar to sustain their lives. Later, as the sun drops, the colors of pink, blue, and orange bless the horizon. A quail family crosses the yard in line. A month ago, the babies looked like little walnuts with legs. Now they follow their mother as she hops on the fence. The whoosh of their wings lifts them into the air as they fly into the welcoming branches of the tree. It is at these moments I wonder how much longer we will be able to enjoy nature's day-to-day happenings and this normal way of life.

Earth Shifts

᯽᯽ One of the things I think is very interesting coming from where I exist is that, in your solar system, a ribbon wraps around your Mother Earth. This ribbon attracts cosmic and universal particles, which protects your earth from cosmic rays. My own energy exists even further beyond those cosmic rays.

Your solar system is special. Where your planet lives in the solar system is perfect for human life. There is something like a great big bubble of protection around your solar system and around your planet as well. When you have this kind of energy from all these beautiful particles, it's important to know how all of this energy is helping to change your planet. This is why, for the first time in thousands and thousands of years, all the planets are lining up—why the sun is throwing out many solar flares. Energy is building to a high and powerful level. When the solar flares and earth changes occur, they pump up the planet's energy. Not only do they increase Mother Earth's energy but your energy as well. You are just as affected as the planet by these energy shifts and changes.

This ribbon of energy has always been. It's like a piece of tape that particles stick to. That is what creates the ribbon and is going to help protect the earth. It might be good to visualize this as a lovely ribbon tied up in a bow wrapped around your planet.

In 2012 the earth will move through what is called the "Disc of the Plane." All planets will move through the center of the Milky Way. Earth will be shaken around, but it will keep moving. At the end of 2012, there will be bigger solar flares shooting from the sun.

This is why you need to protect yourselves. With your earth going through all these changes, the solar system will work its way out of the Milky Way years later. Large solar flares will continue. The energies from the flares will cause natural disasters, leading humankind into the end of an old age. The new age will bring transitions and transformations of a new life.

Earth has never gone through these types of changes with human beings on the planet, and it's best to be prepared. It is not only the economy shifting so quickly, but also the environment. Your planet is changing dramatically. The changes your planet is experiencing are very much like human birth. Physical changes happen when a woman becomes pregnant, and then there is the explosion of the birth experience. Earth, or Gaia as it is called, is in a pregnancy.

Global warming or global freezing does not cause what is occurring. The movement of Mother Earth is creating change within her very core—much like an unborn baby kicking. She has given birth many times. Each time, a new creation is brought into existence.

Earth produces a force field from deep within its core that protects human life. Everything strives for balance. This is a good thing because it protects your planet from space radiation and solar storms.

The magnetosphere is weakening, causing the magnetic poles to shift and new poles to shoot up. This shifting of the planet causes ice to thaw in every icy corner of the earth. The Arctic glaciers, which are the fresh water supply you drink, are melting twice as fast as they did forty years ago. If the earth's surface gets warm enough to melt the ice in Antarctica, your planet will have a big problem. There is not another place on earth that is colder to create balance if the ice caps melt.

Some claim if the ice caps melt, the water level will only rise two hundred and fifty feet. When the ocean heats even a little, it expands enough to notice. A rise in temperature by a half degree has an effect on your planet, and balance is disturbed. You will have global warming of the entire planet.

The biggest cities in the world are on the seacoasts. In the United States, there are Los Angeles, New York, San Francisco, and Miami. If your oceans rise twenty feet, you will need to evacuate due to flooding, especially during storms. When the ocean levels rise two hundred feet, all of these cities will be underwater. Countries such as Indonesia will be below water. It will be a gigantic disaster.

Farmland located at low elevations means crops and land ruined by salt water, produces food shortages. In this case, even if you have the money to buy food, there will be none to buy. Farmers will need to relocate to elevated areas, where the land is rockier and less suited to growing crops.

Diseases such as malaria and influenza will spread because the new standing water will be a breeding ground for mosquitos and other insects.

Wildlife will suffer. Some species may become extinct. Ringed seals and polar bears will become extinct. Snowy owls, lemmings, reindeer, and caribou will migrate north to survive.

Global warming is naturally occurring and it cannot be stopped. It has happened multiple times. The rate of increase in global warming is due to humankind. When the ice caps melt, the global water level will increase. This will change the ecosystem. Earth plates will shift, creating tsunamis and earthquakes. All of these will affect your world.

It will be warm in places where it used to be cold. It will be wet in places where it used to be dry. The melting ice caps and glaciers will not only affect your ocean. The melting will change the ocean currents and the way dolphins and whales live. Some islands are already gone because of the rising waters. The Cape Verde Islands will disappear under the depths. Hawaii will disappear except for the highest tips of the mountains.

You can expect still more weather changes and consequences of those weather changes. I promise you will see hurricanes, earthquakes, tornadoes, and flooding throughout your world.

෴

Q: Will global warming increase, and if yes, what effects will that have within the United States?

DM: Global warming will increase, but so many people will say, "I don't know why they say global warming is even real because it has been so much colder where I live, or so much hotter where I live." Global warming could be considered global freezing. And yes, more of that will occur, and more weather changes will occur in 2012 and beyond.

Q: Will there be any major natural disasters in 2011 within the United States, similar to the destruction of Hurricane Katrina?

DM: There will be more flooding and tornados. Winters will be more than what people are used to in some areas. But as far as disasters in the United States, not currently.

Q: Is it true magnetic north is constantly changing and currently moving toward Russia at a rate of about forty miles per year?

DM: Yes, and your planet is creating new magnetic poles to keep it balanced. Magnetic poles pop up anywhere because the earth's major purpose is to seek balance. The rapid shifts in the earth's magnetic poles have caused the birds and fish to die from a natural poison similar to cyanide.

Q: World scientists have stated the earthquakes in Japan, Chile, and New Zealand in 2011 moved the continents by a few inches. Is the movement the reason why the sun came up early in Greenland?

DM: As the ancient Somalis and the Hopi Indians have stated, this is a transition period of what is coming for your planet. This is the end of one cycle and the beginning of another. The large number of birds and fish dying was the first stage.

Q: Will there be natural disasters in other countries?

DM: There will be disasters in other countries. There will be more earthquakes, more tsunamis, and a big water earthquake will happen in Japan.

Q: DreamMyst, in 2010 you warned us of a tsunami and earthquakes for 2011 through 2012. The tsunami that devastated Japan's coast on March 11, 2011, was the fifth largest recorded in the world. It occurred hours after a massive earthquake. The 9.0 earthquake you predict, is that going to be along the Pacific Ring of Fire?

DM: The great earthquake in Japan created two volcanic eruptions, one in Russia and one in Indonesia, which is a part of the Pacific's burning Ring of Fire, an arc of volcanoes and fault lines encircling the Pacific Basin. In the future, there will be many earthquakes and volcanos. Your planet is waking up. Disasters could be in Russia and any number of places in Asia. This has not happened before.

Plates are shifting in the oceans and on land because of the pressure put on the planet from the magnetic poles balancing this means more earthquakes. The burning Ring of Fire is activated. Look at the volcanoes. Many volcanoes have begun to erupt at the same time. The plates are moving up and down, releasing pressure. The shifting of the plates on your earth creates sinkholes. The pressure creates great cracks and crevices in your earth and literally rips apart your earth, creating a deep hole. These forces build up gases that need to be released.

The Cayman Islands will have another big sinkhole. Florida may also have inland sinkholes. The sinkholes and cracks appearing for no reason are forewarnings of something about to happen.

The year 2011 was the beginning of the rumblings of the earth. Earthquakes, volcanoes, tornados, and flooding will increase in numbers. The solar flares trigger the tornadoes and flooding. The sun and the earth are setting the tectonic plates to shift. Massive amounts of water trigger earthquakes. Plates shift, becoming less stable.

So what happens if some of this water is drained, like the Mississippi River? The United States of America's food sources will go away because the water will drain into the farmlands and ruin crops. It is a difficult choice, but the water needs to be released. A fault line is located under the Mississippi River. A disaster almost like a tsunami could be triggered from the water weight of the Mississippi River.

Q: In 2011, there were fifty-two small earthquakes, registering at 3.0 or under, in Puerto Rico during a seven-day period.

DM: It is a weakened area. Puerto Ricans regularly experience small earthquakes. There will be earthquake activity in South America also. There is a tip of Puerto Rico that is weak. Should that area break off, and slide off into the water, it will cause a tsunami in Florida traveling up to New York, causing flooding. The heated flow of water mixing with cold water makes a big hurricane. Winds from a hurricanes cause damage the yet biggest issue is what is happening in the water itself. The movements of the plates in the subduction zone at the bottom of the Atlantic Ocean are shifting all the way to New York. There will be earthquakes in Mexico, Russia, and Asia. These earthquakes are like a band around your planet, and the cause is the shifting of the magnetic poles.

You will feel an earthquake in New York. (This happened as DreamMyst said. A 5.8 magnitude earthquake in Virginia rattled the East Coast and New York City on August 23, 2011.) The earthquakes in California are averaging over one hundred a day, with some in Oregon, Utah, and the state of Washington.

You need to know these things to prepare for your survival. These events are happening sooner rather than later. If people don't know about these changes, they will have a hard time getting prepared and may not survive. So many humans do not want to look at what is happening in their physical world. Many believe if they pray enough, it is going to change. The cycle will finish.

The earth wobbles a bit differently as it rotates on a shifted axis since the magnitude 9.0 earthquake/tsunami hit Japan on March 11, 2011. The Inuit people in the Arctic, who navigate by the sun, moon, and stars, have clearly noticed a change. The day is shorter, the sunset is not where it used to sit, and the moon seems to be a bit further away. The planet is shifting.

Deep within the bowels of the earth, a spinning, molten, inner core spins faster than the earth above. The temperature of this gyrating core is about the same as the sun. Earth's magnetic field originates from the seething and surging giant spinning magnet that is shifting the magnetic poles. Since 1989, it has shifted by about thirty-five miles a year toward Siberia. If this continues, the magnetic latitudes will shift northwest, and eventually we can expect the North Pole to become the South Pole. Siberia will become the center of a new arctic circle. Until then, we can expect mighty floods, hurricanes, tornadoes, earthquakes, and volcanic eruptions at record levels. Eventually this will correct itself, with the United States getting weather that is more moderate.

Animals and humans will either adapt or die as nothing can alter natural earth shifts. The geomagnetic force maintains the position of the magnetic poles.

Weather patterns have changed. Honeybees are confused about the warm 2012 winter. Flowers bloomed in February, and honeybees were seen in places like St, Charles and St. Louis, Missouri, which would normally have frozen lakes and rivers. Birds were back in New York. In upstate New York, the black bear woke early. In western North Carolina, the daffodils were up, rose bushes had lots of new growth, and the magnolia was trying to bloom.

The US government's Department of Agriculture states that plants that used to grow in New Orleans will now grow in latitudes hundreds of miles further north, in areas like Missouri, Kentucky, and North Carolina.

DreamMyst suggests paying attention to the signs your world is giving you. In this way, you will know when it is time to prepare for the earth shifts ahead.

Within four days of each other there were numerous earthquakes throughout the world. A 6.2 earthquake occurred on August 10, 2012 in the Fox Islands, Aleutian Islands, and Alaska. A day later Iran was hit with a 6.4, and ten minutes later a 6.3 earthquake, leaving over three hundred people dead and five thousand injured. A strong 6.3 quake on August 12 hit China. A powerful 7.7 quake jolted both Japan and Russia on August 14.

Japan is the site of convergence for several of the earth's tectonic plates. It seems when the plates start shifting, there are swarms of earthquakes set off in different areas, with an increase in volcanic activity.

Solar Flares and Geomagnetic Storms

❧❧ Cataclysmic changes are cleansing the earth. Solar flares affect your planet. This is the beginning of a period when the Hopi Indians talk about going under the ground. A change will lead to other changes as the planet lines itself up in a certain pattern with the Disc of the Plane.

It will be interesting to see the extent of the weather changes. As I have stated, there have been a lot of earthquakes and volcanoes on your planet, which began when the earth's core leaked a poisonous gas, and lava flowed from the volcanoes in your Pacific Ocean.

Q: On December 21, 2012, the sun will rise and intersect the Milky Way. Scientists say this planetary event will happen for the first time in approximately 26,000 years. How will the December 21, 2012, planetary event affect people? How will it affect the earth?

DM: Hmm. Everything is connected by energy. On December 21, 2012, as the earth begins its journey through the Disc of the Plane, the planets will align in their proper order for this cycle. While the earth is lining up, your planet will be bobbing up and down, and it will not come through the other side of the Disk of the Plane until many years later. Earth is going to move through a lot of different types of, hmm, planetary debris. Your planet will be rocking and rolling and shaking a little bit. The sun is doing what it needs to do, and continues to become even brighter and hotter. The solar flares will get really strong and big.

Q: Is it true that government scientists and politicians are aware of the major earth changes that are going to happen?

DM: Yes. The government is preparing for the survival of special people, but they are not preparing for the average, dispensable American. Disasters help with population control. As events escalate, move into an isolated area. You are going to be better off.

Q: Do the nine thousand people who lost their jobs with NASA know about the solar flares that are going to hit the earth?

DM: It depends on what their jobs were. Some of them worked in different parts of the program. This is why scientists, astronauts, and NASA are moving away from Florida. Do you really think that your government is going to inform the public that life as you know it is over? The government is not saying very much. It does not want panicked people.

Q: Is it possible to predict exactly when the United States will be hit by a super solar flare?

DM: No, but scientists can track solar flares days in advance. Your sun builds up heat in an area, and it ejects a flare, kind of like spitting. If a human being were to spit, you would have a general idea of direction. The sun doesn't aim. It's just spitting and shooting solar flares off. When it spits off a powerful solar flare, a geomagnetic storm pushes hard and fast toward the earth.

Radiation penetrates the protective shield around your planet. It can hit anywhere, in not only the United States, but other countries as well.

Q: When will the super solar flare activity burn out electricity?

DM: Even if this does not occur by 2014, it will happen in the years after. All it will take is one solar flare hitting one electrical transformer. That will easily create a chain reaction that knocks out electricity in different states, almost like a domino effect. One solar flare hit can put a number of states in different areas of the United States completely in the dark at the same time. When there is no electricity, you will need to do more things in the daylight hours. You will need an alternative light system. Oil lamps are good. Olive oil is good for food and oil lamps.

Expect to see northern lights in the sky where you've never seen northern lights before. Auroras are not caused by solar flares but are the interaction of the earth's magnetic field and the stream of charged particles springing from the sun. Solar flares make them brighter, but auroras exist without solar flares.

There will be other signs, other weather changes. When a solar flare is released from the sun, get ready for earth changes and gamma radiation. You will know it's time to get underground. Cell phones will stop working.

Immediate radiation emanates from the radiated particles that penetrate the earth's magnetic sphere. Humans can do nothing about the radiation. Eat the nutrients that protect you from absorbing radiation, such as algae. Eating nutrients before radiation fallout is best so your thyroid is filled with good nutrients. Then it will not absorb the radiation. Radiation causes health issues many years later as well as present-time health consequences.

Q: How long will people need to stay underground until the radiation dissipates from a coronal mass ejection?

DM: With consideration to dangerous levels of radiation, it will depend on the size of the coronal mass ejection. It might be a few days, or it could be a week, but probably a few days. Then it will be safe to come out until the next solar event. That is when you go back into your safe environment. If people cannot get underground or get in a cave or other such protection, they need to make sure their homes are prepared as well as possible to protect them from radiation, just like they would for a nuclear power plant leak.

Q: Would it be helpful to use duct tape to create a seal around windows and doors?

DM: Not just duct tape around all windows and doors. Use plastic or bubble wrap because bubble wrap also helps to insulate. Place bubble wrap around the windows, then duct tape it. Do the same for the doors. Look at what other areas of your house are open from the outside, such as vents from the dryer and washer. Fill them up and cover. Make sure all openings are covered from the outside the house as well, so nothing can get in. If air can get in, so can radiation. Don't forget your fan that gets rid of the good smells when you cook. Make sure nothing can get inside the air conditioning unit or cooler; cover it in plastic.

Q: What is the best way to cover a fireplace chimney?

DM: Cover the chimney, then go under and cover the flue and the big inside hole. Don't worry; it is not like you will run out of oxygen from having your house completely closed up for a few days.

Q: There is a piece of equipment that can detect radiation called a dosimeter. Would that be a good investment? Should we use the dosimeter to check the air, our home, bodies, and even vegetable gardens?

DM: That would be a good investment, yes. Hopefully people will have created a safe environment outside for their gardens, such as a greenhouse, plastic over the garden, or a garden inside the house.

Q: DreamMyst, what makes radiation dissipate outside to make it safe in a few days?

DM: Radiation flows down on the plants. Water and rain move the radiation around and away. The earth absorbs the radiation. It will be there for years, but you do not want to get the strongest hit of the radiation. Let the plants and the earth absorb the radiation. Stay inside. The radiation needs to dissipate. There will be periods of time you will need to stay underground. It could be for a week or until the levels of the radiation change.

Q: Can we eat the plants that are radiated?

DM: It is better to eat your stored food during this time. You will need to hose the grass and wash all the vegetables in a solution of colloidal silver and water. The washed vegetables that grew outside are better for you than eating animals that ate the radiated grass, which will transmit the radiation to their meat and muscles.

Q: Marijuana, also known as hemp, was used at Chernobyl, where there was a huge radiation leak. The marijuana absorbed the radiation from the ground. Is marijuana effective in absorbing radiation?

DM: Natural plants like marijuana, sunflowers, and a fungus known as mushrooms are good for cleaning radiation to make the soil healthy. Hemp will be one of the best medicinal herbs for humanity. It helps human beings in numerous ways. So yes, that is something you'll be able to freely have when, uh, when you don't have a government paying attention. Human beings should include it in their gardens.

Q: This question is for parents who are concerned about retrieving their children from school. When a car is in the garage, turned off, will the car be protected from a solar flare? Will it run so a parent can pick up his or her children from school or daycare?

DM: Yes.

Q: Is it correct that unprotected cars driving on the roads will have burn damage to their electrical wires? Will they stop moving and block the roads?

DM: Cars, buses, and trucks will stall in the road, so it would be good to have an alternate way of getting to the school or wherever you need to go. Teach your children the best place to meet you based on different possible scenarios. Show your children where to meet you when they are somewhere besides school. Do a practice run.

Another scenario to consider is the solar flare hitting the United States when you are driving your car. Having a bicycle in your car trunk with a "get out of Dodge" bag will prepare you for when you are stuck without a working car, or if you are unable to maneuver your car around a traffic jam.

Q: Will many countries lose electricity as a result of super solar flares?

DM: It is not possible to predict exactly where solar flares are going to hit. The countries closest to where the flares hit will incur the most damage. And yes, the chances are very big that the United States and other countries will take some direct hits.

Q: Electricity will be lost because the solar flares will be so strong that they will burn out the transformers permanently. Is that correct?

DM: In the United States, yes, because the electrical grid in the United States is set up differently than in other countries. So you in the United States are even more at risk of not having electricity.

Q: When you say the United States' electrical transformers are set up differently, are you referring to the fact that they are interconnected with each other?

DM: Yes. The transformers are in a line, kind of like old Christmas tree lights; when one light burns out, the whole line of lights does not work. To fix the lights, you have to test one bulb at a time to find out which one is the problem. So yes, that would be like your electrical transformers. It will be similar to what happened during the summer of 2011 in Arizona, when a man touched the wrong button and it turned out the lights in parts of Arizona and California, too. It gave human beings an idea of what it would be like if it all went down, kind of like when the lights went out in Georgia.

In the United States, there will be a chain reaction when a solar flare hits a good transformer. The power surge will get stronger as it travels down the other, connected transformers, burning them out. The stronger the power surge, the longer and farther it will travel down the wire, becoming more powerful as it hits each connected transformer until it reaches a point where there are no other connecting wires.

It will cost a lot, a lot, a lot of money and years to fix. Repairing and rebuilding electricity will be one of the priorities if loss of electricity happens when the United States has money and a government that will attempt to repair the transformers. If electricity is lost after the economy crashes, it will take longer to restore. It depends on when this event happens. Electrical transformers, wires, and cables are much less expensive now than they will be in the future. In the future, there may not be a working factory, and there may not be a way to ship supplies in. The transformers will need to be ordered, and it will take two years to manufacture them. Other countries will be ordering them as well. So yes, repairs will take four to ten years.

Communication can continue with CB radios, ham radios, and hand-crank generators. In the beginning, landline phone communication may be available some of the time, every few days or every few weeks, until a super solar flare fries the switching stations. Buy a pre-princess rotary phone that does not plug into electricity. Learn Morse code and train carrier pigeons. During times of war, the military has used carrier pigeons to send messages when there were no radio transmissions. Carrier pigeons also delivered tiny vials of medicine when road access was not available. Pigeons can travel up to one thousand miles and can be trained to go between two destinations.

Many of the banks will not be prepared for this event. When the banks' computers burn out and the Internet goes down, you will not be able to withdraw your money. Food purchasing is a concern because cash registers might not work. Grocery store checkouts may have to use pencil and paper or battery- and solar-operated calculators to figure out food totals. These future events are very real.

A computer will be damaged when your energy source, the electricity coming in to your house, is not protected from solar flares. Information not on a disk can be lost within a damaged computer. If you know there is going to be a solar flare coming, unplug your computer. What you can do is create a Faraday box. Place all electrical items inside the Faraday box to protect them. Anything plugged in to an outlet will allow the solar flare to come in and hurt your electrical components and appliances. Place them in a Faraday box, and you will have them safe.

Q: DreamMyst, it would be appreciated if you could make a statement that would help people understand that it will take years to recover from both the economic collapse and the loss of electricity from the solar flares. Is there something you can say to help humans to prepare for a long period of living differently?

DM: Solar flares are the least of your worries. Earth changes, such as volcanoes and earthquakes, are triggered from geomagnetic storms and coronal mass ejections. When the earth moves into the middle of the disc of the plane, its energy will be bigger coming out of the sun. Survival will be more challenging. More earth activity will occur. Be prepared so you can be safe. Knowledge is power. Prepare because so much of it is still unknown.

❧❦

Many enjoy looking at the beautiful and breathtaking aurora borealis. Filament eruptions (the angel-hair-like material that wraps around the sun) and coronal mass ejections (CMEs) breaking through earth's magnetosphere are periods of high geomagnetic activity.

Solar flares[20] are measured in three categories. X-class flares trigger worldwide, long-lasting radiation storms, major blackouts, and global transmission problems, depending on the size of the X-class flare.

M-class flares are medium-size flares, which occasionally cause slight radiation storms and brief radio blackouts. M-class flares affect earth's polar regions.

C-class flares are small and have little noticeable effect on earth.

It takes ten minutes for a solar flare to hit earth. The results from flares come within forty-eight to seventy-two hours. The effect from each flare is consecutive and can last up to two weeks before things get back to normal.

DreamMyst reminds us that solar flares, coronal mass ejections, and geomagnetic storms affect the earth's core, weakening the planet's magnetic field by causing it to fluctuate. As the moon and tides interact, so do the planet and the sun. The earth's weakened geomagnetic field allows radiation exposure to enter from solar flares and coronal mass ejections. We can expect to see extreme weather in many parts of the world due to cosmic fireworks. On

---

20   NOAA Alerts http://www.swpc.noaa.gov/alerts/archive/current_month. html

March 7, 2012, a powerful, earth-directed X5.4-class flare caused extreme weather conditions. Solar activity has been busy since the leap year 2012. The Midwest experienced catastrophic damage in five states, with two towns demolished amid ninety-four tornadoes. Some of the enormous tornados spawned mini twisters, many of which were multiple-vortex tornadoes.

How Solar Flares Affect People

৯৯ Many do not realize the earth-sun connection that causes the earth to shift after a geomagnetic storm affects humans as well. People around the world feel more impatient and on edge from this earth-sun energy connection. There will be fear, violent acts, suicide, depression, riots, rebellions, and war. People do not realize that whatever it is they have not worked on and healed within them is going to jump out big, almost like a volcano or a hurricane. It is important to heal unresolved hurts and emotions and improve how you respond to situations.

Whatever it is you love or fear will be created. People who are working, learning, and growing along their spiritual paths may have a difficult time. As these energies magnify fears, they also magnify intuitive ability and healing. People will be affected according to their radiance. The light of change will shine through them, and they will accept whatever they can receive for learning.

৯৯

Q: Is the geomagnetic energy getting stronger and having a stronger effect on humans?

DM: Well, the outside forces from the geomagnetic energy are having a strong influence on your own personal electromagnetic energy field. You have an electromagnetic energy field because you live on earth. Some people call it an aura, but in reality it is an electromagnetic frequency (EMF). That's the scientific name for it.

Q: What can people do to resist the negative effects on their emotions?

DM: When you wake up each day, decide not to pay as much attention when people bother you. Walk off your irritation or anger. Taking a shower can help. Be aware most people aren't aware. All of you are special. You have big energy, but some of you do not know you do. Big energy is important and helps you get what you want to manifest in your reality.

Q: Scientists have written the sun is coming out of a quiet period that has allowed the sun's energy to build. Is this why we are beginning to experience sensitivity from solar flare activity?

DM: Exactly! Geomagnetic storms, periods of high geomagnetic activity caused by large solar flares, cause clinical depression. Geomagnetic health problems affect 10 to 15 percent of the population. Animals and humans have magnetic fields that surround them the same way the magnetic field surrounds the earth to protect it. The sun's solar storms create weather changes. Humans respond to these changes internally and express this outwardly.

❧◈❧

The sun has moved out of its quiet period into an active phase. This activity is in the form of sunspots exploding and shooting solar flares into the atmosphere. The geomagnetic energy from solar flares affects all life on earth. Their effect on people has been linked to clinical depression. Could our bodies' magnetospheres be picking up on earth changes, which are perhaps charged electrical particles? Since 2009, DreamMyst has explained how humans are growing more sensitive to the energies that surround them, which intensify and amplify all human emotions. Happy people will feel happier. For others anxiety, bewilderment, sadness, and depression will deepen as well. The effect on the physical body will increases sensitivity to toxins or allergies.

To get through this energetic phase, experience your emotion and then consciously release it. Move forward from that moment. The Hopi Indians call this period the Great Purification.

Everything is energy. Every living thing has an aura, a luminous cocoon of electromagnetic energy. The magnetic fields of humans and animals respond to the changes in the sun's magnetic field.

The electromagnetic field (EMF) is in constant motion. It changes with our moods and feelings as it responds to the energy around us. It is measurable, gives off both light and heat, and surrounds us at all times. When we are happy, the aura is large and bright. Clear colors emanate from it with a denseness that reflects solid energy. Sadness or illness shrinks the aura, making it small, with dull, murky colors. It appears thin and jagged if we are angry or fearful. The more energy a person has, the larger and more visible the aura as it bubbles and bulges around the body.

Geomagnetic storms and solar flares affect your auric field because they alter the chemistry in your brain and body. Melatonin is secreted by the pineal gland. The pineal gland is sensitive to magnetic fields and links geomagnetic activity and human health.

The EMF is as individual as DNA or a fingerprint. Each person is affected differently by a geomagnetic storm. People who are sensitive to energies may feel more in tune with their intuitions, initiating the activation of their strongest intuitive ability.

At a physical level, geomagnetic storms affect blood pressure and melatonin. They can increase cancer as well as reproductive, cardiac, and neurological diseases. Other effects are headaches, sinus problems, sleeplessness, itchy eyes, breathing difficulties, dizziness, and disorientation. Scientific research shows the heart is the most powerful generator of electromagnetic energy in the human body, produces the largest electromagnetic field of any of the body's organs, and synchronizes the body's brain waves with the brain waves of the people around us. Solar magnetic activity influences the earth's geomagnetic activity, thereby influencing the human magnetic field.

Animals sense the earth's magnetic field through magnetoception, demonstrated in birds. Sensing earth's magnetic field is important to the navigational abilities of birds during migration. Pigeons and other birds are light sensitive because they have a special magnet in their right eyes. Birds also have a place on their upper beaks that contains magnetite, a small magnet. Because of this, birds "see" magnetic energy field maps, as do fruit flies, honeybees, turtles, lobsters, sharks, stingrays, dolphins, and whales.

A Natural Form of Cyanide
Causes Global Mass Deaths

❧ The Earth is Balancing ❧

In January 2011, the world experienced a mysterious, mass die-off of fish and birds along with unprecedented weather changes such as flooding in Australia and snowfall in forty-nine of the fifty American states. On January 13, 2011, quite unexpectedly, Susan Norgren and her husband, Rob, discovered from DreamMyst the shocking reason for these mass deaths: concentrated clouds of natural cyanide released from the earth's core.

❧ Birds are falling out of the sky. Fish are dying in the ocean. The magnetic poles are beginning to shift slightly. That little shift has changed the earth's core. Poison is evaporating from the oceans into the sky. When the birds fly through the clouds, they die.

❧

Q: Is the poison a gas?

DM: It is a gas like what was used in World Wars I and II: cyanide. It is natural cyanide built up within the earth's core. This is the beginning, one of the early signs the earth is changing. There is no scientific proof. This is new science. This has never happened from the time modern-day science has been documented. Bats died first. Pelicans have died, and turtledoves, crows, blackbirds, and more.

Q: DreamMyst, my research shows that turtledoves have died in Italy. I cannot find any news about bats and pelicans.

DM: Bats have died in Arizona. Look for pelicans in North Carolina. The scientists and doctors who think they know say the pelicans may have died from an oil spill, weather, or other means. They did not. They died from the gas. Birds will continue to drop from the sky. There will be occurrences of fish dying. It took many years of the earth slowly rotating to create what is happening now. The existence of poisonous gas is a sign that planet earth is cleansing.

It is a probability the gases will subside and build up again. The poisonous clouds are concentrated. As they evaporate, they will become less concentrated. They will dissipate. For a while, things could go back to what human beings call normal.

If the earth slows down, there won't be as much gas as what is being thrown into the earth and sky now. With continued shifting of the earth, gas will build up and release again. There will still be occurrences of birds and fish being harmed and things of that nature in 2012. It took years for the gas to build up. If things get calmer and the rotating pattern doesn't continue as powerfully, it will take a while for significant changes to occur. This is one of the early signs of big things happening.

Q: DreamMyst, you have told us that the increased numbers of natural disasters we are experiencing all over the world are signs of the planet changing. Now you have told us that the birds and fish dying are another sign. What will be the next sign?

DM: Volcanoes will begin to heat up and get ready to release their gases because they are a part of the earth also. More volcanoes will get active, as will earthquakes. The burning Ring of Fire will become more active, and volcanoes that are not active will get ready. In 2013, there will be more activity from the Ring of Fire.

Q: How is the poisonous gas reaching the birds?

DM: Because of the magnetic shift of the poles, the earth's core has built up a brew of poisonous gas. The poison is released into the ocean and evaporates into the air.

Q: Does the earth store our human-made cyanide or make its own?

DM: You know how you feel bloated and say, "Uh-oh, I have to relieve myself," and you pass gas? That gas, from the air you breathe in and everything you put into your body, is all turned around, and then the human being relieves the air from the back end. Right? It doesn't smell good. Right? Okay, when you think about it, that is what the earth is doing. The earth is a planet, and all the different mixtures from the shifting of the earth are creating gases. Those gases build up, and you know what it is like—there is more room on the outside than there is on the inside! You know what happens! There is an explosion or a leak. The earth is doing the same thing. It has to have that release.

Q: As the earth releases gas into the ocean, the ocean fish are being poisoned. How are the fish being poisoned in the rivers?

DM: Deep, deep down in the earth, there are tunnels and holes and crevices. The gas is traveling through them to lakes and rivers.

Q: Can traces of cyanide be found if the birds and fish are tested?

DM: Yes. The cyanide from the earth can be found in the animals. This is unprecedented.

Q: If the water is tested where the fish die, will traces of cyanide be found?

DM: Yes, if the water is tested immediately when the fish die. Otherwise, the concentration of cyanide moves on. The poisonous gas could kill the remaining bees. If there are no bees, then there is no pollination. Yes. It is dire. It has nothing do to with overpopulation. It is not a human-made situation. Abuses have not helped the planet, yet taking better care would allow the earth to stay strong.

∂∾∾

(In 2011, DreamMyst spoke about cyanide killing animals.)

Something unusual began on New Year Eve, 2011, and continued a year later: mass animal deaths. Eighteen cows in Elgin, Texas, in late May 2012, died from eating common Bermuda grass planted fifteen to eighteen years ago. The rancher's eighty acres of fields were tested in several areas. The results showed a mix of negative and positive signs of cyanide poisoning. Ranchers across the county tested their fields, which also tested positive—the grass had started venting hydrogen cyanide, a poisonous gas. This is the first documented case of cyanide deaths linked to cows eating grass. Researchers do not know what caused the poison to build up.

Thousands of dead shad washed ashore on August 13, 2012, littering the Texas coast from the Colorado River to Galveston Island. Tens of thousands of dead fish, along with dead seagulls, washed up on the shores of Lake Erie's Pennsylvania panhandle on September 6, 2012. It is interesting that most of the fish to die were not game fish, but rather shad, carp, sheepshead, perch, catfish, and suckers, all of which are deepwater bottom feeders. Is it as DreamMyst said? Is cyanide working its way up through the earth's surface and seeping through the many fissures of the earth's floor? Or could it be a combination of cyanide and earth change? DreamMyst says that with the earth changes, birds, fish, whales, and dolphins are affected by the changing of magnetic north. All four of these species sense magnetic fields well enough to use the earth's magnetism to navigate. They have crystals of magnetite—magnets which respond to a weak magnetic field—in their brains and skulls. Birds have magnetite in their upper bills for a navigational aid. Sea turtles, bats, and bees also have crystals of magnetite to detect the earth's magnetism.

Five Cape Cod beaches experienced 178 healthy dolphins stranding. New Zealand had 103 whale deaths, and 260 dolphins became stranded in Peru. Luckily, some recovered and returned to sea in February 2012.

Nuclear Power Plants and Radiation

≈≈ The most dangerous area is the East Coast, which has the strongest concentration of nuclear power plants. Make your voice heard about the nuclear plants in your area. Warn humankind to take actions to protect itself. Knowledge and preparedness are power. Like a current that flows outward, pockets of people create changes. How can something not work if it uses the butterfly effect? When people protest in large masses, your leaders know things have to change. Lawmakers do not want change because they want the big money nuclear power plants generate.

With the massive radiation in Japan, the area will be known as a dead zone for many years. Americans will begin to feel the unhealthy effects of the radiation. That should be enough to motivate Americans to take correct action. What happened in Japan and to the people there is a major disaster. Americans on the West Coast will suffer some of the poor health effects the Japanese will suffer. Radiation floats over the ocean to the United States. It causes babies to be stillborn. People who breathe in the micro particles of radiation will have lung cancer and other cancers where the particles touch inside their bodies. This should motivate people into taking big action so that there is not more radiation in America.

Because of future earth changes, water will swallow the nuclear power plants built near the ocean. When they are underwater, the water will keep them from overheating. Some of the nuclear rods will stay cool and safe enough that they expand or leak. Who knows? Maybe in a future generation, your family members will look through the bottom of a glass-bottom boat and say, "Hmm, it's too bad my great-grandparents decided to build this nuclear plant, but at least it's underwater."

Hopefully, wise minds will make wise decisions to shut down the power plants before they go underwater. There will be enough warning, enough time. When the water heats, hopefully the nuclear reactors will not break and damage can be averted. It is a good idea to get away from San Clemente, Dana Point in California, and all points in between. Japan will not be the same for hundreds of years. They need to take everyone off the main island.

Oh! In the ocean, mountains as tall as the Grand Canyon is deep are underneath the water. This is what will happen to the islands and landmasses existing now: they will become covered by an ocean filled with radiation, and beneath the waves, volcanoes will give birth to new islands.

Earthquakes and Nuclear Power Plants

ॐ Earthquakes are occurring in areas with nuclear power plants and nuclear waste areas. This is of concern. Some of these power plants are no longer working, but are still dangerous. Many of these plants are in the state of Washington. The power plants dump nuclear waste in the ground at the nuclear power waste sites The earthquakes have been small, but methane gas deep, deep in the crust of your earth is moving up and pushing on the big, deep shafts built for your nuclear power plants. That is why you are having so many earthquakes where there are nuclear power plants. Manmade or natural, it is dangerous for an earthquake to occur near nuclear power plants.

☙❧

DreamMyst said many of the world's earthquake fault lines are located near nuclear power plants. What would happen if an earthquake caused a power plant to crack and leak radiation? Sadly, the world found out when an earthquake struck the coast of Japan, followed by a tsunami. Nuclear reactors leaked high levels of radiation and massive amounts of radiation leaked into the ocean and traveled through the air to the west coast of the United States and beyond. All countries that have nuclear power are facing radiation danger from nuclear plants.

On October 20, 2011, a rare, record-breaking, 4.8 magnitude earthquake struck in south Texas. The epicenter of the earthquake was twenty-one miles from the South Texas Project Electric Generating Station, site of two nuclear power reactors. Another earthquake in Somervell County was only four and a half miles from the Comanche Peak Nuclear Power Plant.

Here is some research on the locations of the five US nuclear reactors in the highest-risk earthquake zones:

1. The Diablo Canyon Power Plant in California

2. The San Onofre Nuclear Generating Station in California

3. The South Texas Project Electric Generating Station near the Gulf Coast

4. The Waterford Steam Electric Station in Louisiana

5. The Brunswick Nuclear Generating Station in North Carolina

» The plant with the second-highest risk is located in Massachusetts.

» The plant with the third-highest risk is located in Pennsylvania, followed by plants in Tennessee, Pennsylvania, Florida, Virginia, and South Carolina.

Here are ten nuclear power sites with the highest risk of an earthquake causing core damage:

1. Indian Point 3, Buchanan, New York

2. Pilgrim 1, Plymouth, Massachusetts

3. Limerick 1 and 2, Limerick, Pennsylvania

4. Sequoyah 1 and 2, Soddy-Daisy, Tennessee

5. Beaver Valley 1, Shippingport, Pennsylvania

6. Saint Lucie 1 and 2, Jensen Beach, Florida

7. North Anna 1 and 2, Louisa, Virginia

8. Oconee 1, 2 and 3, Seneca, South Carolina

9. Diablo Canyon 1 and 2, Avila Beach, California

10. Three Mile Island, Middletown, Pennsylvania

It appears Einstein was right again when he said nuclear power would eventually kill its users.

Chapter 4

Timeline of Events

Recently much bantering has centered on the end of the earth, especially in the year 2012. It is not the end. In fact, 2012 is only one year in a line of many that hold major earth changes for the physical planet.

The loss of government, a fallen economy, and no public-centered atmosphere are what will end life as we know it. Yes, the earth will continue to exist, but the changes will be cataclysmic. Many, many people will die. Landmasses will be destroyed. Martial law will rule.

Where will you be? What will you be doing when the fear begins to creep in because a solar flare rocked the earth upon impact? What do you think will happen when the earth wobbles? Knowing what's ahead can be lifesaving. You can have the advantage at a time that might be too late for some.

For those who survive, a new vibration is on the rise. Instead of a fear-based planet, it will be cleaned up and ready for love. According to DreamMyst, the following represents an accurate timeline of earth changes, economic decline, and government actions. Any variation will be the difference between a period and a comma—one year or less—not ten years.

2010

The world's economy is falling into a deep depression. Governments are manipulating their economies to delay the inevitable. People who are consciously aware know that their governments are distorting the truth about the state of the economy all over the world.

An increase of natural disasters will accelerate the economic depression, a factor not considered by most economic analysts.

2011

The economy will become more unstable. Large numbers of people will be applying for government aid. The president will make comments that will offer a false sense that there will be a pasture of plenty. A large percentage of people will lose their jobs.

The US government prepares for martial law.

*Note: In December 2011, Congress and the Senate quietly passed a law that is designed to strip the constitutional rights of Americans and allow the country to become a military state. Americans can be arrested by the military without cause and held indefinitely without trial. Over a thousand FEMA camps have been built throughout the United States, some on closed military bases. Those who protest are secretly declared terrorists by the US government.

2012

An increase in solar flare activity will create more earthquakes, floods, volcanic eruptions, hurricanes, tornadoes, and tidal waves. Many will occur where they have not in the past. Glaciers melt faster. Safeguard by moving to high ground and away from large bodies of water.

Soft martial law is in effect.

Economy spirals downward. Americans will see a shift in the economy. The year 2012 will be the beginning of major, challenging changes for most Americans and people worldwide. You will want to have everything in place to protect and preserve yourself and your families. During the Christmas season, people will be concerned about buying food, not gifts. The economy slips deeper into its downturn.

*Note: In 2012, an alignment of the planets will be exactly the same as happened 238 years ago, in 1774, the year before the beginning of the American Revolution. The planetary alignment indicates there will be massive public outrage regarding fiscal issues in 2012, the same angry feelings people expressed in 1774.

On December 21, the planets will align with the center of the Milky Way galaxy and be at the center of the Disc of the Plane. When the earth moves through the center of the Disk of the Plane, it will physically shake. The sun will absorb stronger energy, which will create more powerful solar flares.

2012–2013

Numerous X-class solar flares will occur.

Drought and unusual weather shifts will occur.

California continues to have job losses on a bigger scale. People will sleep in tents. Gas prices will rise.

There is an 80 percent chance President Obama will remain president.

2013

Food prices will move higher.

There will be more loss of freedoms from executive orders.

War will occur.

Large and small banks will close in response to Europe's economic crisis. Be prepared by having dollars in your pocket, propane tanks filled, two weeks of food and water, and extra gasoline stored.

The Dow Jones Industrial Average will dip into the 9000s, just as it did in 2008–2009. This time the stock market will not recover. It will continue a downward slide.

The economy will worsen on a grand scale due to a combination of natural disasters. The government will no longer be able to manipulate the dollar. The dollar will crash.

Electricity will become too expensive for most people.

Millions will face foreclosure. Do not move from your home. The banks will be inundated with paperwork. They won't be able to keep up with the foreclosures.

The government may need to create tent camps with water (possibly through FEMA).

Due to inadequate funds, there will be large layoffs of the American police force. Crime will increase. More Americans will be aware that the government has initiated martial law.

The draft will be reinstated. To avoid the draft, families will be forced to move to other countries. Those who are drafted and sent overseas may never see their families again.

A tidal wave will hit Manhattan. This will be the first of many. The storm damage will temporarily halt shipments by sea. Eventually, Manhattan will be underwater, whether in 2017, 2018, or 2019, and will stay this way for many years.

2013–2014

Peaceful protesters and those who speak against the government will be taken away, never to be seen by their loved ones again.

The US government will falsely accuse Iran of actions to fabricate reasons for a war. The United States partners with Israel, which has been sent bunker bombs by the United States.

Super solar flares will hit the earth. At this time, there is no indication where the flares will hit, but when they do, the radiation will eventually travel around the entire earth. During this time period, it will be best to be underground because radiation is harmful to humans and animals.

*Note: NASA has a small team of scientists tracking solar flare activity 24/7. In 2011, a new satellite was launched to observe the sun's activity. Super solar flares will cause loss of electricity, which will take four to ten years to reestablish in the United States. To prepare, think what would happen with an extended loss of electricity—blackouts, looting, loss of mass transportation. Electrical systems in cars could no longer function. Gas pumps will not work. Food, paper products, and essentials will become scarce. Individuals will not have access to banks or their money.

The loss of electricity is not certain. Yet choosing to be prepared is the same as buying insurance in case of illness, death, fire, accidents, or natural disaster.

To find evidence of radiation exposure, look for natural signs. For example, the northern lights will be seen in other areas besides the north.

The damage from the solar flares will increase and impact the earth's temperature, increasing the effect of global warming. Ice glaciers will continue to melt. Shorelines will decrease globally due to the rising water.

Martial law will continue to be established. FEMA camps will be opened for holding Americans.

2014

The stock market's Dow Jones Industrial Average will fall below 1000 points. A twenty-dollar bill might buy some things.

The government will establish roadblocks. Americans will be checked for flu vaccines. If they have not been vaccinated, flu shots will be administered. Those who refuse will be placed on a bus and sent to a FEMA camp. Accept the flu shot to avoid being taken to the internment camp. Chaos will be rampant under martial law. Avoid being gathered into buses by FEMA or the military. They are not there to help you. They will take you to concentration camps to work and be brainwashed.

2015–2017

The economic depression will be deep. By 2015, the country will experience food shortages because of severe weather, earth changes, loss of electricity, and inflation. Grocery store shelves will be empty. During the Depression of 1929, people came together to help and support each other. In 2015, the majority of the population will be self-interested. People will hurt others and even kill to provide food and water for their children. This occurred in New Orleans during the aftermath of Hurricane Katrina.

School systems will not have adequate instruction for students. In many school systems, writing paper, which is essential for elementary education, will become limited. Teachers will experience pay cuts.

2015–2020

During this time, China will invade America when America is at its weakest. It is not determined which country will win or lose this war. This may involve the use of nuclear weapons to cause an EMP, effectively shutting down all electrical-sensitive equipment.

2016–2017

Hyperinflation will continue. The American lifestyle will change drastically. The deepest part of hyperinflation and deflation will exist at the same time.

2018

The volcanoes within the Pacific Ring of Fire will become more active. In later years they will all become 100 percent active, one volcano activating another as if igniting a long chain of firecrackers.

*Note: The Pacific Ring of Fire is an area where large numbers of earthquakes and volcanic eruptions occur. The 40,000 km (25,000 mile) horseshoe shape is associated with a nearly continuous series of oceanic trenches, volcanic arcs, volcanic belts, and plate movements. The Ring of Fire has 452 volcanoes and is home to over 75 percent of the world's active and dormant volcanoes.

2016–2021

There will not be enough people paying taxes. Only a few will be able. Those who can pay taxes will stop. (This may happen sooner because of loss of electricity from the solar flares.)

No taxes, no IRS, and a small government with no influence over the people. This is a repeat of history. There will be complete renewal.

If there is a way for people to vote, and China has not taken over, a president will continue to be elected. The Constitution will be rewritten so it is clear for the people.

2018–2020

Many banks will have already closed due to mortgage failures. Credit unions will last longer because they do not offer the same services as banks. During this three-year time frame, some of the big banks will fail, including Bank of America, Citibank, and Wells Fargo. Details of fraud to their customers will be revealed. Banks that are more honest will last longer. They will have customer support.

Chapter 5

Beginnings and Endings

⊱⊰ As the illusions of safety and immunity crumple, the absolute power of the president and those in authority will increase. The president during peacetime will take control of all large bodies of water and food crops. Why worry about this when you are so worried about making some money to feed your family since the economy collapsed?

One day, the military arrives and orders you to evacuate. They tell you that FEMA will take care of you. When you arrive at the FEMA camp, you realize I'm in a concentration camp on American soil for Americans. When you protest about the fate that brought you here, your neighbor turns you in as a terrorist in exchange for a little food to feed her children.

The Department of Homeland Security comes for you. No one has a weapon. Guns have been outlawed for some time now. Violence and public executions of civilians without trial are commonplace occurrences. The splintering and crashing of your door sounds the alarm. You have no place to hide. Grabbing and pushing, they shove you into the street. Closing your eyes, you wait hopelessly for deliverance.

The loud crack of a gun going off makes you flinch, and suddenly you are awake and drenched in sweat. With tears streaming down your face, you sob, "It was only a nightmare." Only a nightmare. You are safe. You are safe in bed, and this new awareness brings with it extreme alarm, "What if my dream is one of the near future? Will it really happen?" you ask yourself.

Clarity is instant as the blinders of denial fall from your eyes and fear is replaced with knowledge. You know what you need to do. There is still time. To make changes, to overthrow oppression. A way to avoid an American revolution. There is time to prepare, and you can do it.

ॐ‑ॐ

ॐ‑ॐ *The worst lies are the denials you tell yourself.* ॐ‑ॐ

Survival for the Best Prepared

ॐ‑ॐ Insights are like planting seeds. There is new growth where some of those lovely seeds land. Each person takes his or her action and prepares in a way that is best for that individual. Little baby steps are good actions. Some people will follow this advice and spend a lot of money, for example in placing sand bags around their homes in anticipation of a flood in their area. Those people will say, "I hope DreamMyst was right about the future flooding because I spent a lot of money putting sandbags around my house and my property." (The person who said this is glad he did it; his home survived.)

Guess what? It is like having advance notice so you can protect yourself and protect what's yours. Some will do as suggested and move away from the big water and the big cities. Others will build underground. Do what you can. Enjoy the time with your loved ones. Have physical books to read. If there is no Internet, you will want books with you during a period that will be an isolated time in your life. Buy a bicycle and hook it up to a generator. The whole family can get their exercise and have electricity to enjoy.

In the days and hours after the economic collapse, and later when more earth changes begin, there will be rioting and revolts. Do not get involved in the protests. Nothing is going to change the situation for days or weeks. Stay calm, control your emotions, and keep a watchful eye for looters.

What about when the euro crashes and the US economy dominos into a collapse, either from this or something else? What happens when a country decides to shoot a nuclear weapon so high into the sky that the EMP shuts off the electricity and rains radiation down on your head, ending life, as you know it? Do not forget about the resistant superbugs the drug companies have developed which existing antibiotics can't touch. Or the erosion of American freedoms and rights. The earth and its natural disasters are the least of your worries.

Back in your Great Depression, people were able to survive as well. This economic depression will be worse than the 1929 Depression because it is based more on technology and food shortages due to earth changes. The earth changes will cause flooding and drought in farmland areas. America is already beginning to experience this with the flooding of the Mississippi River and drought in Texas.

There will be little or no communication, transportation, food, and water. Chaos will reign. The government will be crippled. It will work and operate for a little while, and then it will crash. There will be no government. But at least there will be no IRS, either, so that's a good thing, right? Income taxes can go away, and a new government can be formed. America can do this sooner, before there is civil unrest in eighteen months or less. This is not the end of the world.

How will you know when it is time to get out of Dodge? First, you need to be prepared. Second is the action of practicing to be prepared. Practice and learn how to use all the things you will need. Do you have the batteries or a certain tool to use with that shiny new camp stove? Make it second nature to use your survival tools. Can you tie a strong knot? Do you have the cord in your supplies? When the time comes, you will be glad you became familiar with your survival tools and supplies. Gather your friends and family and go camping to see how using the tools works in a different reality.

Gather funds and like-minded people together to create communities. There is security in numbers. Have an evacuation plan for how and when it is time to move to your safe place. Find property far away from population centers. Build homes either underground or anchored on high, solid bedrock close to the surface, away from major rivers or oceans. It will be safe and beneficial to build a dome structure that can be grown over and hidden. Make your home self-sustaining by using wind energy, solar panels, solar motors, and generators.

Critical thinking will help you anticipate what is going to happen. Critical thinking is not difficult when you discover and follow this one truth—do not believe anything the media is spoon-feeding you. What Washington denies is usually true. Listen for denials and know the opposite of what is being said is true.

Stay a few jumps ahead of the turmoil when that one little thing tips the scales leading to disaster. It's okay if people do not want to believe, but it is not in their best interest if they want to survive. Not everyone will survive these events.

Q: Is it negative to know this information?

DM: No, it is not negative. If you do not know what is occurring, how can you protect yourself and those you love? You do not have the insights to take action, and this is what the government wants. If you live in ignorance, you may be one of those who does not survive.

Q: What comment do you have about people who say, "Oh well, I'll deal with the emergency when it comes"?

DM: They will be the people looking for food. They will be the ones saying, "Oh my goodness, I wish I had listened." They will be the ones caught with their pants down. They will be the ones who will try to take what is yours.

Protection

⇨⇦ Some people will band together to help each other, but more will be very scared. Fear makes people do things they might be ashamed of later, things they will have bad dreams about. But in that moment, they react from a sense of survival, and they do what they would never, ever do if their world had not changed.

The mental attitude of a survivor is to fight back only when necessary. If someone threatens your family or tries to take what you have, it is a threat of deadly physical violence. Take defensive action in any way you know how. Defending yourself and your family is not bad or wrong. It is your job to defend yourself against desperate people with no qualms about taking away your food and water, or killing you. This may be difficult to accept. They will not care about your life or the lives of your family. People in this situation, in any disaster, will hurt, steal, and take as they can. Be ready to defend what is yours. Aikido, hapkido, and kung fu san soo are martial art styles that focus on street-fighting, self-defense techniques. Choose something that teaches you how to use your body to defend against physical attacks.

Learn how to use a cane or walking stick for self-defense. These items are not weapons, but when walking with a walking stick, you can use it to defend yourself. Put some silver coins inside the hollow tube of a cane—you will have a heavy tool for protection and a fantastic hiding place for your silver.

Learning how to use a bow and arrow would be good because arrows are quiet and are good for distance as well. The bow and arrow will be good for hunting when ammunition runs low. You can make or buy arrows. Mini crossbows are small enough for a woman or an older child to handle but are not good for shooting long distances. Kitchen knives are not just a tool to use for food.

Buy wasp spray; it is more powerful than pepper spray and it sprays farther. With a gun, you can only usually shoot only one person at a time, but with the wasp spray, you can spray several people at once. You do not want to use this on the military. Use it on the people who are trying to take away what is yours, who try to break in to your home to take your food, silver, and weapons.

Buy or make a slingshot. There are always rocks you can use.

Tip: Violent encounters can occur at any time, mostly without warning. Some lifesaving defense techniques to remember are kick to the crotch, eye gouging, biting, head butting, and elbowing. Use direct, maximum force against your adversary's weakest areas.

Surviving Martial Law

☙∽ The greater fear is not a 2012 massive event. It is martial law. The mentality you need to deal with martial law is very much like in all wars where the conqueror takes over. Americans will find martial law difficult to live through because they have not been in a situation where it is necessary to protect themselves and what they own.

When the government declares martial law, the military and the police will be in FEMA's control. FEMA is prepared with tents. Both the police departments and military will be ready. FEMA will have control over Congress once martial law is decreed. Martial law leads to civil unrest and revolution.

Surviving means to live through martial law when FEMA goes into effect. If you revolt while living under martial law, it can lead to your death. This is why living outside of the cities is a better idea. When martial law begins, the police and the military will go first to the largest, concentrated cities where the masses of people live. That is why FEMA is going to put up checkpoints, to keep you in one place. Martial law is not something you want to defy or challenge. There will be police and military everywhere. You need to know how to survive martial law.

One of the actions I suggest when you see the military is to realize they are mostly young men who are nervous and trained to kill. They are between the ages of eighteen and twenty-four. Be very polite to them and *do not* carry anything on you that could be construed as a weapon. Having a weapon is a perfect reason to kill you or, worse, take you to a terrorist FEMA camp.

During Hurricane Katrina, the military and police went into homes to check on people. They acted as if martial law had been declared, confiscating everyone's weapons. Food did not arrive, and the government did not help the people. FEMA did not come through until later, when FEMA decided to take people to the relocation camps.

During martial law food will be scarce. Keep your food in multiple places if you possibly can. If all your food is in your cupboard at home, anyone can come, get it, and take it away. Putting food caches in trees and burying caches in different parts of your property make your food less likely to be discovered unless someone has metal detectors. Most people will not have metal detectors. You can have a special wall or door made that hides your food. Do the same thing with your guns. Most people will only steal what they can see, and they will not look very deeply. The military will not take the food at first, civilians or looters will. What will the military take? During martial law when there is unrest and violence, the military will slam open doors and go through the house. I do not believe your military is going to take your food, at least not in the beginning, but they will take any weapons and any gold or silver they can find.

Bury your guns, ammunition, and weapons. During martial law, any weapon found will get you killed. Store your guns and weapons in PVC pipe. Seal the ends of the pipe. Bury the guns outside of your home. This will hide your guns and ammunition, but a metal detector will detect them if the hole is less than seven feet deep. Realize that if the military or police raid your home, they may bring metal detectors and x-ray machines.

Power corrupts. The military and especially the police departments have more power now, and it is going to go right to their egos. Some are good people with good ethics, but in a time of chaos and civil unrest, they run on their adrenaline. They are as nervous and as scared as you are because they do not know what you are going to do. You do not want to give them any reason to harm you in any way.

If the military comes to your home, and finds your pretend stash of food, let the military personnel have it. Have your real stash of food, silver, weapons, and ammunition well hidden. You do not want to have military personnel find a gun in the back of your underwear drawer or in the far corner of your closet.

Abide by the curfews. Stay inside more than you are outside. It will be safer. Americans have always had the freedom to walk outside any time they want to. Go outside when absolutely necessary.

Do not tell anyone, even your children, about the food you have saved. Eat as sparingly as you can. If you gain weight and everyone else is getting bony, that says you have food, and people will come to find it. Keep this as your secret. People who would not normally take such actions will be more than willing to tell on you, or to tell lies about you, for extra food. This is another reason for being very quiet about what you have.

Martial law is a time to be very private. To stay home with your food, guns, and silver hidden so it is not available for anyone to find. If you use paper plates, burn or bury them after you have eaten. Do the same with your cans and jars if the water is off. Bury the evidence that you have food. People will go through your trash.

Don't take the government's word at face value. What the government says is never true or honest. Do take government officials seriously if they say they are going to kill you. However, if you don't do what they say, they won't have a problem following through on the threat; you are not real people to them. They will not care if you die. Stay away from populated areas, especially during the first weeks of dangerous chaos. Cooperate with the authorities. Keep a low profile, stay in your home, and hide your food and your guns.

What I see is that people will eventually organize and form communities, and there will be a resistance against martial law. There will be Americans and some of the military and police to organize the resistance. The resistance will need supporters. If you can support the resistance, then yes, do that. But unless you are qualified, do not become a part of the resistance. Let those who are trained join the resistance. This is where people who know about survival will be very good to have on your team. They can help to protect the community and the people.

❧❦

Q: When the US government declares martial law, will they also bring in paid terrorists from other countries to help them take control of Americans to attain their goal of a New World Order?

DM: Yes, they will. The changes will be quick. The US government will use the same false blame tactics as they did with Osama bin Laden and 9/11. The American government planned the action, the terror, and the murders so it would have a reason to go to war.

Q: What will it take to cause the military decide to support the people? Will the government mistreat the soldiers? Will they not have enough food or money? What will trigger the military's decision?

DM: The military is made up of leaders, some of whom are not good leaders and some of whom are great leaders. It is about politics, the military, and the secret service that protects the president. When enough people take to the streets and protest, military personnel will also have families they love placed under martial law. The people within the military will very quickly decide this is not what they are going to accept or support. Military personnel from a different country will supersede them. Mercenaries.

Q: Will members of the military disperse and join survival communities?

DM: Yes. Some of the soldiers will disperse because they will want to be with their friends and families and in their hometowns where they grew up. Many will desert. During the Civil War, when the soldiers could, they would go home. Some came back to the army and some stayed home. The same thing will happen during this revolution. At first, there will be martial law. You need to know that.

Q: When there is martial law, will the military go into people's homes, looking to take gold and silver?

DM: I would have to say in the worst-case scenario, that is exactly what will happen. Gold and silver will be taken before the military personnel say, "This is not okay, and I am going away."

Q: Will American soldiers go into people's homes and take their food and water to support the military?

DM: During this period, the military will be protecting the government and not the homeland, not the people of America. The police are currently violating American rights by going into homes without warrants. By law in many states, police are allowed to enter homes as they wish. Americans are experiencing the beginning of soft martial law.

The majority in the military will not like the actions the government directs them to take. They are trained to follow orders and are not given a reason or a choice. They were trained take actions against the enemy. Americans are not their enemy, but they will have to take these actions anyway.

Q: How can communities and individuals protect their homes and families during martial law? What should they do when the military knocks on the door to claim their food or gold or silver?

DM: If you don't answer the door, they're going to crash it in anyway. If you do answer the door, you better have protection, which is a little bit of stuff in a box that you have in a decoy hiding place. You can give that to the military and not reveal your main food or provisions. This is why you should have food under your carpet in a big hole, in your attic, or anywhere it will not be easily discovered. Food is something you need to be willing to protect with your life.

Q: People are having difficulty understanding the enormity of the danger from which they will need to protect themselves. Can you shed light on the danger?

DM: Americans will be protecting themselves from the military and police. People will need protection from rioters. You will need to protect yourself from those who did not prepare. Unprepared people are even more dangerous because they are desperate to protect those they love.

Q: A reduction in police officers is expected throughout the United States because of budget cuts. People will become vulnerable to more crime. When will local and state governments lay off policemen?

DM: Some of that is happening now (2011). By 2013, large numbers of police officers will have lost their jobs due to lack of government money. Some of your states do not have enough money to pay their bills. People are being let out of jail and prison early. You need to know this will happen. It will be about the same time that the 401ks come due.

Q: Will it be advisable to have a gun?

DM: Yes, for protection and for hunting. Everyone in the family needs to know how to use the gun. They need to know how to keep it safe but readily available. Keep guns safe from children. When somebody has a gun and really doesn't know how to use it, or is afraid to use it, then the gun can be turned against him.

Q: Do you suggest hiding a gun in the home or placing it readily available by a door or window?

DM: The gun can be placed close to a door or a window if it is safe from the children who could get hurt. If looters come in and you have the gun on the wall by the door, they could take the gun and run or use it on you. Know how to use your weapon.

అ☙

Americans have been living under a form of soft martial law for a number of years. What is around the corner is worse: the very real possibility of martial law in response to an economic collapse or an emergency the government manufactures. Move from the large cities; this is where the military will be at first. Move to rural areas away from the city.

One of the questions asked of DreamMyst was where to buy the safest property. Her response for the past ten years has always been to buy on the western side of Montana because there would be flooding on the eastern side of the Continental Divide. In 2011, hundreds of people lost their homes, were hurt, or died when the eastern side of Montana experienced massive flooding.

Western Montana is not very populated. Tornados are extremely rare, and earthquakes have historically been small. It is a nuclear-free zone; there are no operating nuclear reactors or fuel recycling facilities located in the area.

Get a Guard Dog

అ☙ Even a family pet that has never been trained will give warning when intruders approach. They will protect their domain and the people they love.

It is better to have your dog trained to stand at the ready to attack if needed. People need to learn to command with hand movements or by snapping fingers. If trained to hand movements, the dog will be able to act at a time when words might mean your death. Trained dogs stand by you and/or go find help.

If you want protection from someone attacking you on the streets, how can you get it? Train your dog to know what it needs to do to protect you. Know how to defend yourself in the event somebody shoots your dog.

The German shepherd is the best dog in intelligence, loyalty, and physical ability. This dog needs training to respect your authority and that of your family, including the youngest family member. A dog can stand guard, protect your children when they are playing or working, and get them home safely. A dog will be a great help in a hunt and will defend the home if someone tries to break in.

Secure Your Home

శ~ళ Connect an alarm that sounds inside your house. Keep the fence charged with solar energy. Put up security cameras, even if they do not work. When your home looks protected, looters will think twice about breaking into your home.

శ~ళ

Q: How do people protect house and building windows that are low to the ground?

DM: Well, in the pioneer days, wooden shutters were placed over the windows. The shutters could be left open, and then closed in the event of danger. Put locking shutters or protective bars on your windows. Think about how you can escape your home if there are bars on the windows.

Q: How would people reinforce their doors against looters?

DM: Be prepared before panic hits. Buy a solid wood door, a solid metal door, or something similar. Upgrade your locks and the frames of your doors. Be sure that the door has a peephole. A pet door for a large animal will allow other animals to come inside, as well as human beings. Cover dog doors so people cannot use them to enter your home.

Q: Would you suggest a tall fence around the entire house for those who live in areas that allow fencing?

DM: Yes, or put up another kind of fence. Have an electrical horse fence so that when an invader touches it, he gets shocked. Have a big speaker to amplify the sound of an alarm. Use solar energy to keep it charged and turned on. Fences will be important for those who live in a town or city with a lot of people.

Even if you don't have a big yard, an electrical fence can be installed on the house if you have a porch. This offers protection too. It can be at the end of your yard and up close to your house. If you are limited as to where an electrical fence can be placed, it can be placed close to or on the porch.

Put security signs on your windows. Have a video cam (a nanny cam will work) installed on your home, even if it does not work. A big "Beware of Dog" sign will help too.

Hiding Places within Your Home

A hiding place for your valuables, for the silver you've been collecting, is very important. Valuables should be placed in little spaces in your home. Do not put your valuables in your bedroom. If you use a safe, get one that is old and too heavy to carry and then try to hide it.

Valuables can be hidden in unused heater or air conditioning vents. Hide gold and silver in a wall behind a pretend outlet. In an emergency, hide things in your washing machine or dryer. Use the drain hose or the tub of the washing machine. You can use your dryer's vent hose or tape items on the back of your washing machine. Open a stuffed animal or doll and put silver in it. Turn a book in the bookcase into a box to put treasures in. This way you can hide it in plain sight.

Bury your silver and put flowers or a birdbath over it. Dig a hole in the ground, put a refrigerator in it, fill the refrigerator with food, and cover it up. If you live in a mobile home, make a trap door that will let you climb down under the home. Store food down there too. Not too many people will think to look underneath. Even if you have to lie under your home, you are at least safe until the danger is gone. PVC is good for storage. Remember where you hide your gold and your silver so you can have it later.

After you put away your valuables, make a pretend stash. Include a broken gun and some worthless dollar bills. Perhaps add a tiny bit of silver. Hide this in plain sight. It's better looters take the pretend stash than find the real valuables you will be using to provide for your family.

Your valuables need to be well hidden in places where they will be difficult to find.

☙❧

Wrap your coins in plastic with a silica pack to avoid dampness. Seal them in a waterproof container. Use your imagination. On hundred ounces of gold is about a double handful. There are many dead spaces and places to hide your valuables.

The police may use special equipment like metal detectors, x-ray machines, or ground-penetrating radar, and will have unlimited time. But freelance thieves do not have fancy equipment or the time to tear apart that baseboard or the kickboard under your sink. A thief would not have the time to go to the effort of looking behind mirrors for a hollowed-out space. Nor would he think to dig around in the gravel of your fish tank for your stash.

Where would a thief search? You can bet he would head to the bedroom and rummage through the closet, the drawers, and between the mattresses. Next, he would head to the bathroom to see what medicines you might have for the taking, never noticing the window air conditioner you gutted and stashed valuables in.

What are some other places he would never take the time to look in? Maybe the last step on your stairs, or the space at the bottom of your bookcase. Never would he think about the shower, or the clothing rod in your closet, or the hollowed-out leg of your chair, or the taped stash under the dresser. Would he think to check your child's swing set, or the hollow legs of patio furniture, or the roof of the doghouse?

A concealment construction specialist can transform areas in your home, including but not limited to fake walls for the concealment of a safe or food and weapon supplies. Build an outdoor shed, pool house, or garage and bury your safe under it. Then put a refrigerator or something heavy on top of the access way. What about building a false back in a closet and relining the closet with cedar paneling?

The more gold or silver you have, the more you need to investigate other areas for redistributing your treasure. If you have a vacation home, you may want to put some of your precious metal in safe places throughout that home. Another choice would be to pay someone to hold a box for you.

Hiding Places

» Grease gun: Place the stash at the bottom, packing the gun with grease.

» Vaseline or cold cream jar: Scoop two thirds of the contents out and insert the stash. Heat the scooped-out contents and pour back in the jar.

» Paint cans, creosote, or any other thick, opaque liquid: Seal stash in a heavy plastic bag with weights inside to insure it sinks to the bottom.

» Bicycle pump: Remove the piston assembly from the inside, shorten the rod, and insert the stash.

» Drainpipe: Lift the cover; attach a string to the stash and the cover.

» Candle: Make a candle using a glass jar or other mold. Tie the wick to your protected stash. Add a crayon to the melted wax to color it and make it opaque. Pour the colored wax into the jar until it is halfway full. Insert your stash. Pour in the remainder of the wax, and let it cool.

» Base of lamp: Open up the base of a lamp, insert the stash, and close the base.

» Pillows or zippered cushions: Unzip the zipper, put in the stash, and rezip.

» Birdhouse: If you are handy with tools, build a birdhouse with a removable top and put it in the backyard.

» Compost pile

» Furniture: Take out the staples holding the fabric underneath a chair or couch, hide stash within the padding, and restaple the opening.

» Hollow-core door: Cut a slot at the top, drop in the goods, and then fill the slot with wood putty then repaint.

» False roof vent: Buy a roof ventilator, attach it to the roof, and put your stash inside.

» Old hot water heater: Be sure to make it look like it is hooked up for use.

» Dummy plumbing/ stovepipe: Look for existing connections and add sealed dummies to them.

» Beams: Ceiling and walls can have hollowed out beams. A lot of work, but safe.

» Fence: Dig a seven-feet-deep hole next to a fence with a post-hole digger. Fill the bottom twelve inches of the hole with jars full of coins. Then place a capped six-foot length of PVC pipe vertically in the hole with more of your stash. Above the pipe will be dirt. The fence acts as a decoy for metal detectors.

» Septic tank: Seal your silver and gun in waterproof packaging, wrap with nylon cord, and attach them deeply in the septic tank.

» Garden statue: Find a hollow garden statue and load it up. Put it in plain sight in your backyard or as a decoration on the patio.

> » Tree: Climb a tree and secure your stash in a tube on top of a branch.

The worst places to hide valuables are in closets, dresser drawers, night tables, mattresses, or old clothes, and under carpets, couches, or jewelry boxes.

Do not:

> » Bury any item you may soon need.

> » Put items in a spare tire if there is a possibility someone in the family may decide to clean the garage and haul it off.

> » Hide your valuables where the neighbors will suspect something is going on. If you are going to do some midnight gardening, it is a good idea to plant trees, shrubbery, or flowers at the same time.

> » Forget where you buried your treasure. Use a corner of the house or a bird fountain to direct you to your stash.

> » Tell more than one trusted person where your treasure is located. It is better to attach a map to your will in a sealed envelope for next of kin.

> » Send in the consumer card that came with your safe when you bought it.

> » Hide your stash under a mattress or box spring.

> » Involve the children or tell them you have coins.

Avoiding Conflict

❧ Bewilderment, anxiety, and fear do not empower a person. Rather, they immobilize him, like a deer staring into a car's oncoming headlights. Awareness of events and possibilities to expect helps to lessen human fear and vulnerability. For many, these first steps will be small and slow, and for others, nonexistent.

In a collapsed environment, innocent, scared, desperate refugees who did not prepare will approach you. The best solution is to hide. Your challenge is to stay alive. If you are not prepared to help, don't risk your welfare or your family's.

In this new society, no one will be entitled to anything other than what they have prepared for their family's survival. If there is no police force, a thief will feel safe stealing from you. Decreasing your home size is a good idea to keep it energy- and cost-efficient. A smaller home lessens the possibility of becoming a target.

Blend with the crowd to avoid unnecessary conflict. You don't have to do anything wrong to be targeted by the police, or later by the military during martial law. Blend in and avoid conflict by dressing the same way as the people around you. Wear what they wear.

Do not wear a lot of jewelry or expensive watches. Do the same with your vehicle: get one that blends in. Anything expensive draws attention and says you might have money, which is not a smart move during an economic collapse.

Avoid public protests. Getting involved in conflict during this time of anger, fear, and frustration may be very tempting. When the riots begin, do not get involved. Stay at home and be safe. Backing down from confrontation will prevent you from being injured or arrested. Anticipate the fight or conflict and get out of the way. How can you tell when things are about to escalate? Is there yelling and pushing? Watch the body language. Leave when it starts to get rowdy.

Safe Shelters

Q: How can people plan to get home safely when electricity no longer exists because of a super solar flare?

DM: Drive to your planned evacuation route and plot alternate routes on a map in case main roads are blocked or gridlocked. Have your "get out of Dodge" bag ready and with you at all times. Walk with friends; there is protection in numbers.

Q: What guidance can you offer to humans who become unexpectedly homeless because they need to leave their houses for safety? How will people best survive?

DM: Find a cave. If you have to, stay in your car; it is protection. If there is a subway, get down into the subway. Even if you have to be in your sewer for a while, it's better to be down low in the sewer passages than it is to be on top of the ground during chaos, danger, or a life-threatening situation. If you can't escape from a dangerous area, go to wherever you can possibly be safe. During World War II, they had shelters where townsfolk went to be safe. Have a "get out of Dodge" bag for each family member and keep those bags with you at all times.

Q: Should we have our own generators?

DM: Having your own generator is a good idea, except the noise and physical presence of the unit are a sign to looters unless you can hide them. Solar panels and generators will draw people to you who will say, "Oh, they've got this. Find the people." If you can camouflage the solar panel or generator, then it is a good idea. Solar electricity will be needed. Wind turbines should be many and small so they are easier to hide and control. Protect what is yours.

Q: Will some other countries restore their electricity faster than the United States?

DM: Maybe. It will depend on the amount of changes and how they have their electricity hooked up.

Q: Once electricity is restored in the United States, will people buy their electricity from power companies?

DM: Unfortunately, right now and into your future, electricity is not affordable. Unless a different form of electricity is created, people will not be able to afford it. Some developers are coming out with easier ways to harness solar and wind power. There are many ways to create electricity using wind power. It's important to inform people. All they know is when they enter a dark house, they flip a switch—lights on. They flip a switch—lights off. People do not even think about how harmful it is to generate electricity with nuclear reactors, although some woke up when the reactors cracked and leaked in Fukushima.

Your president wants you to forget about any radiation threat. After all what can you do about what happened? Human beings think, "It happened in Japan, but it won't happen in our home. It won't happen in our land or in our city." It is very easy to do nothing to change, and change is not affordable for most people. They don't know they have other options.

Q: Will large numbers of people buy solar panels and wind turbines, or will they be too poor?

DM: Most people will be too poor to purchase solar generators.

Q: For those who will have money or items to barter, will electricity-producing solar and wind products be available, or will they be scarce?

కళ

Cities will become unsustainable and uninhabitable. A city has to bring in everything from outside itself—water, food, and electricity. This is a starting point for disaster.

Los Angeles New York City Las Vegas Phoenix and Boston, to name a few, are death traps. They do not have three fresh water sources surrounding them. If you live in or close to these areas, please consider moving to a safer area. The scared, seething mass of humanity will be desperate when the municipal water supply is not operating and the storehouses of water are depleted.

2012 America's Top 10 Most Dangerous Cities

1. Flint, MI
2. Detroit, MI
3. St. Louis, MO
4. Oakland, CA
5. Memphis, TN
6. Little Rock, AR
7. Birmingham, AL
8. Atlanta, GA
9. Baltimore, MD
10. Stockton, CA

25 Most Dangerous Metro Areas for Violent Crime

1. Detroit, MI
2. Memphis, TN
3. Sumpter, SC
4. Fairbanks, AK
5. New Orleans, LA
6. Miami, FL
7. Myrtle Beach, SC
8. Las Vegas, NV
9. Victoria, TX
10. Florence, SC
11. Stockton, CA
12. Shreveport, LA
13. Pine Bluff, AR
14. Lafayette, LA
15. Jackson, MO
16. Saginaw, MI
17. Phoenix, AZ
18. Tucson, AZ
19. LA County, CA
20. Baltimore, MD
21. Albuquerque, NM
22. Vineland, NJ
23. Montgomery, AL
24. Little Rock, AR
25. Charleston, SC

Most Dangerous Metro Areas for Earthquakes

1. Mexico City, Mexico
2. San Francisco/Oakland, CA
3. Los Angeles basin, CA
4. Anchorage, AK
5. Seattle, WA

Top 10 Most Dangerous Nuclear Targets in or Near a Metro Area

1. Washington, DC, and related bases (major command and control for the president)

2. Colorado Springs, CO (Cheyenne Mountain Complex, two space command/communication bases)

3. Omaha, NE (secondary command and control bases)

4. Seattle, WA (Trident missile submarine base and numerous naval bases)

5. Jacksonville, FL/Kings Bay, GA (Trident missile submarine base, major East Coast naval center)

6. San Diego, CA (largest West Coast naval complex)

7. Norfolk, VA (major East Coast naval complex)

8. Kansas City, MO (Whiteman Air Force Base, B-2 nuclear bombers)

9. Cheyenne, WY (Warren Air Force Base, Minute Man and Peacekeeper MX missiles)

10. Great Falls, MT (Malmstrom Air Force Base, Minute Man missiles)

ARE YOU SAFE IN YOUR HOME?

Take the following quiz about the security of your home.

1. Do you know how to keep your house from freezing in the winter if your electricity is off for several years? Do you have some type of wood-burning heater?

2. When natural gas is not available because of a disaster situation, what backup cooking facilities do you have? Do you have a way to heat water?

3. When a natural disaster strikes and you do not have natural gas, propane, or electricity, do you know what to do?

4. Can you survive with candles and batteries for more than a year? Do you have any solar-powered items to use in an emergency?

5. When public water supplies become contaminated, do you know how to collect and filter water for drinking? Do you have six months of water stored for each person in the family? Do you know where in your home you can find potable water for washing? Do you know how to ration your water?

6. If a storm damages the windows in your home, do you have enough plastic sheeting and repair materials to enclose the area to retain heat?

Your home and family are *not* protected for the loss of electricity from super solar flares if you answered no to any one of the above questions.

City Dwellers

ى‌ه Move out of cities. They will be targeted by looters and the government when there is a state of emergency. When the economy crashes or a natural disaster lasts more than a week, you do not want to be one of the people scavenging and looking for food. Those who are not prepared will be stealing from those who have more than they do. Move as far out into the country as possible, to a secluded area at least seventy-five miles from a major city. The larger the city, the farther you will need to move.

ى‌ه

Something that can make the gut clench is putting together the pieces of how the government is preparing for martial law. Puzzle piece one is the National Defense Authorization Act (detention of US citizens on US soil). Piece two is the Department of Homeland Security buying enormous amounts of ammunition and weapons.

Piece three is about to be implemented with FEMA preparing for mass fatalities on US soil.

When a national crisis such as nuclear war, violent and widespread internal rebellion, natural disaster, or civil unrest occurs, expect martial law.

Those who live in the cities have the illusion of being self-contained when the fact is that no city can feed its own people. At most, there is only one week's worth of food supplies in the grocery stores. Every single life-preserving resource is trucked into urban areas. Sickness from lack of garbage and sewage disposal and living with no electricity or running water are issues of vast importance. If there is no electricity, the banks will be closed, so money for food and water will be unavailable.

During a time of collapse or natural disaster, there will be rioting and the very real possibility that within days, all major routes in and out of the city will be blocked.

More than half the cities in the United States have had to make budget cuts for essential public services. In 2011, cities that have been hit hard include Detroit, New York City, Philadelphia, and Los Angeles. They have chosen to cut basic public services such as road repair, trash collection, and the fire and police departments.

Cities all over the United States will become hotbeds of crime and homelessness.

Learn how to live safely in a city, an apartment, or the suburbs. Urban planners did not build with natural emergencies or social unrest in mind. People living in the city usually have very little in the way of supplies or skills for survival. Cities are the worst place to be during an economic collapse. Buy a good multitool and enough plastic and duct tape to insulate your windows.

During a time of collapse or natural disaster, rescue organizations and emergency responders may not be nearby to help. Panic will be contagious. Expect rioting, with the very real possibility that within days all major routes in and out of the city will be blocked. Later, the cities will become death traps during the years of major economic and earth changes. Cities will be monopolies for scumbags who become the natural leaders with no scruples or morals.

Survival depends on preparation and planning an escape route before disaster strikes. What are the escape routes you can use that are *not* major routes? How will you defend your home? What is the best way to defend your person?

Have a water filter and plenty of bottled water and food stored in a closet, the laundry room, or under the bed. Have cash hidden that is equivalent to at least the monthly amount of your paycheck. How will you stay warm in winter and cool in summer?

You can create an area to grow food, like a sunny little space, a windowsill in your kitchen, or a small patch of lawn or patio. Plan an aboveground garden. Use pots or make a square-foot garden from an old bookcase or two by fours and plywood.

Hang some of your plants. A bucket with a hole drilled in the bottom can be used to grow a plant upside down. Place the plant ball inside the hole you drilled in the pot. For smaller plants, you can use an empty soda pop bottle that has part of the top cut off.

Plan and utilize the space you have. If you have a private space outdoors, collect rainwater and filter it for use. Create a greenhouse by enclosing the porch with plastic. This will help to keep the cold from entering your home as well.

Emergency Food Storage

To prepare for a disaster, buy some calorie-dense food, not just nutrient-dense food. Fruits and vegetables do not have enough calories in them to sustain you if you are burning energy under high stress.

Here is a list of foods to store:

> » Peanut butter.

> » Honey is healthy. It gives you quick energy and is a sweetener. It lasts for thousands of years in the can.

> » Twenty-five pounds of quinoa in an airtight container.

» Oil—have a few bottles of olive oil and large cans of coconut oil, because coconut oil doesn't go bad very easily. Oils burn long and slow for sustained energy.

» Omega-3-rich foods.

» High-quality fish oil in gel caps.

» Nitrogen-packed fish oil that can be stored at room temperature until opened.

» Chia seeds and flax seeds.

» Canned fish, especially sardines and anchovies.

» Salt holds fluid in your body. Your body cannot survive without salt.

» Sprouting seeds provide tremendous nutrients your body needs. Practice sprouting now.

Children: The Future of the Planet

෧෧ Do you know why you are so special? It is because the rays of love and open-mindedness allow me, DreamMyst, to come into your hearts and souls. Without you, universal light beings such as me would not be able to share our vision of how special and unique you are, not only to us, but also to the people in your world.

Many beautiful little energies are coming into this world now. In future years, when the earth has changed from the world you know, children will continue to experience the miracles of nature on earth.

As more babies come into this world, they need to be protected. These children are coming in with their DNA strands connected so they can help humanity survive. The younger generation is being born for a specific life purpose. These children will begin the new world with all of their abilities intact. There will be many more people with the ability to deep-trance channel.

When you think about DreamMyst, my energy gets even bigger and surrounds you, creating an energy of abundance, wellness, and peace.

Children do not have the bias, or disbelief that something cannot be or cannot happen. Their lives are impacted in a very positive way because of their belief, their sense of wonder, and the naturalness of trance channeling. Teaching children to ground and protect their energy, if done as a game, will help them learn about trance channeling. If done often enough, it can become second nature, allowing them to open, to receive, and to know that no matter what, they are always divinely loved and protected.

It is up to the parents to decide when a child is ready to trance channel and to record the session. Sometimes children will say very wise things. Children do not necessarily need to go into a deep trance to be a channel. Children teach their parents as the parents teach their children, keeping the family unit strong and allowing for communication. A child will not have to think, "Oh no, I can't tell my parents what I am experiencing. Otherwise I will get in trouble. They will believe I am pretending and that I have an active imagination." You know what? An active imagination is a beautiful, fantastic ability.

Transitioning from their current lifestyle will be easier when parents adjust to the situation. Children always need toys. They may not have all the battery-operated toys or the electric toys, but children always need toys of some kind. They can recreate and reproduce in their playtime the skills for their future. Little girls are the mommies and they like to nurture. But, you know what? During the period you're coming into, little boys will nurture and mother as well.

Those who are ten and younger will adjust more easily to the new family dynamics and lifestyle because they will not have had many years of experiencing everything at their fingertips. Older children will have a harder time. Although children who have video games like a Wii will really, miss them, what is nice is that children continue to be children. They desire and need toys and tools that show them they are responsible and a very important part of the family unit or community. Older children will learn how to build fires and use their minds in different ways instead of texting, watching television, and playing video games. Living a different lifestyle, children, and adults will not have the obesity problem. There will be exercising—not exercising like going to the gym, but in doing the things that are natural and physical for the body.

Explain to children beforehand how the world and economy are changing. You don't want to make children afraid. It is important to explain what is occurring naturally. Let them know they will be safe and with you. Talk to them. Introduce the subject at the dinner table or let them act it out during playtime. You do not want to sit the young children down and tell them that they are going to live in the dark and under the ground. Let them know it is going to be good. They can be happy because you are going to be with them. For very young children, keep it almost like play and playing house. Show what it will be like in their new world, and how the world will change from the world they live in now. This approach makes change seem not as scary.

Older children, preteens, can be given a little more information. Let them know that with the changes in the economy, they might not live in their house anymore. Tell them it may be decided that the family will go camping or to the mountains. Give the children information as they can understand it. This is dialogue. I like that word!

Dialogue is a conversation of what ifs—if this happened, what do you think the best solution would be? Or what do you think of this? This is where communication with your family comes in, so they are not afraid of the changes that are coming but, rather, prepared.

With teenagers, tell them what is going to happen. "We need you to do your part, because we are all a team and a family. We need to stay united. Yes, things change, and I am sure you can handle whatever happens. You are very good at change." In this way they will feel that they are an important part of the family unit.

All children, to the extent they are able, will feel confident and know they are a part of something that is going to help the people they love.

Give children the story of what life used to be like before the changes. Point out how positive their lives are now. You can tell them America is alive again, and they will be healthier and happier. America will not have a government that says, "I am going to keep all your money and other wealth. I am going to take away all your toys." The government will not be doing that. There will not be any taxes, so there will be more money.

You will work through the recovery in stages. Have you ever had an injury that required physical therapy? Well, the recovery will be kind of like that. The economic crash and earth changes will be like getting an injury. Physical therapy, which is the recovery process, is not always easy. It may not feel wonderful. In fact, most of the time you may say to yourself, "I don't know if this is really working." But you keep doing it, and then you notice it gets better, and *that* is recovery. Then you maintain your recovery and get stronger for the next steps of the recovery process.

Eventually your world and living will become better and better until the people in communities and towns decide what they are going to do in regard to the government. Government is not always a bad thing; the American people gave away their rights. If Americans decide not to have a government, that will be okay too. New businesses will spring up, and a thriving community will bring healing. People will have simpler lives.

Educate your children to grow their wealth and teach them leadership skills. These lessons will change their destiny and history. The economic turmoil may last four to ten years. Even with earth changes and natural disasters, young people who survive will create a better, stronger United States.

Your land and the people who can grow food from the ground won't have to worry about getting in trouble for it. Farmers who grow vegetables can eat raw food again. People who raise animals can eat eggs again or drink raw milk, not homogenized. They can consume goat's milk and cheese that is natural, or meat that is healthy for humans to eat. Life does not have to get harder.

Use the environment. Teach young people wilderness skills and military hand signals. Learn the plants for eating and healing. Teach children how to make tools from trash and rope from material. Preservation of knowledge and culture will be of primary importance. Children will learn trades that are best for the lives they live. They will learn healing.

෧෨෧

Q: We would like to travel with our children to different parts of the world before the solar flares take away electricity. Will our travels be safe?

DM: Right now you can take them. See where they are having many earthquakes. If a country is having many earthquakes, do not go. On December 21, 2012, the planets will be lining up, and we do not know all the changes that will occur after that point.

෧෨෧

Schools

෧෨ Homeschooling will be a part of the recovery until your communities become reestablished. In some areas, if a teacher wants to open a school in her house, she will be able to, but most children will need to be homeschooled. It will be important to have physical books and a computer that is kept safe.

Purchase teaching software for various subjects and many grade levels. It is possible your area will be without electricity or a public school for ten years. Have all the information you want on a CD or a DVD—all of your backup information, so it can be easily accessed during the recovery process. During the recovery process, computers can be repaired and reloaded with information from your backup discs.

There will still be doctors and nurses who can teach, but there won't be big medical schools. Everything will be on a less grand scale, simpler. Children will be able to learn, but perhaps not at the university.

Older children may be taught at what used to be a small elementary school or a building that was a church. It will just depend. There will be enough humans and enough variety to teach and show children what they need to know. Teach them the history of what the world used to be like for their parents and for their grandparents. All of this is important, and it should be taught to the children.

People who love children and want to teach will be very important. Saving and having some physical books will be important for your children. Teach your children at home so they can become wise young people.

There will be a period where you will need to either get into your home and stay there or have a safe underground home so you can live for days and sometimes longer. For children who are growing up during this period, and later after the government is reestablished, there is one more piece of information to consider. There is a good possibility that in 2034, 2035, or 2036, an asteroid may hit the earth near Rome, Italy. If this happens, it will be children who had parents that built an underground home who will have a safe place to escape the asteroid.

Schools will go away because they will be unsafe after 2015. Large school buildings could be used again later; it will depend on the community and what is available. Those big buildings can be used for sheltering people who do not have homes anymore. They can be used for many different purposes.

Education goes back to the basics of reading, writing, and arithmetic, in addition to learning about how best to take care of the new environment. Education will not include technology and the Internet. It will deal very much, though, with what is currently happening in the world. It will take a long time to bring technology back. Some may go away forever. Learning skills will be in many ways as it was in the nineteen-thirties and -forties.

Technology- wise, it may be like that for a number of years. As more people in the world get themselves and their lives back together, they will reach out as parts of a community to bring in the things they feel are important to have. Have information on CDs or DVDs for your computer. The information, the programs, and pictures, can be used for rebuilding America.

Q: Do parents have to worry about the schools brainwashing our children into believing in the New World Order?

DM: History books are not based on truth. If the New World Order overthrows America, the side of the winner will be the story that goes in the history books.

The children on this planet will grow up to be the people the new federation chooses to oversee the new system. The events that will change the monetary system are already happening. The consequences from the corrupt and damaging monetary decisions that began about forty years ago will keep getting bigger, with inflation and deflation occurring at the same time. Your economy will enter a downward spiral, and later it will level out. People involved with the new federation will be raising children and teenagers until they are old enough to become your future bankers and government leaders.

❧◦❦

Does preparing your children in a normal, healthy way for future life changes harm them emotionally? Many people think survival preparedness is to the equivalent of being paranoid or emotionally unstable. In a worst-case scenario, teaching your child to survive if something happens to you is a wise choice to make.

Survival skills date back to the beginning of time, but in this day of technology, there are fewer people to teach our children a different way of living. It is a real possibility that our children could be forced to live without the technology of electricity—without video games or microwaves. The time may come when their lives will depend on knowing how to hunt, fish, and store food. Knowing which wild plants, like dandelions, to forage for food and how to cook what you have found may keep you from starvation. Mending your gear, weaving blankets, sewing clothes, and working with leather to create shoes and waterproof bags may also become a source of income. The skills of weaving and knot-tying will come in handy to make nets to catch fish and to make strong rope, and may be life-enhancing skills.

Prepping and practicing survival can be fun, especially for children. Part of preparing for coming earth changes and survival in a post-collapsed world is learning and practicing new techniques. These are not a one-time play activities, but rather lessons in survival. If a situation were to arise, children who have learned those lessons will be prepared to face any challenge.

Teach your children how to text with their cell phones. Program your number and emergency numbers into the phones so children know who to call in an emergency. Let them pack their own survival/explorer bag, filter water, or discover how to make their water from living breathing trees by tying a plastic bottle on a branch with leaves. What child doesn't like to play in the dirt? Why not help them to plant a garden of quick-growing vegetables, such as green beans? Even very young children can be involved with planting a garden. Teach your child how to cook easy, simple meals. Learning how to cook using a solar oven is not only fun but also teaches them how to harness the sun's rays for survival.

Activities such as Boy Scouts and Girl Scouts, karate, 4-H, camping, horseback riding, and swimming seem like good learning opportunities. Encourage children to stay physically active and fill the hours of the day with positive activities rather than sitting in the house playing video games and watching TV. When free hours arc filled with activities, there are fewer opportunities for your child to be involved with the wrong group of friends. Activity helps them to say no to drugs and helps keep kids out of trouble.

Sewing is not just for girls; boys can enjoy it too! Sewing and mending are important skills to have. Older children can sew bags to keep in their –"get out of Dodge" bag. Make a child a safe archery set or a toy slingshot. Both boys and girls will enjoy finger knitting. Children have made forts and tents since time began; extend this skill in other ways to protect them from the elements. Show your child how to bury himself in a pile of leaves for warmth. Children need a child's versions of adult survival skills. These skills are effective and fun, and if practiced on a regular basis, your child will be prepared for any emergency. The experience of learning how to prepare does not have to be scary—it can be fun.

Making and practicing these projects teach children self-reliance, confidence, and self-esteem. Survival activities create memories your children will carry with them into their adulthood.

Forming Communities

&*& Everyone will have friends, neighbors, coworkers, and family members who may not know the world is undergoing changes. Human beings are survivors and industrious. Sometimes adversity brings out the best in people. I would have to say many times chaos brings out the worst in people, and you will see a lot of that. Your friends and family may not have your beliefs, or maybe do not know anything other than what they read in the newspaper. They want to be prepared, yet they won't be.

Human beings have an innate capability of accepting whatever's happening at the time and getting through it. Some of those people will get through the challenging changes, and they will thrive and be happy. You can thrive and prosper when your life, and your world, has changed.

Within the survival community, you will have several people who can provide support and assistance during emergencies and disasters. Having between fifteen and fifty people of varying ages is best to make up your community. Each person can offer a variety of skills. If your community is too small, you will not always have a way to protect it. Some areas will have larger communities and that is good, too.

Communities need guidelines and people need to be part of a team. It is not necessary for one person to know how to do all survival practices when there is a community of people who share skills. Consider individuals with a natural talent, experience, or education in growing food, harvesting seeds, caring for small farm animals, repairs, natural healing, hunting, or protection. People who write or who tally numbers can use their skills to keep track of stockpiled items and amounts of supplies. This will be important. You are not only creating your community, but establishing a brand-new government or a brand-new way of life. It's pretty special.

Life without electricity could be four to ten years or more in some or all parts of the world. Dig cellars. Use solar energy and alternative light and heat sources. Cooking and preserving food with solar ovens and dehydrators. If there is enough wood, keep a fire for cooking.

Doctors who are not in a community will travel to other communities to help. Hospitals and medicine will be scarce or unavailable. A dentist, doctor, nurse, herbalist, holistic healer, or chiropractor will be valuable to have in your community. Acupuncturists and different healers would be good to have in the community. People will be needed to do other things, such as take care of the small children or teach them. Look at the roles required. Everyone in the community will need to pull their weights and do their parts. Sometimes somebody is very good at cooking and can make a meal from nothing. This is a skill, an ability. Somebody else may be good at building and welding. Somebody is going to be the historian and take notes. Perhaps the person who is good at keeping history is also good at keeping records. So look at what you do, what you are good at, and turn that into a skill that will benefit your community.

Everybody needs to have enough food of their own to last anywhere from two to five years. Everyone will need to be responsible for their families. The community will decide if everybody keeps track of their own food or if it goes into the community stockpile. Each person must work in the garden or at other tasks.

Your community may decide to have a leader, and I recommend that three be chosen based upon their knowledge and skills. Will your new leader or leaders be male or female? It is up to the community to decide and vote. In a community, work with people's strengths, not their weaknesses. Each member in the community has a say-so about what should be done and what shouldn't.

There needs to be a way, even if it is drawing straws, to make a decision. Excellent decision-making within a community is about people putting aside egos and differences, assessing situations together, and keeping themselves and their families safe. Community members don't always have to agree, and they don't always have to be close or love each other. They do need to keep as a priority their desire and passion for protecting their community, protecting their water source, and protecting the land and crops.

What is the best way? Who is the person who is good at thinking of what to do and creating solutions to develop what you want? These are important questions. Who is going to explain the community to your children, and who will homeschool the children? Who is going to cook? Will there be a rotating cooking schedule, or will everyone cook their own meals? This depends on what kind of community you want to create. You could create a neighborhood where everyone buys their own properties, yet in the case of emergencies they'll go to a fort or structure to defend their mutual safety.

Get involved with your community to re-establish law and order. Hmm. When a stranger walks into a community and says, "Help me," what are you going to do? Depending on your community and depending on the community rules, if strangers arrive, you may want to consider not allowing them in, especially in the beginning. If you invite a stranger in and he decides to be mean and nasty, the protectors within the community will need to be willing to get rid of the intruder one way or the other. When a band of people comes upon a single household, there will be trouble. I do not recommend that a single mom live by herself, exiled. I recommend she get in a community with like-minded people who want to preserve an environment of abundance and safety. If she has family, she should stay with them. The closer you are to your friends and family—the more you trust them, the more you know them—the safer it is for you to be with them during this time of change and chaos. Search on the Internet for different groups living in communities within the area she is considering. Have information about people she can meet.

Humans need to look at their family environments. If they have aunts, uncles, or distant cousins whom they can join, this is good. Decide if you plan to stay where you are or join a larger family unit. The trust and love that families and good friends share are why it is a good idea to join as a family unit. If you have a home that will allow multiple families or extended families in your home, that is a good idea. In other countries, the grandmother, great-grandmother, mom, dad, and children all live in one home. Many times, you don't need all the space you normally enjoy in your home. Extra rooms can be made into living spaces for your family members. When family members contribute, that's good, and it keeps the family strong.

Even if you have to live next door to each other, at least that is better than being far away. Three blocks, a mile, or whatever distance is too far away. During a disaster period, what would happen if you couldn't get to a family member's home? You can always wait for rioters and looters to go away and then return to your home, yet if there are earth changes and disaster, it may take you too long to get there.

Single people with no family, or relatives will need to talk to their friends. Discuss your interest in creating a safer environment.

There is protection with greater numbers of people. There are more hands available to do tasks that need to be done. If there is a small number of people, everyone will have more to do. Depending on where you live, necessary tasks may include keeping the home secure, which could mean rotating day and night watches for intruders. It could mean patrolling the property, tending the garden, and charging batteries and solar items. There will be any number of tasks like garbage disposal. Where and how will trash be disposed of? These are tasks a community decides.

Learning how to make shoes is a great skill to learn. At least learn how to make moccasins and put some kind of a sole on them. Susan always wanted to make a pair with used bicycle or cart tires. Those would last a long time. You can learn how to make your own sandals or your own shoes.

Learn how to work with leather. This will be important. Leather can be used to create canteens and holders for liquids. This is the time to collect the information on how to skin an animal and tan a hide, as well as construct boots and moccasins. People who like to sew will be able to create clothes and bedding. In the beginning, it won't be so important because there are so many clothes. Skills such as crocheting blankets, soap making, and candle making may be beneficial, and many of these tasks can be group activities.

Some communities will be very far from each other. It is always best to have a community that provides for most everything it needs. Have people in your core community who can provide the needed items. Again, knowing who these people are and being able to trust them will be important. A next-door neighbor community may be very good but if you don't have a trusted relationship with other communities, you need to be careful.

America has an abundance of things. Bottles of shampoo or samples of perfume are good trading items. If people already have food and water, then they will want to trade for some of the things that make people feel good. Somebody like a peddler who wants to travel from community to community could take these things for trading. These items will be good for enjoyment, playing, or escape.

Time will slow down. You will go to bed earlier because you will work with the sunlight. You will become more connected with the seasons and the earth's patterns because your life will depend on being in tune with the new world, your new lifestyle. The earth will finish doing what it needs to do, and there will be a time of rejoicing. It's going to be such a traumatic change for so many that they aren't going to feel like rejoicing, but the time will come.

Allow your beautiful, unique human imagination to go to a space of endless possibilities for what you can create and what you, as a person or as part of your collective community, can do. This is a matter of how much you want to prepare or how much you want to wait until the last minute. Unfortunately, many people will say, "Oh, whatever. When it happens, it'll happen, and I'll just die." Or, "God will take care of me." Chances are you are not going to die, but survive. Why not thrive and survive?

So let's think about it. If you have a community, you can gather your neighbors and say, "Okay, it's time to build a building." All your neighbors can get together and raise the wall. You can make your own earthship house, using all of the plastic and glass bottles, old tires, and items you would normally have thrown away. It will help your environment, clean up your planet, and give you a place to stay warm or cool, depending on the season. If you all unite, help each other, create, and dream and work together, all things can happen for the good of everyone.

ॐ·ॐ

Q: DreamMyst, should there be a daily ceremony of gratitude, or perhaps dancing, to bring members together and create a community feeling?

DM: After the work is done, it is a good idea to come together, play music, sing, dance, and be happy and grateful. Another day has ended, and a beautiful day begins tomorrow. Celebrate life.

As far as connecting, there will be those who want to join in and those who will not. In a like-minded community, then yes, if you want to, have ceremonies, storytelling, music, and dancing. Again, it is up to the community to decide what they want, what kind of entertainment, what's important for their community. What are the rules of the community?

Q: What will happen to churches?

DM: As times get worse, people go to church. It is important that people have hope. They go back to their spiritual roots.

Q: What will happen to the movie industry?

DM: While there is still electricity, more people will go to the movies, just as they did during the Depression and World War II. This is important; it helps to escape. There will be songs of hope to uplift people in times of trouble. Lyrics will be about America's recovery. Safety in numbers happens when people come together as one for their ultimate goal, which is to survive and thrive.

Bunkers

Spending time in an underground bunker can be stressful. Emotions resonate to colors, and colors have different resonances of energy. You will want lavenders and some purples, or you may want all the colors. Do not use a lot of red in a bunker; the energy of red is anger or passion. You want colors to be warm and soothing. Consider a blue sky on the ceiling.

You want to have—hmm, you know how you hang a picture up on the wall? You do not want anything hanging on the walls in a bunker because it could fall off when you are in an area where earth shakes occur. Glue pictures onto the bunker walls, or use screws to hold them in place. Paint pictures of places you have visited and events in your life. Paint nature scenes, happy scenery. Paint a beautiful mural of what it used to be like when the earth was the way it was as you were growing up. Paint stories about what it was like before everything changed. Have paintings of real trees with birds in them. Create a living mural for your children. Just as in primitive drawings in caves, or even the more elaborate Egyptian drawings, paint pictures to show your children about the surroundings from before earth changes. They will know their home. Even when the world changes, they will have those memories on your walls that will help them remember the life they lived from an earlier time. They will remember what it was like. (For inspiration, look at the book *All Things Bright and Beautiful by Cecil Frances Alexander.*)

Display physical photographs or copies of paintings and pictures. Those memories are going to create hope. Those beautiful photographs are going to create a new and better world. Many people save important photographs on their computers. There may come a day when computers, not placed in a Faraday box will have burned wires from the solar flares. Physical books and photographs will be important.

When gamma radiation comes from heavy solar flares, you will want to be inside and, even better, underground. Store food you enjoy. Salty food makes you want to drink more water, and then you have body functions. Foods to store would be canned foods, which can be eaten out of the can and any kind of food that is easy to eat. Packets of dehydrated survival food are good if you will be able to have warm water.

Have things you love to do. Start playing games with your family now. Bring the ones your children love with you. You do not want electrical games because there may not be electricity and batteries run out. Puzzles, board games, and cards are nice choices. Bring paper to draw on, crayons, paint, and books to read—fun books, comic books, anything that is lighthearted as well as those things that will help you to survive. It will be important to be able to do something different for entertainment, after or in between hard work. Have books for the children to study, home study courses for children at different ages. Let them create food. Have available a number of different things they can do.

Make room, if possible, so children can move, jump, and stretch in the room or house instead of being quiet. Children have boundless energy. A mini-trampoline or rebounder would be perfect. If you don't want them running and fighting, keep them busy. Plan an exercise routine for the children three times a day.

For many people, the reality of creating a safe home and underground bunker is frustrating and challenging. This may involve a number of big actions, such as selling a home, buying a home, building a home, renovating a home, finding the best remote, safe property, securing financing, and actual construction.

I understand humans have emotions; they know what they know. It is hard for them to believe what they don't know or what they haven't been led into. Your government knows how Americans have become complacent. Because of this complacency, the government has been able to gradually, very slowly, in a very sneaky way, take away many of your freedoms. Americans have a let-it-happen attitude because they believe government knows best, yet the government is not looking after the best interest of its people.

Now you have this information. It is different from what you are used to hearing. It is frustrating. If you have a home in a city and you cannot leave it, then you need to protect your home. When you are expecting solar flares, you may have to stay inside your house for a number of days and put up plastic in your windows. Fill up, cover all the air vents, and stay inside. Anywhere that radiation can leak into the house, you want to have those areas filled to prevent radiation from leaking in.

Q: For those who are building a new safe home, should it be constructed with both electricity and candleholders secured on the walls?

DM: It would be a good idea to include the wall candleholders. I recommend having solar panels or a solar generation system. So many people have not thought about other sources or other ways of doing something.

Stockpiling Survival Supplies

Stockpile and save survival items now. They will be difficult or impossible to obtain after the economic collapse and when super solar flares hit earth.

The highest priorities are water and filtration. Have the necessary supplies to produce clean water, such as bleach, filters, storage containers, and water purification tablets. Remember that you can put a couple of silver coins in a five-gallon water container to keep your filtered water pure. Another consideration is to have an underground water tank or well for water.

Survival Items

It can be overwhelming to consider the survival supplies needed to provide your own water, food, heat, and electricity or light. In an economic collapse, loss of electricity, or both, it is wise to plan to be self-sufficient for many years. It is anticipated that those who lose electricity will have it restored by the government in four to ten years. Once it is restored, electricity will be too expensive for most people.

Preparing for the future means living a different lifestyle, in some ways it will be easier than it was to live one hundred years ago. It will be important to have stored food and water as well as to be able to grow food and obtain water from a source.

Here is a list that is circulating among the survival community of one hundred items to disappear first when there is war or chaos.

1. Generators (Good ones cost dearly. Gas storage is risky. They are noisy and are a target for thieves.)

2. Water filters/purifiers

3. Portable toilets

4. Seasoned firewood. (Wood takes six to twelve months to become dry enough for efficient burning.)

5. Lamp oil, wicks, and lamps (Buy clear oil if at all possible, but if that is scarce, stockpile *any*!)

6. Coleman fuel (Impossible to stockpile too much.)

7. Guns, ammunition, pepper spray, knives, clubs, bats, slingshots, wasp spray

8. Cords (Para cord, twine, string, nylon)

9. Honey, syrups, white and brown sugar

10. Rice, beans, and wheat

11. Vegetable oil (for cooking)

12. Charcoal, lighter fluid (Will become scarce suddenly.)

13. Water containers (Urgent item to obtain. Any size. *Hard clear plastic only*.)

14. Mini propane heater head (Without this item, propane won't heat a room,)

15. Assortment of tapes (duct, electrical)

16. Propane cylinders (Urgent: shortages will definitely occur.)

17. Survival guide book and *Mother Earth* magazines

18. Mantles: Aladdin, Coleman, etc. (Without this item, longer-term lighting is difficult.)

19. Baby supplies: diapers, formula, ointments, aspirin, etc.

20. Washboards, mop bucket with wringer for laundry

21. Cook stoves (propane, Coleman, and kerosene)

22. Vitamins

23. Propane cylinder handle-holder (Urgent: small canister use is dangerous without this item.)

24. Feminine hygiene, hair care, and skin products

25. Thermal underwear (tops and bottoms)

26. Bow saws, axes, hatchets, wedges, honing oil

27. Aluminum foil, regular and heavy duty (Great cooking and barter item.)

28. Gasoline containers, plastic and metal

29. Garbage bags (Impossible to have too many.)

30. Toilet paper, tissues, paper towels

31. Milk—powdered and condensed (Shake liquid every three to four months.)

32. Garden seeds, nonhybrid (a *must*)

33. Clothespins, clothesline, and hangers

34. Coleman's pump repair kit

35. Tuna fish in oil

36. Fire extinguishers or large box of baking soda for every room

37. First aid kits

38. Batteries (All sizes. Buy furthest out from expiration dates.)

39. Garlic, spices, vinegar, and baking supplies

40. Bigger dogs and plenty of dog food

41. Flour, yeast, and salt

42. Matches (Strike anywhere preferred. Boxed wooden matches will go first.)

43. Writing paper/pads, pencils

44. Insulated ice chests (Good for keeping items from freezing in winter.)

45. Work boots, shoes, belts, jeans, and durable shirts

46. Flashlights, light sticks, torches, and No. 76 Dietz lanterns

47. Journals, diaries, and scrapbooks (To jot down ideas, feelings, experience, and historic times)

48. Garbage cans, plastic (Great for storage and gathering water—also for transporting if they have wheels.)

49. Men's hygiene products—shampoo, toothbrush, toothpaste, mouthwash, dental floss, nail clippers, etc.

50. Cast-iron cookware

51. Fishing supplies and tools

52. Mosquito coils, sprays, and creams

53. Duct tape

54. Tarps, stakes, twine, rope, and spikes

55. Candles

56. Laundry detergent, liquid

57. Backpacks, duffel bags

58. Garden tools and supplies

59. Scissors, fabrics, safety pins, needles, thread, awl, metal knitting needles, crochet hooks

60. Canned fruits, vegetables, soups, stew, etc.

61. Plain unscented bleach (4 to 6% sodium hypochlorite)

62. Canning supplies—jars, lids and wax

63. Knives, sharpening tools, files, stones, and steel

64. Bicycles, tires, tubes, pumps, chains, and other parts

65. Tent, sleeping bags, blankets, pillows, and mats

66. Carbon monoxide alarm, battery powered

67. Board games, cards, dice, puzzles, and real books

68. d-CON rat poison, roach killer

69. Mousetraps, ant traps, lice hair and body treatment

70. Paper plates, cups, and plastic utensils

71. Baby wipes, oils, waterless and antibacterial soap (Saves a lot of water.)

72. Rain gear and rubberized boots

73. Shaving supplies—razors, creams, talc, and after shave

74. Hand pumps and siphons

75. Soy sauce, vinegar, bullions, gravy, and soup base

76. Reading glasses, hearing aid, extra set of dentures

77. Chocolate, cocoa, Tang, and punch (water enhancers.)

78. Survival "kit in a can"

79. Woolen clothing, scarves, earmuffs, and mittens

80. Boy Scout Handbook and Leaders Catalog

81. Roll-on window insulation kit

82. Graham crackers, saltines, pretzels, trail mix, and jerky

83. Popcorn, peanut butter, and nuts

84. Socks, underwear, and T-shirts

85. Lumber, all types

86. Wagons and carts

87. Cots and inflatable mattresses

88. Gloves—work, warming, gardening, and latex

89. Lantern hangers

90. Screen patches.

91. Teas, Coffee

92. Salt (buy 25-pound bags)

93. Cigarettes or tobacco

94. Wine and liquors

95. Paraffin wax

96. Super glue, glue, nails, nuts, bolts, screws, etc.

97. Chewing gum

98. Atomizers (For cooling and bathing)

99. Hats and cotton neckerchiefs

100. Goats and chickens

101. Birth control

102. Medicines (prescription and over the counter)

103. Bic lighters, flints for Zippo-type lighters, and butane to refill lighters

104. Cleaning supplies, disinfectant, soap, mop and broom.

105. Animal feed

106. Dental repair kit and clove oil, floss and lots of toothbrushes

107. Sling shot, bow and arrows and supplies to make and repair

Other Necessities

» Light Sources as many as possible, a light with a magnifier to wear on your head, solar flashlight, LCD lights, garden solar lights

» Solar-powered or hand-cranked anything, such as a dynamo and solar outdoor lights solar generators solar lantern radios, flashlights, solar calculators, hand-cranked cell phone and computer chargers, hand-cranked meat grinder, nonelectric hand tools, Grain grinder, Hand-operated can openers, hand egg beaters, whisks,

»   An extra hard drive for your computer

»   Extra parts for your car and if it has a computer, and extra computer

»   Coconut Oil (it stays good for years)

»   Colloidal Silver Maker (replaces antibiotics, and for water storage instead of bleach.

Food Storage

Food storage is for a transitional time. The purpose of stored food is to get you through until you have enough food in your garden. Stored food is also fresh food that can be pickled, fermented, canned, smoked, dried, dehydrated, and used to make jams and jellies. This is the way our grandparents lived; it was a way of life. Buy the highest quality food you can afford. Store some vegetables in the basement—cabbage, squash, apples.

Have two years of supplies stored underground and inside your home: packaged survival food, grains, dried meats, and freeze-dried food. Freeze-dried food has been flash frozen with the water removed. Once rehydrated, its taste and texture is that of fresh food. Freeze-dried food is the solution to your long-term food storage needs. Emergency food storage has a shelf life of twenty-five years and is lightweight. Store grain.

Store lots of sea salt for canning, to preserve meats, to season food, and to mix with water to brush your teeth. Sea salt for dental hygiene will keep your gums and teeth healthy.

Clothing

❧ A different way of life brings changes in styles. The most significant point about clothes is not going to be style. It is going to be about what is useful and what works most easily for you. Women may wear more pants because dresses and skirts get in the way. Dress to blend with your environment. A beautiful, bright purple or lime-green jacket would stick out like a sore thumb to let others know where you are located.

Aprons are a good idea. Wear durable clothes. Layer clothes when it's cold and there's no heat.

If you have children, buy clothes and shoes in larger sizes for when they grow larger. This way they will have enough clothes and shoes that fit. Buy the clothes on sale or at a thrift store. When your child outgrows the clothes, they may be handed down to another, smaller child or made into a quilt or something useful.

The machines to make clothes are in other countries like Asia. Stores that sell clothes, your department stores, will be looted or empty. When this happens, people will need to make clothes. People will remake clothes or alter clothing from a big size to a smaller size. Cotton has too many toxins and chemicals, so I suggest stocking up on linen and hemp material. There are people who spin wool, as well as people who have sewing machines. If you sew, look for a nonelectric sewing machine.

Gloves

 It will be important to have different kinds of gloves. Protecting your hands will be of primary importance. You don't want to get an infection and die from a little cut or poke. Stock up on latex gloves. Whenever you need to deal with anything that could be infectious or messy, use them. If you do not have them available, you can use kitchen sink gloves for those tasks, but kitchen gloves are more bulky. Gloves will be an important clothing item. Buy gardening gloves and leather work gloves, and have them in your stash of provisions.

Hats

ক্ষ A hat keeps you warm in winter and protects you from burning in summer. The sun will be hotter. In the winter, you will need something to keep the heat inside of you. So have hats as well as gloves.

ক্ষ

Tip: Thrift stores are a good source for inexpensive hats, gloves, blankets, jackets, wool, cashmere, and other naturally warm, used clothing in a variety of sizes.

Bandanna Uses

1. Bandage
2. Tourniquet
3. Sling
4. Eye patch
5. Cleaning wounds
6. Bind a splint
7. Ice pack
8. Cover a sunburn
9. Signal flag
10. Mark a trail
11. Collect food
12. Carry food
13. Cover food to keep away insects
14. Tie food bag to tree
15. Clean fruit
16. Water filter
17. Coffee filter
18. Pot holder
19. Dish towel
20. Napkin
21. Washcloth or towel
22. Hobo pack
23. Waist pouch
24. Wrap breakables in backpack
25. Toilet paper
26. Fire starter
27. Lamp wick
28. Canteen plug

29. Sink drain plug

30. Open stuck jar

31. Feminine hygiene

32. Diaper

33. Hang flashlight from tent ceiling

34. Clean firearm

35. Neckerchief

36. Dust mask

37. Cover head from sun

38. Chest warmer

39. Face warmer

40. Earmuffs

41. Sweatband

42. Wipe off sweat

43. Tissue for blowing nose

44. Clean glasses and other lens

45. Tie a ponytail

46. Pillow cover

47. Blindfold for sleeping

Barter

When you need to stockpile items to barter, consider collecting items you would give away freely during an economic collapse. Help others with a bigger need than yours. Give until it hurts, but keep enough for you and your loved ones to help balance the need for self-preservation.

Trade goods that are difficult to get or manufacture have more value. Unfortunately, you will have to defend your stock of trade items from those who want to take them. Useful tools, goods, and services will be more valuable than money when there is a currency collapse. Bartering is extremely valuable for survival in a long-term disaster situation. Learn how to barter safely in the post-collapse economy.

Basic Yet Important Skills

- » Know what you are buying.

- » Don't flash high-dollar gold coins; people may think you are rich. Pull out a silver dime instead.

- » Compliment the person or item and then point out what is wrong with the item.

- » Dress the same as others around you dress. Practice at flea markets and garage and yard sales.

Trade Goods to Barter

- » Distilled wine, beer, and moonshine

- » Tobacco

- » Worked leather items

- » Coffee

- » Medicine

- » Aspirin and antibiotics will be worth their weight in silver coins. If you only have one bottle of penicillin, seek wisdom in your rationing.

- » First aid items

- » Salt and sugar for preserving food

- » Luxury items—people will trade needed food for perfume, cologne, nice soap, toothpaste, makeup, and nail polish.

Offering skills or services to people who are eager to barter will be safer than trading goods because no one can take your skill away by force. Develop your special skills and offer them to those who have something of value to exchange. The skills or services you offer take up little space, other than the tools you will use to perform the job. Skills are easily learned and can be used anywhere. The more exposure your services receive, the more they will be in demand. Your skills will increase in value, and people will compete for your consideration.

Packing for Positive Action

༺ᨆ Thrive and prosper in this emerging new world. Grow strong and flourish. Many people in the United States have the erroneous belief that they live within a robust system. They have an opulent American reality that your government will care and provide for you. This is not true. Your government is not concerned about you.

The natural and fabricated disasters your planet and economy are experiencing are very real. This is not a Hollywood survival reality show, nor is it a hardcore end-of-the-world movie. Those are not genuine. You and the world are snared in the middle of an economic collapse. In fact, the breakdown began many decades ago. It will take only one event to cause the infrastructure of your society to implode.

༺ᨆ

"Get- Out- Of- Dodge" Bag

Q: DreamMyst, what is a "get out of Dodge" bag?

DM: A "get out of Dodge" bag has the supplies you need to grab quickly when you have to get out.

༺ᨆ

If you need to evacuate, you'll want to have a bag for each person in your vehicle. Have a "get out of Dodge" bag at home for each family member so you can quickly pick up your bag and go. The bags should include food for your animals, food for yourselves, and an emergency blanket. It is important to have your medicines in the bag. Store all your important papers in a spot where you can get to them. Have all papers in a protective file folder or envelope. If your laptop is working, you can take it, but keep a paper copy of all of your important papers.

Documents to include are loan agreements, social security cards, birth certificates, real estate titles, stock certificates, bank account statements—the type of papers your state or federal government deem important. Basic services such as electricity, gas, water, sewage treatment, and telephones may be cut off for a week or longer. Remember the rule: two is one and one is none. If the one item you have doesn't work, you are out of luck. The items you want two or more of are knives, light sources, lighters, and cord. Buy good quality equipment and make sure the clips on your flashlight and knives are well made and readily available when you want to use them. Keep two of the critical items in each of your survival bags.

Design different kits and packs for your needs. Having a number of emergency packs is recommended. For home, pack up a couple of storage totes and place them in an area of your home that is easy to access even when it is dark. Food for you and your family might be on a shelf or in one of the totes. Have a tub or container of medical supplies. Tuck into the storage area the other items you will need, like sleeping bags, a lantern, and sleeping pads.

For personal emergency, make a survival backpack for each person in the family. Include in this pack food, a folding shovel, three types of fires starters, matches, a magnesium block, a lighter, kindling (dryer lint), water purification tablets, multitool knives, a two-burner stove, a first aid kit, a whistle, a compass, a mirror, electrical tape, an emergency blanket, a rain poncho, and a gun. Adjust this list to suit the age of the person who will carry it.

Survival Kits and Preparing Your Crucial Survival Gear

Your "get out of Dodge" bag is only going to have value if the bag is with you at all times. Keep it in your car and keep it where it will always go. Create a new habit of keeping it with you at all times, as you do your wallet. A natural disaster or the collapse of society probably will not happen when you are home.

Most bags are made of bright colors to make them easy to locate. You do *not* want this. Use colors that blend in with your environment, like beige or muted green, to camouflage your bag. You do not want a bag too heavy and difficult to carry. (It is difficult to under fill a bag). Try carrying your pack for a couple of hours to determine if you need to lighten the load. If your kit is too big and heavy, you will not carry it around. Find a backpack that allows you to move quickly within your environment without snagging on branches.

Decide how much you need to pack and what the weight will be. The items mentioned below should be in your bag. Add food and other personal items that are important to you.

In a survival situation, you will eat or drink whatever you have, but given a choice, use a ceramic water bottle because the water leaches minerals from the bottle. The bottle also insulates your water, keeping it cool. The first item to place in your bag is water. Consider how much you drink, but plan on a half liter because your bag will get too heavy if you carry much more. Place your bottle in a woolsack to further insulate and protect your water.

Tip: Use the bottom of a ceramic bottle to sharpen a knife.

Water

Pack a half liter.

Wool Thermal Underwear

Your base layer is your thermal underwear. Wear this base layer when you sleep or when the weather is cold. Wool is the best you can use to protect your body and keep it warm, even when it is wet. Wet cotton works against you by making you sweat and takes away your body heat.

Neck Gaiter

A neck gaiter is an insulated, long wool tube you can use for many purposes. Pull it over your head as a scarf, or pull it up over your nose. You can use it as a bandanna or tie it around your head. This would be a great item to wrap around your face against a dust storm, bad smells, or radioactive fallout. Wet the neck gaiter to help you stay cool.

Wool Gloves

Choose good quality, fingerless wool gloves. Depending on the weather, you may need to pack two pairs of gloves—one regular and one fingerless. Fingerless gloves are extremely functional and allow you to use your fingertips for tying knots, cooking, or sharpening knives.

Wool Hat

Pack a wool knit hat with earflaps. A hat is extremely important. It protects you from the elements by keeping your body heat inside. If your feet are cold, put on your hat.

Wool Leg Warmers

Leg warmers cover your pulse points and keep your body temperature regulated. You might want to have a couple of pairs: two for your legs and another for your neck. When you are not wearing them, you will use them to wrap fragile items in your bag and to insulate your water. Make your own wool leg warmers by cutting off the sleeve of a wool sweater where it joins at the shoulder. Weave a drawstring through the top of the sleeve to tie around your leg. Use the cuff for the bottom of your leg warmer. Wool is a natural substance and lightweight, so it packs up small and will not weigh down your survival bag. Any 100 percent wool will work. Wool insulates when it is wet and keeps you cool in the summer. Synthetic clothing holds body sweat.

Maps

With a map and compass, you can navigate to find water and the quickest alternate route out of town. A city can be a death trap if you are not prepared for a natural disaster. Discover how many ways you can get out of the city. Get a declination map and make small adjustments to your compass so you can find true north when you are in different areas of the country. A declination map can be printed from the Internet and laminated. Buy a map of the area where you live and put it in a waterproof case or get it laminated. A Ziploc plastic bag will work if it is not raining or snowing. Place a pen with your map to take notes about good water locations, the location of your food surplus, and your route.

Lights

Keep a ten lumen, thirty-six-hour LED light that can be turned or squeezed on. Attach your light to a cord that you can wear around your neck. Put light where you want it with a headlamp. For night vision, consider getting a lamp with a red light.

Add extra batteries. A high-powered flashlight is great for self-defense and is something you will want to have on your person at all times.

Lighters and Matches

A box of strikeless matches is worth its weight in gold.

Instant Hot Packs

These packs are great for cold weather, frostbite, and muscle tightness.

Loud Whistle

A whistle is good for calling help. The sound of a whistle carries long distances in the wilderness.

Sewing Kit

Buy a sewing kit and include a high-gauge needle. Use the needle to sew up your pack, remove splinters, or to do a bit of repair work on yourself or someone else. Pack a small pair of scissors. Pack some white thread and a couple of Band-Aids in your nail-care kit.

Compass

Buy a compass with a mirror and a small magnifying glass. A good compass will have a ruler measuring 1–3 inches, which comes in handy for charting your course.

Magnifying Glass

The magnifying glass serves a dual purpose. It enlarges small names and numbers on a map and can be used to create a fire.

Small Knife Sharpener

To sharpen any kind of tool that needs an edge.

Little Pouches and Bags

Keep your coins and items protected in pouches that are easy to find.

Dry Sack

This sack holds your wallet and phone to keep them dry.

Cord

A cord comes in handy for tying things down. Pack 550-P cord, which is rated to hold 550 pounds of weight. You can buy this at an army/navy surplus store, outdoor or backpacking store, and online. Buy a couple of yards and loop one end, stick the cord through the loop, and continue the process until the cord is braided. Now all you have to do is pull gently to unravel the cord and cut off the size you need. Keep some cord in your pack at all times. Cut a couple of smaller pieces to tie up your pants around your knees.

Knives

A multi-use tool for living in the city is important and needs to be made from good steel with locking blades. The multitool has several blades, screwdrivers, a lifesaving can opener, pliers, a wire cutter, and other tools you may need in an urban environment. Heavy, but worth its weight in gold, is a wilderness knife with a leather sheath to carry it in. Look for one that has one-quarter-inch steel for the blade. The steel should run all the way down the handle of the knife. You can use this knife for a technique known as batoning, or embedding the knife in a tree and using a strong piece of wood or small log to hit the top of the knife. This will split or break the tree. If you can only have one item to help you survive in the wilderness, your wilderness knife is the tool you want to keep.

Some other items you may want to consider putting in your pack are duct tape and condoms for carrying water.

Preparing for a Disaster Emergency

Much of the information about preparing for a disaster emergency comes from the FEMA[21] Web site. It is good information. Does this mean I believe FEMA is the one to turn to during a disaster? Absolutely not. At all costs, avoid a FEMA government roundup. FEMA has many internment camps throughout the United States. While it appears that FEMA is an organization designed to help citizens that is only an appearance. This organization has been given tremendous powers of control by various presidents through executive orders. FEMA has the ability to control Congress and the power to control the military.

Emergency Shelter

Make sure all family members know what to do in an emergency, whether they are at home, school, work, or outdoors. This includes knowing the number of an out-of-town friend or relative who has agreed to serve as an emergency contact. It can be easier to reach someone out of town during an emergency than to reach someone locally, including family members. The contact can collect information on where and how everybody is and help reassure and reunite families.

Let children assist in preparing for an emergency. This will help them know what to do in an emergency. Ask them to think of items they would like to include in a disaster supplies kit, such as a favorite comfort food, a book, a puzzle, or even a doll or stuffed animal. Children can help the household remember to keep the kits updated by making calendars and marking the dates for checking emergency supplies. Allow them to assist in rotating the emergency food and water or replacing it every six months (also replacing batteries as necessary). Children can enjoy preparing plans and disaster kits for pets and other animals.

When disaster strikes, your child can take actions to remain safe and find shelter. "Shelter-in-place" means to take immediate shelter.

---

21   Rex 84: FEMA's Blueprint for Martial Law in America http://www. globalresearch.ca/rex-84-fema-s-blueprint-for-martial-law-in-america/

Home Shelter

To safely shelter in place in your home, you will need to plan on ten square feet of floor space per person. This amount of space will provide enough air to prevent carbon dioxide buildup for five hours. Keep on hand a roll of duct tape, scissors, and plastic sheeting which has been precut to fit your shelter-in-place room openings. You may need to seal the room to prevent outside air from entering. Access to a water supply is desirable, as is a working hard-wired telephone. Cordless phones will not work if there is no electricity, and cell phones may be inoperable as cellular telephone circuits may be overwhelmed or damaged during an emergency.

If you are at home and hear a warning signal, be ready to act quickly. Listen to your local radio station or television station for information.

1. Bring children and pets indoors. If your children are at school, do not try to bring them home unless instructed. The school will shelter them.

2. Close and lock all outside doors and windows. Locking may provide a tighter seal.

3. If there is danger of an explosion, close the window shades, blinds, or curtains.

4. Turn off the heating, ventilation, and/or air conditioning system. Turn off all fans, including bathroom fans operated by the light switch.

5. Close the fireplace or woodstove damper. Become familiar with proper operation of flues and dampers ahead of time.

6. Get your disaster supplies kit. Make sure the radio is working.

7. Take everyone, including pets, into an interior room with no or few windows and shut the door.

8. Pets should not go outside during a chemical or radiation emergency. If you have pets, prepare a place for them to relieve themselves where you are taking shelter. Have plenty of plastic bags and newspapers, as well as containers and cleaning supplies to help deal with pet waste.

9. When instructed to seal the room, use duct tape and plastic sheeting, such as heavy-duty plastic garbage bags, to seal all cracks around the door into the room. Tape plastic over any windows and vents, and seal electrical outlets and other openings. As much as possible, reduce the flow of air into the room.

10. Call your emergency contact and keep the phone handy. Stay off the phone.

11. Keep listening to your radio or television until you are told all is safe or you are told to evacuate.

12. When the emergency is over, open windows and doors, turn on ventilation systems, and go outside until the building's air has been exchanged with the now clean outdoor air.

Shelter in a Vehicle

Taking shelter in a vehicle may be an uncomfortable experience, especially in very hot or very cold weather, but it is safer than exposing yourself to chemical or radiological contaminants in the outside air. Keeping a disaster supply kit in each of your vehicles will help to make this experience more bearable.

Have a water filter. Keep a can with a lid and a big candle in your car because it will create heat. Have a blanket in your vehicle. If anything happens, a blanket can be turned into a tent or wrapped around you to keep you warm. You can pull and carry your stuff on it.

When you hear a warning signal, listen to local radio stations for further information. You will be told what to do, including where to find the nearest shelter when you are away from your shelter-in-place location.

If your nearest shelter is too far away, pull over to the side of the road and park in the safest place possible. Park under a bridge or in a shady spot to avoid overheating. Turn off the engine. Close windows and vents. Seal the heating and air conditioning vents with duct tape or anything else you may have available.

Listen to the radio periodically for updated advice and instructions. Stay where you are until it is safe to get back on the road. Be aware that some roads may be closed, or traffic detoured.

Supplies for your vehicle survival kit could include:

» Bottled water and nonperishable foods such as granola bars

» Seasonal supplies: Winter—blanket, hat, mittens, shovel, sand, tire chains, windshield scraper, fluorescent distress flag. An empty coffee can, a large candle, and matches will keep you warm and alive in cold or freezing weather. Summer—sunscreen lotion (SPF 15 or greater), shade item (umbrella, wide-brimmed hat, etc.) and a battery-operated, handheld fan

» Flashlight, extra batteries, and maps

» First aid kit and manual

» White distress flag

» Tire repair kit, booster/jumper cables, pump, and flares

Preparing Your Pets for Emergencies

☙☙ Stock up on your pet's food. On those days that you know there is going to be a solar flare, bring them inside to avoid radiation. Do not leave your pet behind. Arrange in advance where you will stay with your pet.

Many evacuation shelters do not accept pets, and rescue officials may not allow you to take your pets if you need to be rescued. Do not wait until the last minute to evacuate. Hotels, motels, campsites, and other facilities around the country now allow pets.

As you create your "get out of Dodge" bags for your family, you will want to create one for your pet(s) as well. Include enough food for two weeks in airtight, waterproof containers, and drinking water for each animal. Include bowls for food and water. Gather first aid supplies for your pet, small garbage bags and plastic bags for disposing of waste, a toy, and a blanket.

In a plastic zip bag, place current photos of you and your pet for identification purposes and a physical description of your pet. Include details or markings. Include a list of medications, vaccination records (especially rabies records), and a list of friends' phone numbers and addresses to return the animal if it gets lost. Include a list of emergency phone numbers (veterinarian, local animal control, animal shelters, Red Cross, etc.).

» For dogs—include a leash, harness, and sturdy carrier large enough to use as a sleeping area.

» For cats—include a litter box, litter, and a sturdy carrier large enough for transport.

» Fasten a current identification tag to your pet's collar with the phone number of a friend or family member in case your pet gets away from you.

» Transport pets in secure pet carriers and keep pets on leashes or harnesses. A harness is safer because an animal cannot strangle.

» If you and your pets cannot stay together, call friends, family members, veterinarians, or boarding kennels in safe areas to arrange foster care.

» Never leave pets in a car, even with the windows down.

» If possible, pets should be kept indoors during excessive heat or cold. Allow access to the coolest part of your home.

Disaster Supply Kit

A disaster supply kit is a collection of basic items that could be needed in the event of a disaster. Assemble the following items to create kits for use at home, the office, at school, and in a vehicle:

Water—one gallon per person, per day (three-day supply for evacuation, two-week supply for home)

» Food—nonperishable, easy-to-prepare items (three-day supply for evacuation, two-week supply for home)

» Flashlight

» Battery-powered or hand-crank radio (NOAA weather radio, if possible)

» Extra batteries

» First aid kit

» Medications (seven-day supply) and medical items

» Multipurpose tool

» Sanitation and personal hygiene items

» Copies of personal documents (medication list and pertinent medical information, proof of address, deed/lease to home, passports, birth certificates, insurance policies)

» Cell phone with chargers

» Family and emergency contact information

» Extra cash

» Emergency blanket

» Map(s) of the area

Consider the needs of all family members and add supplies to your kit. Suggested items to help meet additional needs are:

- Medical equipment (hearing aids with extra batteries, glasses, contact lenses, syringes, cane)
- Baby supplies (bottles, formula, baby food, diapers)
- Games and activities for children
- Pet supplies (collar, leash, ID, food, carrier, bowl)
- Two-way radios
- Extra set of car keys and house keys
- Manual can opener
- Whistle
- N95 or surgical masks
- Matches
- Rain gear
- Towels
- Work gloves
- Tools/supplies for securing your home
- Extra clothing, hat, sturdy shoes
- Plastic sheeting
- Duct tape
- Scissors
- Household liquid bleach
- Entertainment items
- Blankets or sleeping bags

Pack the items in easy-to-carry containers. Label the containers clearly and store them where they will be accessible. Duffel bags, backpacks, and covered trash receptacles with wheels are good candidates for containers. In a disaster situation, you may need access to your disaster supply kit quickly—whether you are sheltering at home or evacuating. During and after a disaster, having the right supplies can help your household endure home confinement or evacuation. Make sure the needs of everyone who would use the kit are included, especially infants, seniors, and pets.

Stock up on food and survival supplies. Make this your new way of life. Use this information to prepare for any catastrophic event. As DreamMyst says, knowledge is power. The knowledge contained within this book will allow you to make choices to live in harmony with nature and to be healthy, safe, and happy in a post-collapsed community. The transition into this new world may be challenging, yet it is guaranteed to be the greatest adventure of your life. When we all do our parts, we transform the destiny of humankind.

Chapter 6
Elemental Survival

Water, Earth, Air, Fire, Metal

Every day we warm ourselves by fire. We wash ourselves in water. We feel the wind in our hair. We walk and eat the food upon the earth and exchange the energy of metal for shelter and security. Everything in nature is made of these five basic elements. The proper respect and precautions you take in regard to these elements replaces surviving with thriving.

Water Element

Water is the world's new gold and the seedbed of all life.

❧ Water is transformed by pharmaceutical drugs as the drug residue, which is sometimes fluorescent in color, is eliminated through feces and urine. This all goes through a filtering system to become drinking water, yet the system does not filter out all the chemicals. The pharmaceutical companies know this but do not care. Fluoride and other chemicals will continue to be put in the water.

Rainwater or water from your faucet will need a water filtering system. You will need to filter or boil your water. If you have this information, then you can use it. Running your water over charcoal will help make it clean.

Find property that has two or three sources of water. Do not live near big water, like oceans, lakes, or rivers such as the Mississippi.

If you have a well, buy a nonelectrical hand pump and filters because if you have a well or water source, you can pump water into your home. When the water companies no longer produce water because there is no electricity and their computers do not work, you will have a way to get the water out of the ground and into your pipe. People should have a hand pump filter with them at all times. If you do not have clean water, a hand pump like the ones used for camping will purify water for drinking.

Start collecting water now. Get five-gallon containers to fill. Test your water with a swimming pool tester kit that balances the pH of the water. Then put colloidal silver in it because colloidal silver will keep your water clean and pure. Collect a lot of water. Everyone can go without food, but no human or animal is going to live long without water to drink.

Do the simple and most important things first. Buy or make a water filter. This does not have to be a filter that hooks to the faucet. Water is more important than food. You can always eat grass, but you cannot drink water that is not clean and purified. As long as there is not a lot of radiation in your area, you will be able to wash your vegetables and they will be safe to eat.

➤➥

The old saying "Water, water everywhere, but not a drop to drink" has a new meaning in the world today. Water is the life-force nutrient we drink. Without water, life dies. Your body is seventy-five percent water. Your cells live within this element of water. Healthy water creates a healthy, thriving body.

All the water on the surface of the earth has been contaminated with oil leaks, industrial agriculture, pharmaceutical drugs, sewage, urban storm runoff, and industrial waste.

Clean, pure water is our most precious resource, but where can we find it if the water on the surface of the earth is polluted? Look underground. Find an underground spring. No, you probably will not find it in that plastic bottle that claims to be spring water. Most of the bottled water advertised as spring water comes from a well. Underground spring water is free unless someone owns the water rights. It doesn't have radioactive particles in it because it has been underground for thousands of years, locked in underground lakes known as aquifers. When the water bubbles above the ground, it flows freely from one rocky stream to another. Spring water is the cleanest and best water for drinking.

The other purest water is natural hot mineral spring water. It is not only pure but hot out of the ground and filled with minerals. Mineral water may take some getting used to, but all of the minerals found in this water are great for your body. Try diluting it with natural spring water to add more nutrients. Another great choice is well water. Drilling a well can cost thousands of dollars, but once the drilling of the well is paid for, the water is free and clean. If you drill a well, be sure you have a manual hand pump installed in case there is no electricity.

What happens if there is a water emergency in your city? Hopefully you have found a spring and have stored up some fresh, healthy water to use in an emergency.

During an emergency, and for days after, there may not be access to water for people who live in the city. If you use tap water, consider buying a hand pump filter at a camping or backpacking store. This filter can be used not only with your tap water but for any water source besides floodwater. Sanitize your water for use by boiling it.

Learn where the water intake valve to your home is located. If you hear reports of broken water or sewage lines, or if local officials recommend doing so, shut off the water to your house by using the incoming water valve to stop contaminated water from entering.

Safe Use of Water Containers

1. Wash containers with dishwashing soap and rinse with water.

2. Sanitize by swishing a solution of one teaspoon of liquid household chlorine bleach per one quart of water on all interior surfaces of the container. Rinse thoroughly with clean water before use.

Store enough high-quality drinking water (two gallons of water per person per day) for everyone in your family, including your pets. If you have found a spring, fill water bottles with nature's purest water and seal. Or go to a place that offers reverse-osmosis water. If supplies run low, do not ration water: drink the amount you need today and look for more tomorrow. Don't risk dehydration.

Treat your water like you would a fine wine!

Protect your water from light, heat, and oxygen. With pure spring water, keep it out of the sun. The water will begin to turn green with life forms if left in the light. Store your water in a carboy bottle or ceramic bottle. Cork it and melt wax over the cork to seal it from contaminants. Place the bottle in a cool, dark area. Water will store well for at least a year. If you use plastic bottles to store your water, look for those that have been rated number one.

Your drinking water is not for bathing. Use other water sources for bathing. Use the water in your hot water heater, pipes and faucets, ice cubes, the tank located on the back of your toilet, and even the toilet bowl. If you have enough time to prepare beforehand, fill the tub and other large containers with tap water.

To use the water in your hot-water tank, be sure the electricity or gas is off and then open the drain at the bottom of the tank. Start the water flowing by turning off the water intake valve at the tank and turning on a hot water faucet. To use the water in your pipes, identify and turn on the highest faucet in your home to let air into the plumbing. Then you can get water from the lowest faucet.

Finding Water Outside

When you need to find water outside your home, try rainwater, streams, rivers, other moving bodies of water, ponds, lakes, and natural springs. If you own a pool, cover it to protect it for future use. Create a pond with a child's plastic swimming pool. A flat roof will hide your pond. If you have a lot of rain, collect the water in a barrel. You can filter it and use it for drinking, cooking, or bathing.

Be cautious about solar flare damage and gamma radiation in rainwater. This is when a dosimeter comes in handy to detect radiation. It also highlights the importance of owning a water filter. If you don't have a dosimeter, always filter your water. Clean water is critical. Those who do not have purified water will die.

Water is heavy. It weighs seven pounds a gallon, and you will need plenty of both drinking water and nondrinking water. A five-minute shower uses between ten and twenty gallons of water. Take sponge baths. Your toilet uses one to two gallons of water to flush. Line a five-gallon plastic bucket with a plastic bag and place a toilet seat on top of the bucket to use during a transitional period. You can do the same thing with your toilet at home. Line it with a plastic bag, and at the end of the day the waste can be buried.

Ways to Make Outdoor Water Safe

These instructions are not for treating water to be stored, but for emergencies when no other water is available. Untreated water can make you very sick. Besides having a bad odor and taste, it can contain toxic chemicals, heavy metals, and germs that cause such diseases as dysentery, typhoid, and hepatitis. Before drinking outdoor water or using it in food preparation or for hygiene, make it safer to use by following these methods.

Straining water: Pour the water through paper towels, a clean cloth, or a coffee filter to remove any suspended particles.

Boiling water: In a large pot or kettle, bring water to a rolling boil for one full minute. Cool it and pour it back and forth between two clean containers to improve its taste before drinking it.

Chlorinating water: Use household liquid bleach that contains 5.25 to 6.0 percent sodium hypochlorite (listed on the label) as its only active ingredient. Add sixteen drops (one-eighth of a teaspoon) per gallon of water in a large pot or kettle. Stir and let stand for thirty minutes. If the water does not have a slight bleach odor, repeat the dosage and let stand another fifteen minutes. If it still does not smell of chlorine, find another source of water and start over.

Distilling water: Fill a pot halfway with water. Tie a cup to the handle on the pot's lid so that the cup hangs right side up inside the pot when the lid is in place over the pot. The cup should not dangle into the water. Boil the water for twenty minutes with the pot lid in place. The water that drips into the cup will be distilled.

None of these methods are perfect. The best solution is to use all of them. Boiling and chlorination will kill most microbes but will not remove other contaminants such as heavy metals, salts, and most chemicals. Distillation will kill or remove most of any remaining contaminants.

If you plan to buy property, try to purchase land with a spring. If not, have a well drilled. This way you will own the water rights to your property. When the local town's water is cut off because they did not have a manual pump installed, you will have plenty of water to use, share, or sell.

Stay away from places and land where the water is shipped in from great distances, like Los Angeles, Phoenix, or Las Vegas. Should you live in an area without three sources of water (municipal, well, lake, or stream), then plenty of rainwater is critical. Otherwise, you may want to relocate to an area with three sources of water. What happens when water does not flow into your city? Water wars. Water will be the world's new gold.

Tip: Salt water must be distilled before it can be drunk.

Items to Consider Buying Before an Emergency

Rubber water bladders are good for transporting water from one place to another and can be found cheaply in army/navy stores.

Solar showers are great because they use a water bladder suspended in the air. Place your shower in the sun. In a few hours, get ready for a hot shower. For a hot shower in your home during transitional times, find a portable shower that has a propane tank hooked to it to run a continuous flow of hot water for your bathing needs.

Hand pump ceramic water filters are for home or camping. They have a ceramic element you clean with sandpaper and can be reused many times. A pump like this can be the difference between life and death.

Be prepared with numerous strategies for preparing safe, healthy water.

Healthy Ways to Filter Your Water at Home

ॐ◈ Put colloidal silver or some junk silver coins in your water to keep it safe. A colloidal silver maker is a good thing to buy. Water treated with colloidal silver helps you stay healthy, is pure, and is also an antibiotic.

When you need to filter and clean dirty water, use different-size stones, little rocks, sand, activated charcoal, and zeolite. Layer these and pour your water through. You will need a bucket with holes in the bottom and a container underneath for the water to drip, drip, drip into. You may want a five-gallon container with a lid to put water into after it is filtered. When you have no drinking water from the faucet because a solar flare has hit or the electricity has gone down, there will be little or no water in the pipes. If you do find water, it might be contaminated. You will need to clean out the invisible bugs in the water that make you sick.

Get a plastic bottle, like a big soda pop bottle. Fill it three-quarters full of dirty water and then put the lid on it. Don't fill the bottle all the way because you've got to shake it for twenty seconds. Shaking the water bottle creates bubbles that oxygenate the water. Then take something that is dark, like one of those *big* black plastic bags, and lay it out in the sun. Lay your soda pop bottles with water in them on the plastic in the sun. Leave them there for six to twelve hours and you will have good drinking water. That's amazing, huh? The plastic bottle brings in the heat from the sun. Shaking puts oxygen in the water and gets rid of all of the icky germs in there.

You could also put your bottles up high on the roof or anywhere you like. After the water has cooked in the sun, you can pour it into whatever you want. Fill those same bottles again the next day. When you are collecting water, some days you might not have as much water to shake up. You don't need to boil it because the water is being cooked in the plastic bottle that got hot.

❧⸱⸱☙

DreamMyst had the right idea about creating a healthy water filter with items you can buy inexpensively or may have around your home. This filtering system is cost-effective and easy to make. Even if your water is muddy and dirty, it will turn out clear and purified of heavy metals and toxins. When you combine both water treatments DreamMyst describes, the impurities will be removed and your water will be ready to drink. You will have healthy, pure water.

Depending on the quality of both the storage and the water, you may need to add peroxide, a bit of bleach, colloidal silver, or, as DreamMyst recommends, few silver coins to the bottles to purify the water. This will prevent pathogens from colonizing in the water.

So are you wondering why zeolite? Zeolite is a supplement that works by trapping heavy metals and toxins out of the air, water, foods, or vaccines. Zeolite is extremely effective in removing radiation and was used to remove radiation from the ground, cattle, humans and from the air in the Ukraine after the Chernobyl nuclear accident.

Earth Element

Walk and eat the food upon the earth.

❧⸱⸱ Support your local farmers.

Farmers are the keepers of heirloom food and seeds. ❧⸱⸱

❧⸱⸱ Right now Mountain House, a survival food manufacturer and internet store is not the only company your government uses to buy food. In 2011, the US government had contracts with at least three different companies to purchase ninety percent of the freeze-dried survival food from the survival food companies. FEMA is one of the branches of the government authorized to purchase about $500 million in survival food. The US government is not putting all the food in bunkers. It is going to sell the food to different countries and make money on it. None of the money will go back into what Americans need. It will go back into the greedy pockets of your government.

Some of is the food will be for the government's storage, but most will be sold to other countries. The government will buy up the inventory in stores because it knows things are changing. Meanwhile, the government will make it difficult for regular people to have a garden, to keep cows and goats for milk, or even to gather rainwater on private property.

The Food and Drug Administration does not want Americans to have gardens or to have raw milk out of a cow, which is better for you than milk that is homogenized. Definitely plan on buying your animals soon.

One suggestion is to buy your food in cans when survival food packets are not available. Cans are heavy and go bad over time. So take them out, use them, and rotate new cans into the stockpile. That's how you keep your canned food fresh. Another suggestion is to dehydrate food. You can buy the foods called freeze-dried, which will last for many years.

&⤑

Q: DreamMyst, the United States Congress had an argument about how much money to give FEMA. FEMA is a government organization that gives help to people in disaster areas. The Internet reported that the government is buying huge quantities of freeze-dried food—survival food—through FEMA. Is that why it was important for more money to go to FEMA?

DM: The US government is buying survival food to stock bunkers through FEMA. That's one of the corrupt spokes in the wheel, yes. The government buys through that facility. It has other programs that it uses. The survival food has to be allocated to certain government sectors and then sold to the highest bidder.

Q: DreamMyst, one of Susan's clients says she has been stockpiling for the future. Recently, when storing new purchases in her survival closet, she became excited by the realization of how much had accumulated. Then she had a series of thoughts. "I am collecting all this stuff! What if nothing happens?" Followed by, "It's okay, because at least I have it." Do you have a comment for her?

DM: During and after a disaster, it will be vital that you and your household, including your pets, eat enough to maintain your strength. Preparing is the key to surviving. When you buy that extra roll of toilet paper, toothpaste, floss, soap, food, or medicine, I can promise you that you will save on the cost of these items in the very near future.

❧❦

Nature provides balanced nourishment. Earth is the soil and provides the healthy food needed to thrive.

Worldwide food shortages are a reality, and Americans are living those shortages today. There will be no more days of cheap food. Between 2014 and 2015, the constant flow of food to the stores will end. Shelves will be empty because of severe draught and inflation.

Buy heirloom seeds and plant your gardens now. Learn how to save seeds from your harvest. Use any spare space, inside or outside, that has sun for growing your own food. Acquire knowledge about wild foods and know how to gather and prepare wild foods found in your area. Wild food will supplement your own food stores. In the future, this valuable skill will allow you to gather food for trade or money.

Your body needs salt to survive, especially if you are a vegetarian. Salt holds fluid in your body and is needed for many things. Humans and animals cannot live without salt. Himalayan salt and sea salt are healthier than iodized salt. The feed store sells twenty-five-pound bags of iodized salt for about eight dollars. Salt will be extremely scarce and valuable in the new world. Salt is an investment. You can use salt and trade it. Buy as many bags as you can.

Gardening

❧❦ People with money and influence are not eating GMO foods. The government is not necessarily buying heirloom seeds. The government doesn't really care what types of seeds it buys as long as it can sell the seeds. The government is not worried about recreating a new, green environment. If it was, it would change how energy is produced to eliminate nuclear power plants.

Buy wheat seeds and a hand grinder to grind the seeds for flour. Have as many five-gallon containers as you possibly can of wheat. A hand grinder for making flour can turn wheat into flour for bread, or you can sprout wheat and eat it. Did you know when you sprout wheat, it is wheatgrass? Stock up on wheat.

∂∼∽

Keep your organic, heirloom seeds in a cool, dry place. Choose a variety of organic heirloom seeds for your climate. Avoid commercial hybrid seeds; they have little flavor. With whole foods, the most nutritious vegetables and fruits have the best flavor. Get instructions from a book on how to save seeds from vegetables, or print instructions from the Internet.

Begin to plant your gardens with heirloom seeds. Use any spare space that has sun for growing your vegetables. Plant a garden and hide or camouflage it to keep it protected and safe. Grow your food in patches or clumps, so they blend with the landscape. Drones above and people below will be searching for neat rows of planted vegetables.

Food prices will continue to rise. The destructive weather in 2011 and 2012 established that the time is sooner rather than later to produce your own food. It is important to create and maintain your own gardens. Determine the size garden needed to grow enough food for each member of the family. Eventually it will be a main food source. Be sure to include orange foods for beta-carotene. Working your land will help your environment to thrive and help the bees stay healthy.

The Iroquois and other Native American tribes in the northeastern United States planted three crops together that grew synergistically on a flattened mound. The Indians planted corn, beans, and squash and named them the Three Sisters. The corn stalk serves as a pole for the beans. The beans add nitrogen to the soil which the corn needs, and provide amino acids the corn does not have. Squash provides a ground cover that creates shade, so the soil retains moisture. The tradition of interplanting corn, beans, and squash in the same mounds is a sustainable system and works extremely well.

Plant vegetables in large pots, reused household items, or a garden box above ground. Instead of sending plastic containers to the landfill, recycle them in your garden. Reuse and recycle to keep the cost of your garden at a minimum. Cloth shopping bags and cut milk containers work well as pots. A plastic trash can or tub is perfect for plants that grow under the ground. Think potatoes, yams, onions, carrots, parsnips, garlic, and horseradish, to name a few. Use a bag of potting soil by cutting an X in the bag and planting the seedlings in rows on the bag of soil.

Sprouting

When you cannot grow vegetables by a window inside your apartment or home, grow sprouts. Sprouts are a live food and considered a complete food because they contain high levels of protein, vitamins, minerals, and enzymes. They are pure nutrition for the body.

What you will need to grow sprouts at home:

> » Cheesecloth or a stainless-steel screen
> » Quart-size Mason jars
> » Tray to prop up the sprouting jars
> » Rubber band or a canning ring to hold the cheesecloth in place
> » A selection of seeds, beans, or grains
> » A cupboard or corner of your counter out of direct sunlight
> » Five to ten minutes each day to care for your sprouts

How to Grow Sprouts

Fill a jar with water. For alfalfa, clover, or other small seeds, put two tablespoons of seeds in the jar and let soak in the water for eight hours. Beginning the soaking process at night develops an easy rhythm for daily maintenance. Check them in the evening, then again in the morning.

After the soaking time (in the morning, if started at night), empty the water out and rinse the seeds with fresh water. Cover the mouth of the jar with a square of cheesecloth or a sprouting screen and set the jar upside down in a tray or bowl to catch any water that drains out.

Rinse the sprouts every eight to twelve hours by filling the jars part way with water and then draining them thoroughly. The water from soaking and rinsing the sprouts is great for houseplants, gardens, or for the compost pile.

When the sprouts have reached a size you prefer for eating, rinse them thoroughly and place them in the refrigerator until you're ready to enjoy them alone, in a smoothie, in a sandwich, or in a salad. They will keep up to a week.

> » Wheat berries—delightful, slightly sweet sprouts that, if planted, supply wheatgrass. Soak one cup whole wheat berries for eight to twelve hours.
>
> » Spelt berries—similar to wheat in appearance and taste, only a bit nuttier.
>
> » Flaxseeds (golden or brown)—can be sprouted in spite of a waxy coating. Flaxseed has beneficial fats and protein, and is delicious.
>
> » Alfalfa seeds—soak two tablespoons for four to eight hours.
>
> » Raw hulled sunflower seeds—soak one cup for six to eight hours.
>
> » Chia seeds—soak one cup for six to eight hours.
>
> » Sesame seeds—soak one cup for six to eight hours.

Many seeds and nuts may be soaked and then eaten without fully sprouting them. A favorite is sunflower seed milk made by blending soaked and rinsed raw sunflower seeds with water until they are the consistency of milk. Honey or maple syrup may be added for a sweetened version. Using the same method of blending the seeds, but only adding a little water, creates a base for dips and spreads, which taste great with chopped, fresh vegetables and herbs.

Construct a Greenhouse

Construct an inexpensive greenhouse with plastic sheeting and PVC pipe. Building a greenhouse in this way allows you to dismantle and move it if needed. Create an indoor garden in the sunniest room of your home or use indoor garden lights. Consider community gardens, roof gardens, or greenhouse gardens.

Water Wicking

Create a self-watering system using a two-liter plastic soda bottle and a strip of felt or material. All you need to do is to cut off the top part about halfway down the bottle, flip the top part spout- down, and thread your wick (the piece of felt or strip of material) through. Tie a knot in the wick to keep it from pulling out. Fill the bottom part of the bottle with water. Place the top part of the bottle wick-down into the bottom part of the bottle. Fill the top part with soil and plant your seeds or a small starter plant. The wick will keep the plant watered. Water the plant as you normally would.

Hydroponic and Aquaponic

Both hydroponics and aquaponics are soilless agricultural methods that use water with a blend of nutrients for crop growth. Hydroponics is an alternative method of planting your garden. It offers abundant fruit, fewer bugs, and can be set up indoors, outdoors, or in a greenhouse.

Aquaponics is based on the same principle except it incorporates fish, which help to keep your plants healthy. The byproduct of aquaponics is having fish to eat and being able to use the pond scum as an alternative fuel source or as mulch for the garden.

Hydroponic and aquaponic systems use a pump to move the water, tubes to bring water to the individual plants, and an air stone which oxygenates the water so the plants thrive. Your system can be simple or more advanced depending on your needs.

Livestock

చం-త Plan on the government buying livestock. Under the executive orders Obama has signed, the government has full authority to take control of livestock, farms, and farm equipment. Anything they want, they will take. So yes, the government will be buying animals, but it is not going to share with you. I recommend buying livestock soon. Buy small livestock like chickens, goats, rabbits, and homing pigeons if you have a piece of property that allows you to have animals. These animals are small enough to bring inside your home if necessary. All provide fertilizer for the garden. Train the homing pigeons to receive messages outside of your community. Chickens can grow on a quarter acre or less. Check with your town or city to see if you can raise chickens.

Chickens eat ticks, and the chicken litter is critical for composting. Chickens eat garden scraps and leftovers. Chickens will eat just about anything, including meat. If you are feeding birds or chickens in your yard, rinse, dry, and crush up eggshells and add them to a dish near the feeder. Female birds that are getting ready to lay eggs or have recently finished need calcium.

Eggs are good. Yolks are nutrition-rich. Eggs create sulfur in your belly, and that is good. Sulfur helps to digest your food and keeps you from getting as much of the radiation poisoning. Begin to store food now by canning. Purchase survival food. That is one thing that you can plan on—radiation will become more and more predominant.

Rabbits eat wild grasses, herbs, flowers, leaves, and twigs, and enjoy a treat of fruit and grain. Give them water. A baby bunny needs a diet high in fiber. Don't give them the treats!

Make a trap for small wild animals. You can catch fish with a basket. When they swim inside, close the lid really fast. Learn to skin an animal and tan the hide for leatherworking. Hides can become bowls or canteens to carry liquids. Tanned hides can make a very soft bed for a baby and can keep you warm. Turn a hide into a bag for cooking food. You can do these things, but you need to begin practicing now, before radiation contaminates your environment.

చం-త

Tip: You do not have to refrigerate eggs. You can keep them on the counter in a bowl for weeks and months just as they are. When you buy eggs, buy extra. When you get home, oil the eggs in the shell, put them back in the carton, and store them in a dark, cool area like a root cellar. They will last for months. Turn over the container of eggs once a month. The best eggs to use are unwashed, fertile homestead eggs. Washed eggs from the grocery store do not last as long. Refrigerated at 35°F to 40°F and they will last up to a year. Their whites may runny looking, but they will smell good, taste good, and have a good texture even after seven months. Do not use stored eggs for whipped egg whites. Did you know that if a raw egg floats, it is spoiled? However, spoiled eggs stink, so you do not need to float them.

Air Element

Source of Life

*Air makes life on earth possible and provides
the oxygen life needs to thrive.*

The air you breathe is filled with strontium-90 caused by radiation fallout from nuclear weapons testing, automobile exhaust, and other air pollution.

Air, the source of life, can be a terrible force of destruction when out of control. We call this force hurricanes, storms, tornados, and solar flares. The element of air can be a teasing, gentle spring breeze or the freezing winds of midwinter.

In the new world, air will sweep away respiratory ailments such as asthma and allergies, bringing back the freshness of clean air and the sweetness of robust health.

A strong immune system removes toxins and damaged cell material. Use heat and fire to sweat radiation and toxins from your body by building a sweat lodge. Use a heavy metal detox to clear the body of the toxins you breathe. Consider buying a gas mask and masks that filter airborne pathogens. To prevent radiation poisoning, fill the thyroid with proper nutrition, like brown algae.

Tip: Buy the kind of gear backpackers and climbers use to prevent a strong wind from blowing their tents away. Search for tents with simple pole structures and get a waterproof cover to store your tent during bad weather.

Bees

𝕰𝕰 There is a bee crisis and humans are not interested in bee keeping as a hobby. This is sad because the bee needs your help. Backyard beekeepers keep bees healthy. Local bees strengthen the bee gene pool. Create a buzzing bee garden free of pesticides to help stop colony collapse.

Hopefully the bees will go where there is not as much radiation when this becomes a problem. With all the magnetic changes within your earth, bees will be led into a different migration pattern as well. Insist that your government take interest in bees. Healthy bees equal healthy humans.

Mud bees will survive better than the ones flying around until radiation becomes a problem. If the honeybees die, you can still pollinate plants. Take a cotton swab, touch one plant on the flower, and then touch another plant on its flower. That will help the plants pollinate. It is easier to make healthy bees. Keep the bees safe. Your life depends on it. Give bees a voice. Like me, they need a human to have a voice.

𝕰𝕰

Honeybees are dying. DreamMyst says this is due in large part to all the cell phone towers and earth's magnetic shifts. There are many possible reasons. Among them may be genetically modified plants, pesticides, or earth shifts. Whatever the cause, if this continues to happen, human life may become extinct. Bees pollinate the crops and plants. Bees also produce wax for candles, honey, and royal jelly.

Bees' eyes are sensitive to polarized light, which penetrates thick clouds, so they are able to see the sun in poor weather. Bees use the position of the sun, and there is evidence they have sensitivity to the earth's magnetic field.

Electrical Power Grid Outages

The need to prepare for electrical grid outages is urgent. Due to the recent sweltering heat wave, extreme heat warnings were issued in fourteen states in 2012. Areas hit the hardest included Virginia, West Virginia, Indiana, Ohio, Maryland, and Washington, DC. One in three Americans baked in temperatures of over 100 degrees Fahrenheit across six hundred thousand square miles.

Imagine how having no electricity will affect you. What if there is no electricity to run fans, air conditioning, and refrigerators? A run to the store for ice may be out of the question, as the ice will be gone with no way to make more.

» Make a paper fan and use it to move the hot air.

» Wear a hat and lightweight cotton clothes that cover your arms and legs if you are in the sun.

» Spray your clothes with water to keep cool.

» Fill the tub with cold water and soak in the tub.

» Spray water on your head and neck.

» Soak your feet in cold water.

» Wet a bandanna and place it around your neck.

» If humidity is not an issue, open the windows on the side of your home that is in the shade. Then crack windows in other areas of your home for airflow.

» Go outside. Sit under a nice shade tree with your spray water bottle, and have a glass of water or sun tea to drink close to hand.

» Get in a pool or play in the sprinkler or squirt a hose and have an old-fashioned water fight.

» If it is safe, sleep outside or within a screened porch if you have one.

» If there are pockets with electrical power, gather at the library or other public buildings to stay cool.

» Before your meats turn bad in the freezer, cut in strips and dehydrate them in the sun for future use.

» Cook your food on a barbecue grill or eat your canned fruits and vegetables straight from the can.

While the outage of the electrical power grid system is not a natural disaster, there are disastrous consequences for not preparing for electrical emergencies.

The reality is we cannot alter our physical universe. Mother Nature does not concern herself with how humans fare as she creates raging storms, fires, earthquake, hurricanes, and heat waves. So expect climate shifts to the extreme.

Modern human civilization depends on electrical power grids to provide light and coolness at the flip of a switch. When these manmade devices go down, as they will do, we are unprepared.

In areas prone to storms, power outages may occur at any time of the year. It may take anywhere from a few hours to several days for electricity to be restored to residential areas. Without electricity or a cold source, food stored in refrigerators and freezers becomes unsafe.

What to Do before a Weather Emergency[22]

The great resource information below is from the USDA website and can be freely used. It is not Susan Norgren's or DreamMyst's information.

» Keep an appliance thermometer in the refrigerator and freezer. In the case of a power outage, it can help determine the temperature of the food.

» Make sure the freezer is at 0°F or below and the refrigerator is at 40°F or below.

---

22   http://www.usda.gov/wps/portal/usda/usdamediafb?contentid=2012/10/03 36.xml&printable=true&contentidonly=true

» Freeze containers of water ahead of time for ice to help keep food cold in the freezer, refrigerator, or coolers after the power is out. Freeze gel packs for use in coolers.

» Freeze refrigerated items such as leftovers, milk, fresh meat, and poultry that you may not need immediately. This helps keep them at a safe temperature longer.

» Plan ahead and know where dry ice and block ice can be purchased.

» Have coolers on hand to keep refrigerated food cold when the power will be out for more than four hours.

» Group food together in the freezer to stay cold longer.

» Store food on shelves that will be safely out of the way of contaminated water in case of flooding.

What to Do after the Weather Emergency[23]

» Keep refrigerator and freezer doors closed as much as possible to maintain the cold temperature.

» The refrigerator will keep food safe for about four hours if it is unopened. A full freezer will hold the temperature for approximately forty-eight hours (twenty-four hours if it is half-full) and the door remains closed.

» Discard refrigerated perishable food such as meat, poultry, fish, soft cheeses, milk, leftovers, and deli items after four hours without power.

» Food may be safely refrozen if it still contains ice crystals or is at 40°F or below when checked with a food thermometer.

» Never taste food to determine its safety.

---

23   http://www.usda.gov/wps/portal/usda/usdamediafb?contentid=2012/10/03 36.xml&printable=true&contentidonly=true

» Obtain dry or block ice to keep your refrigerator and freezer as cold as possible when the power is going to be out for prolonged periods. Fifty pounds of dry ice should keep a full, eighteen cubic foot freezer cold for two days.

» When the power has been out for several days, check the temperature of the freezer with an appliance thermometer. If the appliance thermometer reads 40° or less, the food is safe to refreeze.

» If a thermometer has not been kept in the freezer, check each package of food to determine its safety. If the food still contains ice crystals, the food is safe.

Fire Element

Fire is the energy of summer sun, flame, lightning, and solar flares.

It gives us warmth but also destroys.

Whether you turn a dial to heat your oven or heat your house, fire is a tool for staying warm, for cooking, and for light. When your normal heat source does not work, it will be important to know how to use physical fire to purify water, cook, and stay warm.

A good source of light is the most important item to have in your survival kit, house, and car, as well as upon your person. A small light on your key chain or clipped to your purse can aid you to see in the dark. Flashed in an attacker's eyes, it can temporarily blind him, allowing you to escape to safety. A small flashlight kept in the pocket is an effective self-defense tool even for children to use.

Buy and stockpile any light source that is solar. This will be a great barter item. A light that straps on your head provides hands-free light.

Consider the sun as a free heat and light source. Light a fire using a magnifying glass to focus sunlight onto tender leaves or paper. If you are building your home, face your house south for solar heat. Make or buy equipment for solar cooking and food dehydration.

Without electricity, there will be no air conditioning. For those who live in a hot climate, when you are inside remove as many clothes as possible. If you are outside shade your space to stay cool protect your body from burning. Place water or a wet cloth on your pulse points, over the back of your neck, and on your head to keep you cooler. A diet low in fat and calories will keep your body cooler when you sleep.

No matter where you live, it gets colder at night. For those who live in a cold climate, use anything you can to insulate your body from the cold. Warming pulse points will keep your core temperature up and keep you alive. Put something over your nose and mouth, like a ski mask, when you sleep.

A sleeping pad keeps you warm when you are sleeping on the ground. Have sleeping bags, hats, a down jacket, and warm wool clothes to use if you find you are unable to heat your house in the winter. An emergency space blanket works like a mirror to reflect your body's heat back into your body, and should always be in your car and survival kit. Heat up hot water bottles and take them to bed with you. Share your body heat with others in a small space. Use the cushions of your couch to stay warm.

Turn a phonebook into a nest by tearing out the pages, or use newspaper, crumpling the sheets of paper and stuffing them into your clothes. Fill a plastic trash bag full of leaves and lie on the bag or wrap yourself in it. Using some of these techniques will insulate and protect your body from the elements.

Fireplaces are not designed to efficiently heat a house. Invest in a wood stove for your home and stock up on wood so you can switch over when you need it during the earth shifts and economic collapse. A wood-burning stove gives you warmth that can be vented into all your rooms and creates a light source. You can also cook with it. Invest in some of Grandma's cast-iron pots and pans to use in a fireplace or on a wood-burning stove. You can cook a complete meal, including dessert, by stacking them one on top of the other and placing them in a hot fireplace or campfire.

> *Tip:* Look for good deals on wood-burning
> stoves during early spring and summer.

Element of Metal

Prosperity, Security, and Future Abundance

Gold is financial insurance. Metal is associated with money, wealth, and protection. It is a symbol of organization, power, strength, creativity, and goal achievements.

❧ Copper will be another precious metal. Buy guns and a lot of ammunition now. Soon the government will not allow it.

❧

How to Prepare for Economic Collapse

❧ The government has plans for the New World Order, a one world government. Unite throughout your United States, as a group, as a collective, and overthrow whatever the government has begun. This is called a convention. Civil unrest, with Americans fighting Americans, will come. There will be a revolution. It will not be peaceful, but at least you will get your world back. There is not going to be an easy way to do this. Writing polite letters to your government is not going to change anything.

At this point, you really do not have a democracy. If you look deeply enough, you will see the true happenings changing of your world—a world without freedom, a world where your government can tell you everything you have to do. Your economy needs to collapse so your government can dissolve. Because your economy is so deeply in debt, it will take years and years of economic depression to get out of your country's debt. Many Americans will file bankruptcy.

There will always be computers. Even if EMPs hit computers and information on mortgages is lost for many years, some will survive. How the information is saved will determine whether or not the information survives. If an EMP hits your computer, goes in, and fries everything, you will not have the information, and you will not have a computer. You can rebuild a computer. Some will come back, and some will go completely away.

❧

Hyperinflation is a period of rapid inflation that leaves a country's currency worthless. Such an economic period is marked by disastrously high increases in prices (50 percent or more a month). It is caused by the almost total collapse of a country's monetary system due to excessive deficit spending by a government. By 2014, hyperinflation will be one of the reasons people will be more angry and ready to take action to create a revolution. A revolution does not always lead to a physical war.

If you have anything of value, you might want to consider selling it now, unless there is an emotional attachment. These items may not have the same value after an economic collapse. Examples of some of these items are artwork, cars, coins with value above the price of their precious metal content, collectibles like baseball cards, stamps, and coin collections, and diamonds and other gems.

Many have asked DreamMyst how they can possibly afford to prepare for the coming collapse. DreamMyst suggests, "If you can't pay cash in full, do not buy it."

Get Out of Debt

ॐ Get out of debt, right now, today. Begin to stock up on silver, gold, and junk silver coins. Buy as much as you can afford. Junk silver coins are worth their silver value; they are not worth only a dime. You are not paying a lot of money for a dime. The dime is silver. All silver will increase in value. It is what will help you survive and reestablish your life in the future.

Gold and silver are for saving. For bartering in the future, make sure you have silver dimes because you do not want to pull out silver dollars. People will think you are rich. If you have a silver dime, you will be able to negotiate for some of the bigger items you may need, or purchase medicine.

I don't recommend you keep your money in the bank. You don't want to keep your gold or silver in a safe deposit box. When the bank, for whatever reason, can't open, you will lose everything. You would no longer be able to get your coins, valuables, or money.

Q: DreamMyst, for those with limited money, you've given the advice to pay off credit cards, then use those credit cards to buy gold. The explanation for this advice is because at some point, the banks will fail and any loans that are owed to them will go away. Yet, during a different conversation, you said banks would come back and open up their records.

DM: This is true. Many banks will come back. With gold in their pockets, people will be able to pay off the bank debt and still have a whole lot of gold left over.

The banks will work with the people. When you buy property or land now with borrowed money, you will have to be able to keep up the payments until the economy crashes and the bank fails. When you buy gold and silver it is yours and no one can take that away.

അംഗ

Make a List of your Debts and Assets

അംഗ It is possible that loan information, the actual promissory notes on paper, will be lost. The super solar flare will take out most of the country's electricity for many years. The EMPs produced by the solar flares will fry computers. Loan information banks stored on a CD will be safe. Some of the loans will come back eventually—many years from now—when electricity is restored and computers are rebuilt.

You do not want to stop paying on your mortgage if you plan to stay in your house. If you need to, look into refinancing if you're on an adjustable rate. If you have a flat rate, pay the minimum payment required.

Because of your economy's inflation, more and more of your paycheck—that money in your pocket—will be spent for food, gasoline, and necessities. Less of that paycheck will be left to pay your mortgage. Refinance if you can.

Many human beings think of their houses as being their asset. What they do not realize is that it is not an asset unless it is owned free and clear. If your home is not paid off and it is going into foreclosure, leave it. Walk away from it and rent, or get in a transportable home like an RV. One of your government's schemes is to make it so most people will have to rent a house from the government in the future. The government sells farmland and homes to other countries and the banks would rather have empty houses.

❧❧

How can you pay down your debt and continue to purchase necessary supplies? There is no time to waste. Pay off debt. Your preparation timetable should be as short as possible. If you cannot afford to pay down your debt, start storing food and resources instead. Sell anything you don't need. Buy more food. Do not get further into debt. Pay with cash instead of a credit card. Pay off high-interest debt, loans with adjustable rates, and unsecured debts first. Sell expensive vehicles and buy cheaper replacements using cash. To prosper during a total economic collapse, you need to have assets, not liabilities. Buy silver. Change cash savings into silver and gold.

When the dollar collapses, having precious metals will preserve your future. Use it as currency, or exchange it for a currency value after the economy restabilizes to pay off loans or property. As the dollar continues to lose value, silver dollars will preserve or go up in value. Protecting your assets in the event of an economic collapse allows you to prosper during a recession or depression.

Physical gold and silver will skyrocket in price as the economy worsens. Prices are still low because banks are manipulating the prices. This works in your favor. Buy as soon and as much as you can afford. Be prepared for the euro to crash. After that the US dollar will be next, starting a domino effect.

Remember, credit unions do not have the same sophisticated technology for storing their loan information as large banks. It is more likely your loan will go away permanently if you get it through a credit union, whereas a large bank will have your loan data on backup CDs. Once electricity is restored and computers are repaired, large banks will proceed with collecting loan monies. School loans will probably not need to be paid back. For those who want to go to school, begin now and get the education.

Thriving with Limited Financial Means

∾∾ Silver is king in the new world—physical silver, because it has many industrial uses. Retirement funds with stock investments will lose most or all of their value. If you have money in a retirement fund, take out a loan. Buy silver and gold coins.

∾∾

Q: Will more people default on their mortgages?

DM: The unemployment rate in the United States is higher than it ever has been. As this happens, people will not have paychecks, and they will lose their homes. I recommend that if your home goes into foreclosure, stay in your home and demand to see the original loan documents.

∾∾

Silver and gold are your best investments. To get out of debt, use cash. Be thrifty. Deposit only enough money in your bank account to pay bills. Withdraw and hide your savings.

Do not purchase any item that depreciates rapidly, such as an RV or boat, unless you plan to live in it. Purchasing an RV would provide a place to live. Living in an RV park is usually less expensive than buying or renting a home or apartment. Should you sell your home to buy an RV and have extra cash, buy junk silver coins or the one-ounce silver eagle.

When banks fail and close their doors, credit card debt will go away. Credit unions will eventually crash, yet they are safer places to have a checking account than big banks. Credit unions are required by law to carry more cash than big banks. It is possible that in 2013 big banks will take a "holiday" and unexpectedly close. You will not be able to access your account or use a credit card associated with a closed bank.

When the economy crashes, big banks will survive longer than credit unions. Most or all of the credit unions will be unable to reopen. Taking out a loan with a credit union is beneficial to you because there is a solid chance the loan will disappear when the credit union closes. Big banks will be able to reopen once the economy stabilizes. They have loan information saved on paper and on CDs that they will be able to access. Banks will eventually expect loans to be repaid. Otherwise, your assets will be seized or repossessed.

Large and small commercial banks will not give advance notice when they are going to fail and close their doors. Once they close, it will not be possible to withdraw your money. The small amount of interest you can earn from savings accounts or CDs are not worth the risk of losing your money.

Silver will appreciate by 25 to 50 percent. People who bought silver coins for $17 in 2010 have already earned double the value of their investment. Hide your silver coins. Hollow out a book and fill it with silver. Place the book in a bookcase or on a shelf. An empty tin of chocolate would be another hiding spot, or stuff a doll or pillow with packets of silver and gold.

Get creative and think of how you can store your precious metals in ordinary places no one would think to look. A safe is what looters look for and can be easily found. A small safe is easily carried away, or you may be forced to open it.

Sell anything you do not need. Buy food and silver with the money. Stock up on food. Go to the food banks and stock up on your food supplies. It is critical you invest in a water filter, which you can find at a camping store.

Buy an older car model year 1970 or earlier with cash, one without an electrical computer. These cars are easily converted to run on natural gas.

Get Rid Of

- » Municipal and government bonds
- » Cable and satellite TV (Use the satellite to make a solar oven.)
- » Vehicles with computers or computerized engines
- » Toys from China and other countries

» Luxury items such as paintings and jewelry (Remove the diamonds or other stones, and sell the settings for their gold value.)

» Lawn chemicals, pesticides

» Kitchen appliances that break easily

» Cheap, throwaway household items

Reduce Your Cost of Living

» Downgrade lifestyle expenses wherever possible

» Stop eating out

» Sell a car

» Get a cheaper car

» Carry minimum insurance

» Use public transportation when possible

» Find a way to be close to everything you need

» Decrease electric bill—turn off all power-draining electronics

» Use air conditioning and heat as little as possible

» Turn down the water heater

» Wash clothes in cold water

» Shop sales and clearance racks, eBay, and craigslist

» Use coupons

» Evaluate your cable TV, phone, and Internet expenses (Skype and Magic Jack are less expensive alternatives for long-distance phone calls and the Internet.)

Items to Buy Now to Prepare

» Farmland

» Fresh water source and a water filter

» Silver and gold coins

» Storable food, two-year supply

» Tent, sleeping bag, backpack

» Medications

» Sugar

» Salt

» Coffee

» Toilet paper

» Seeds

» Shortwave radio

» First aid kit

» Sewing kit

» Extra pair of glasses, extra contact lenses

» Dental work (Complete any dental work you have been delaying.)

» Clothing a couple of sizes larger for growing children

» Rifle for protection and hunting (Remington model 700–308, 9mm pistol, junk guns)

» Ammunition

Tip: Save your nickels. They are actually made of nickel and worth a nickel.

Gold Shouts Higher Inflation Ahead!

∾∾ If you can't afford to buy gold, buy cans of tuna fish or sardines and large bags of salt. When there is no food, these items will cost as much as gold.

Gold is *real* money and is a friend of the people. For all of history until the twentieth century, money was gold and silver coins. Buy as many coins as you can now before the price of silver and gold skyrocket. In a few years, after the values of gold and silver peak, their values will level out in the free market system. Silver is currently undervalued at about thirty dollars per ounce. For saving, keep the larger, pre-1964 silver and gold American coins for when the United States begins to get back on its feet. You will be able to build your wealth during this time.

∾∾

A good rule of thumb is to buy gold coins if you have ten thousand dollars or more to invest. With less than ten thousand, buy silver coins. For those with a thousand dollars or less, buy junk silver coins a few pieces at a time. For those who do not have disposable income, buy as much silver as you can. Trade in your gold jewelry and buy silver with the money you receive. Buy and save pre-1965 and Canadian maple leaf silver coins.

"Junk" silver coins are not collectors' items but are usually priced slightly over the value of the silver. Junk silver coins are dimes, quarters, fifty-cent pieces, and silver dollars. Dimes are easy to carry and stash. Junk silver coins will be good to have for barter because they are small. Smaller coins are better to use to survive until the recovery period. Use the bigger coins to rebuild your life in the recovery period.

Where do you buy gold or silver coins? DreamMyst suggests going to your local coin dealer. Purchases can be more expensive on the Internet, especially when you have to pay for insurance and shipping.

Gold and Silver

ক্স•৯ Gold And silver are your golden egg.ক্স•৯

In 2014, gold will go up to at least three thousand dollars per ounce.

In 2016, gold will peak at between six and eight thousand dollars per ounce.

In 2018, the economic depression will get very deep. Gold's value will stay about the same. It will rebalance after the economy gets better. People won't use their gold for anything until after the economy stabilizes.

In the future, the dollar will be worthless. Buy gold and silver in small measures of coins. Pay cash for precious metal. Hide it. Bury it. Do not put it in a bank. Gold and silver will be used to trade for food, shelter, and medicine.

Be alert to your surroundings when you buy gold or silver. Drive to the police station if you suspect you are being followed when you leave the coin shop.

The Seven Phases of a Country

1. The country is established, backed by gold and silver. The United States is strong.

2. The country has money. Everything is good. The government has influence, so it starts social programs such as food stamps.

3. The country continues to have extra money. Massive amounts are spent to establish a big military.

4. The country funds a war to make more money.

5. The government of the country decides to go off the gold standard. The reason is that too much money has been spent on war. The government is stealing from the people when it goes off the gold standard.

6. Inflation is created. Everything costs more money. It is financially wise to buy as many precious resources as possible, like gold and silver.

7. The money bubble bursts. The dollar crashes. The government tries to make it look good. The government will save the economy of the country if the government buys enough precious resources, including gold and silver. The country starts all over again.

Twice the United States has gone through these seven phases. Americans are now experiencing these phases for the third time in history. America is in the middle of the sixth phase. When the economy crashes, the value of gold will go up and will keep going. Most people will not be able to purchase gold because they will not have money to buy it.

Silver Is the Working Man's Gold

❧ Keep silver coins in your pocket when there are other things or services to use in trade. It is good to have silver dimes and quarters because then people will not know you have bigger coins. If you use a fifty-cent piece to purchase something, then people will have to give you change, and those watching will think you have a lot more. Dimes and quarters are easier to hide and weigh less. Bullion silver is for saving, like gold coins. Use gold coins when the economy stabilizes.

❧

Q: Which size should I buy? Do I really need to buy silver coins?

DM: Buy silver coins dated pre-1964: dimes, quarters, fifty-cent pieces, and silver dollars. When you have a nice, big, shiny silver dollar, guess what? Somebody is going to think you have a lot of money. You want to have a supply of little junk silver coins in your pocket to buy things, or for bartering and trading. It will not take very long to establish a new government, and later on, the banks will want their money for mortgages and loans. This will be the time to use your silver, to pay your debts. Silver will be your savings account, your retirement fund. Silver will allow you to create a better life or business for yourself after the economy crashes. America will go through what it needs to go through for its growth.

Q: Junk silver is a great investment?

DM: Yes; you want junk silver coins in your pocket. Old silver coins are no longer junk. They are valuable. Collect silver jewelry. It can be melted down.

Q: Please comment about investing in the stock market.

DM: The stock market is going to go away. You don't want to have anything in the stock market. It is best not have any stock investments. You want the real thing in your pocket—silver and gold coins.

❦❧

Silver will go up in value. Gold is not used as much as silver. Silver is used for many items produced in manufacturing.

Silver will get to three hundred dollars per ounce in a short time and will continue to rise. Silver coins can be used to barter, but a better idea is to save them. Junk silver includes dimes, quarters, fifty-cent pieces, and silver dollars that are dated prior to 1964. These coins contain 90 percent silver. Collectible silver coins are more expensive than regular silver coins because they are valued for their rarity and antique value. Do not invest in collectible silver.

Within the next two to five years, silver will peak at about one thousand dollars per ounce.

Gold and silver coins will be what people use in the future to re-establish their lives, buy new property, pay off loans, etc. Silver will be at its highest value when the economy begins to stabilize and rebounds. Its value will continue to rise, and it has many uses. This increases its value.

Chapter 7

Thrive and Prosper

ॐ Preparing for your future will assist in awakening your consciousness and getting your energy to vibrate at a higher level. As this happens, you will create improved opportunities and outcomes in all areas of your life.

The surging price of fuel and the poor economy will see a trend toward more physical exercise. Because of food shortages and the price inflation of food, many people will grow their own, healthier food for their families. Learn how to can food and freeze vegetables. Create a healthier lifestyle.

More and more people will decide to move away from large cities to create safe havens for their families, especially in 2013 and 2014 when police officers throughout the United States are laid off.

This period could well launch a grassroots movement for a new America. The beginning of a difficult cycle in 2011 will continue for many years in regard to the collapse of the US economy, food shortages, and soaring fuel prices. The economy and eventually the government will fall.

Human beings are not very adaptable as far as what is happening now and how the world is going to change. They see through blinders or filtered glass that does not allow them to see what will be.

Everyone will need a place to live. They will not all be able to stay in their houses. If your home is foreclosed upon, stay in your home as long as you can or walk away from it and rent a house. Owning a home is not an asset if it is not paid off.

Despite economic and earth changes, humans are self-organizing, and order will be restored a few months after this temporary shift. Humans have a good sense of what is right and wrong. Having experienced what does not work, they will manifest a renaissance of creativity in the reorganization of society. Those who are willing to adapt will adjust to a more primitive lifestyle.

❧✍

Q: What indications will there be to signify the United States has moved from the devastation phase into the recovery phase?

DM: It depends on the extent of the devastation. Some of the signs in life will be that more animals will start to emerge. Animals that are able will protect themselves from the gamma radiation of the solar flares, the earth changes, and the manmade disasters such as radiation fallout from nuclear reactor leaks. Animals know before human beings when something is going to happen.

❧✍

Knowledge is power. Desperate people do desperate things. "Prepare" is DreamMyst's message to humanity. What is your plan? Where are you going? What is the weather?

Do you live in a small town? You might want to stay. Traveling will be risky, so if you can, stay where you are. The closer you can get to your survival supplies the better—same thing with food. If you have your food with you, you don't have to worry about starving. You want to have the important things close to you. Even if you have to put supplies or valuables up in a tree or buried in the ground, know exactly where everything is. It is important to keep items close to you because semitrucks eventually will not have the fuel to carry supplies to stores.

In the collapsed environment, innocent, scared, desperate refugees who did not prepare will approach you. The best solution would to lie low and not let others see or hear you. Your challenge is to stay alive. If you are not prepared to help, don't risk your own or your family's welfare.

In this new society, no one will be entitled to anything other than what they have prepared for their family. A thief will feel safe stealing from you when there is no police force. Decreasing the size of your home is a good idea to keep it energy- and cost-efficient. It will prevent you from becoming a target.

Trades and Services

He that hath a trade hath an estate. —Ben Franklin

 People will still have jobs. In the beginning, the economy will not completely crash. Then everything will just go away. Some areas will be okay, and people will still have jobs and money to pay rent. Learn a new skill or create a home business.

Q: How will people earn money?

DM: Society as you know it will end. There will be no banks. People will need to learn skills that benefit and help others. The older people will have to teach the younger people those skills—how to create and make things. How to make alcohol, for example—not just for drinking but also for sterilizing. It will actually be a benefit to have somebody in your community who knows how to make a still and create alcohol.

Start survival training now. It's like having insurance. Be prepared and hope these events never happen. Do you have insurance in case something happens?

Susan Norgren

Here are some skills to learn or improve to make sure you are always able to work and have an income:

» Bicycle messenger	» Bicycle repair
» Repair	» Appliance repair
» Farming	» Day labor
» Health and healing	» Martial arts instruction
» Sprouting	» Boxing instruction
» Security	» Interpreter
» Leatherwork, clothing repair, sewing	» Selling produce roadside
» Tool making and metal work	» Handyman
	» Marine mechanic
» Wild food crafting (edible plants)	» Auto repair
» Welding	» Salvage
» Scrap management	» Small engine repair
» Veterinary skills	» Hairdresser
» Canning	» Massage therapist
» Organic farming	» Selling firewood
» Cobbler	» Food sales
» Fishing and fish cleaning	» Junk removal
	» Nursing
» Gardening	» Butchering
» Snow removal	» Sewing
» Building trades	» Metal detecting

Overlook no resource in time of need—no matter how improbable.

Dowsing can save your life and will create an easier transition into a new way of living. After the crash, a good, reliable dowser will be worth his weight in gold, as wells may need to be dug out by hand. The need for dowsing to create wells for people is a viable and valuable skill to develop now for use when we are living in a post-collapsed environment.

➳⋑ Service jobs, hunters, seamstresses, massage therapists, acupuncturists, midwives, herbalists, Chinese medicine practitioners, dentists, nurses, teachers, actors, singers, chiropractors, and doctors will have skills everyone needs and will be looked up to in the new world.

Butchers will be needed for people who eat meat. Whether it's wild or domesticated, meat will need to be packaged for eating. If you are in an area that has no electricity, then you will be faced with dilemmas such as, "How do I dehydrate this meat? How do I store this meat? What do I do with it?" Many people go to the grocery store and get red meat in a plastic container, correct? It will be important to know the person who has the special skill to cut, hang, and butcher the meat. Butchering will not to be a wasted skill.

Somebody who has been in the military or martial arts can offer his or her services for protection, or can teach others how to protect themselves and their families. That's an important skill.

Knowing how to sprout your own vegetables is valuable knowledge. Many people do not know how to do this. What herbs are good to eat? What herbs are good for medicinal purposes? Somebody who has knowledge of plants and the herbs will be very valuable.

Somebody who can tell a story will be very popular entertainment, for it will not be possible to turn on a television. Or you might only be able to use it for a little bit, if you have a generator. When people visit each other, everybody in the new society will want to hear stories that create hope. Human beings need to escape from the reality of coping. People who play music, who tell stories, who can draw beautiful pictures of what's happening in this new world— these talents create history, but they are also entertainment and become what is passed on to the next community.

➳⋑

❧ ❧

Q: What are we going to do with ourselves in the future? What kind of skills, talents, and abilities do we learn now to thrive and prosper? What can we do to sustain ourselves so that we're not just dancing around and making baskets all day?

DM: Making baskets will be a good thing. If you weave baskets in a certain way out of pine needles or different fibers, they will not leak water. Consider all your abilities when you assess your skills and talents. Should you have a question as to what might be your real talents, ask your friends. Don't ask negative people. Ask people who love and support you what your real gifts and abilities are. If you were to ask somebody who is negative and puts you down, he might not be truthful because that is his belief system.

Those who love, nurture, and support you will give you good feedback as to your special ability or talent. You may even be surprised to learn you have a talent that you did not know about.

Even though life may become simpler, that doesn't mean you will just sit around and do nothing. If that were the case, then you would not be able to thrive during this time. Assessing your skills and discovering your abilities will allow you to see the possibilities. Then you can consider what you want to do and what you might be good at, as well as what you aren't good at.

Q: Would shoemaking be a valuable skill?

DM: That would be good, as well as leather working, spinning, weaving, and sewing. At least learn how to make moccasins. If you get the information you need now, you can learn how to make your own sandals, shoes, or moccasins. Have the printed instructions and tools for tanning leather.

Q: How can people determine what career to have or how to make a living in the future?

DM: What is your passion? If what you enjoy doing can work to help create extra money in your pocket now, and silver and gold in your pocket later, then doing what you enjoy is something to look forward to. Having a service you can offer people may not make very much money, but it will be a valuable skill. The service or skill will be good to barter during a most difficult time period, and it will also be profitable in the recovery period.

৵৽৽

Communication

৵৽৽ Your planet is in a vulnerable cycle. As the earth changes, it is as if the planet is going to either give birth or be cleansed and cleared, blowing all the stuff away. What exactly will happen to your planet is not completely foreseeable. There is so much that could happen that will change everything. It is almost like, "Hang onto your hat and enjoy the ride!"

It may be that television goes away, or is available for only sporadic periods, depending on your electrical sources. There will always be those who will communicate via ham radio or other sources of that sort. I do recommend that you get a ham radio and that all of you learn how to use it very well. Learn to use Morse code also. If there is no electricity and no way to mail a letter, how do you think information will be communicated? Tap, tap, tap, tap, tap.

For the Internet, you need to have enough satellites up and running. With all the earth changes, scientists may not have the satellites working. Technology is going to be very primitive. It is not going to be as you know it now. There are so many variables as to what is going to happen.

Maybe you could look at the results and see what happens after the economy crashes and comes back again. But as far as your planet, the recovery process is almost unforeseeable. Some areas on the earth will not be accessible later, and some land may not even exist in the future. If all the electricity goes down, it could last anywhere from four to ten years. If that is the case, then you won't have the Internet very much at all either. I suggest everybody gets a ham radio. Walkie-talkies will be okay for shorter distances.

৵৽৽

Q: Are you saying it is a possibility the Internet will go away?

DM: Yes, for a long time. That is the way it will be with your banks. The banking industry is connected worldwide. When there is no electricity or limited electricity, and sporadic or no Internet, you will not have access to your bank. Life will return to somebody saying, "Okay, let's open a bank. I'll be the banker." History will backtrack to a time when people actually went to the one and only bank in their town. It goes back to individual businesses.

Q: After the loss of electricity, will we ever be able to use technology to have information and pictures stored on DVDs?

DM: A computer and other electronics can be plugged in to an inverter with batteries, using a generator to charge the batteries now DVDs can be viewed.

Q: Will cell phones come back when electricity is restored?

DM: Cell phones will probably go away. All of the technology will still be there; however, cell towers and satellites won't necessarily exist. Because of volcanoes, earthquakes, or nuclear power plant leaks, there will be bigger things to take care of and worry about besides cell phones.

Q: Will landlines work? Will phone companies be able to repair phone lines before the electrical grid is repaired?

DM: Yes. It would be easier with a landline. All they would have to do is go back to the earlier phones. The princess phone without the light in it would be good to find now. Phone companies will have to go back to the basics and figure it out, but at least they will have old knowledge they can put into effect. So, yes, I would say you could have a phone and that would not be as expensive. Many people are going to be in the dark, with no telephones. This is all going to be very challenging, especially for those who are so used to the conveniences.

Q: People will experience a lot of emotions if they are not able to connect with their families and loved ones ever again because of no phone service.

DM: Yes, that could be possible. Phone service will not be set up to call across the United States. It will be set up to call within your district or area, right there directly. This will occur after things begin to stabilize in your economy and after some of the earth shifts start to change. There will be earth shifts for a long time. This is the beginning of them, and your planet will experience very big earth changes. Life is going to be simpler.

Q: Will people write letters more because of lack of phones, or will paper be scarce?

DM: There will be very little communication, especially in the early stages of recovery. You will need to realize it took about one hundred years for you to come to this place of having cars, cell phones, and computers, which is good. Those who survive through and beyond the changes of the economy and the earth shifting will at least have some of the information to put everything together, but it will still take a long time. It will take getting people together to do all of that. It will take many years to recover long-distance communication if there are earth changes. If the only thing that happens is that your economy crashes, you are looking at five to ten years to have everything back up and running again.

Q: Currently the United States Postal Service is downsizing. People are losing their jobs because there is not enough government money.

DM: No. The postal service will not go away. It will get reestablished as quickly as possible. They won't be able to, maybe, send mail around the world, but they will be able to set up and communicate to some degree.

Q: Will mail be delivered by pony express or will gasoline become plentiful for mail delivery by truck?

DM: Depending on the amount of earth changes that have happened, eventually you will have an alternative fuel source. People who can create their own fuel sources will be able to drive their vehicles. People will be able to send messages by cars. There probably won't be too much in the way of airplanes except for your military.

Q: Will Americans ever be able to send a letter from California to New York State?

DM*:* Eventually, yes.

Q: Is that because roads and bridges will be repaired after the natural disasters or earth shifting?

DM: Only the roads and bridges that are absolutely necessary will be repaired. Yes. Communities will have to look at what are the most important roads to fix. To some degree or another, everyone will play a part in creating a new world.

Q: With fossil fuel being scarce in America's future, how will mail be delivered across the country?

DM*:* Communities will need to come together to create long-distance mail delivery. Communities will look into alternative ways to create gasoline for the post office. It is in the recovery stage that people will band together to create a way to communicate with each other again. There will be more walking because unmoving cars will litter the roads; but they can be moved.

Q: It is sad to know that we won't be able to see other parts of the world.

DM: Yes, for a long time. Other people will be taking care of their own communities, their own parts of the world. Those communities will eventually come together to create a government, but it's going to take years.

Paper and Paper Products

 School systems will not have adequate help for students. In many school systems, writing paper is beginning to become limited, and paper is essential for elementary education. Later there will not be enough paper. Teachers will have pay cuts.

Q: DreamMyst, when people are preparing to educate their children during this period of economic depression, will paper be available for children to learn to write? Should we begin to stockpile paper at home?

DM: Buy a chalkboard. Buy things that children can practice on, like magnetic letters and numbers that stick on metal. Children's work doesn't have to be saved if they're writing their alphabet over and over. Use paper for what is important, which may eventually be to mail a letter. Stockpile your paper. You'll have many resources to create and recycle paper over and over again. Paper can be recycled into more paper; this way you are reusing your resources. In the beginning, that's not going to happen. Later on, it could, but not in the early stages of the devastation or the recovery period. Nobody's going to be worrying about paper, except for the kind that they use privately, for body functions. Just as toilet paper will go away, regular paper will go away as well. Stockpile your paper. Start collecting telephone books now. Those old telephone books may be toilet paper later.

Q: Will the person who owns the company that manufacture toilet paper be important?

DM: Yes, if they can make and distribute the toilet paper. The person who owns the company and has lots of toilet paper will get very rich if he has people around him who need it. Think about it—how much toilet paper do you use in one week? How many rolls? Did you ever count them? Then you will understand how many rolls are needed for two years. People will want some of those conveniences, some of those things that they are used to having.

Some of those convenient things will be made again as early as possible. Toilet paper will be one of them. Toilet paper will become everything—it will replace Kleenex and baby wipes. You might want to save the old telephone books to use when there is no more toilet paper. Rags will be used to wash and be reused and recycled. People will want to have toilet paper again.

Q: So those who have babies, or are going have babies—they should prepare to use cloth diapers?

DM: Cloth will be used for diapers. There won't be any baby wipes or disposable diapers. To make cleanup easier, you might want to save used dryer sheets now to line your diapers later.

え～め

Travel

え～め Travel will change. Gasoline will be scarce and expensive. People will use roller skates, bicycles, those kinds of things. Put a motor on your bike and you can go for a ride without using much gas. You won't have to go real fast because there will be no reason to go fast anymore.

え～め

Q: During the early twentieth century, there were both cars and horses on the road. Not everyone had a car. Is this what it will be like after communities recover?

DM: Yes. Horses can be ridden and can easily pull a wagon or car. Wagons will need to be designed for the existing roads. Roads will still be available, but they will be cracked and have grass growing on them. Clear and fix the roads. When this is done free, trade and commerce can begin again.

Those with far sight will realize how they can create methane gas for their vehicles and create a way to solar-charge batteries. People will learn how to think, discovering within themselves new abilities and solutions. This is why your new America, will become strong and healthy again, for this to happen there will need to be a complete collapse. During the recovery, there will be martial law. There will be riots in the beginning, during the transitional time. The military will realize they need to support the people, not the politicians who carry the power, and the government will be overthrown.

Q: How will future earth changes affect roads and bridges?

DM: Flooding, volcanoes, and hurricanes will damage and destroy roads and bridges. Damage will mean bridges may not be safe. You may have to find a way around or take a boat across if you can. It depends on where the most damage hits as to how difficult it will be to get to the other side. The roads will become broken, cracked, and not easily driven on. Cars may be stuck in the middle of the road, with no way other than manpower to push them out of the way.

Q: What will happen to the supply of gasoline?

DM: Gasoline will become unavailable. You need to have a backup plan. If you roller-skate or ride a bicycle or shake your legs and go for a walk, those are good things. People who live in the cities don't have a place to store fuel, and storing gasoline can cause a *big* fire! People talk about a future that will be a thousand years of peace. Well, part of the reason for peace is because no one can get to the other person to start another war.

Q: When will gasoline run out? Will gas stations have backup generators to pump gas?

DM: Yes, some gas stations will have backup generators. Some of the big companies already have a good idea of what is going to happen, and they are preparing. Some will have backup generators, but gasoline will be prohibitively expensive. When electricity is lost from the solar flares, it will take a while to put the backup system in motion. It will be a problem moving through all the stranded vehicles on the road. When there are stranded cars and trucks on the road, you can use a hose and suck the gasoline out of the stranded vehicles to put in your car or in a big metal gas can.

I would highly recommend you look for alternative sources you could use, like plants that are fast growing, so you can make your own methane fuel. When you compost vegetables, they ferment. You could create methane. It doesn't have to be only apples and potatoes. There are different ways to create methane, which is a very good source of natural fuel for your vehicles.

Q: If a community wanted to plan their recovery on a big scale, should they consider growing a large crop of apples, corn, or potatoes that can be turned into fuel?

DM: Yes. Grow a big crop to sell to others for food or for gasoline. Yes.

Q: In the future, will it be possible to create cars that do not use fossil fuel?

DM: People say, "Okay, this is what we have. Let's see what I can create." Batteries can have solar power. That is alternative and green technology, which is something good to have. Human beings have ideas to create solutions. They work with mechanical things, turn them over, study them, and consider how to create the reality of their ideas. There are a lot of people, some of them without jobs, who know how to build cars now. If those people were to get together, thinking about a better way, cars of the future could be created.

Q: DreamMyst, are you suggesting that those with automobile knowledge invent cars now for people to have after the recovery?

DM: Inventors and scientists can get started now. It may be easier to get one of those three-wheeled bicycles with a motor and a cart. You could just sit in it and go for a ride.

Q: There is no real point to developing electric cars?

DM: Not unless you have a way to charge your electric car. Again, somebody who is great at inventing things could create a completely solar-powered car that is charged from the inverter and a solar generator.

Q: How will we purchase new cars? With silver and gold coins?

DM: Silver and gold coins are for a future time when the government is reestablished and you're ready to invest in your country and yourself. You will be able to use gold and silver, once they revalue, on those things you desire.

Q: Will we live in America for an extended period without cars before solar-powered automobiles are invented?

DM: Yes. Your current new cars have computers in them. When the solar flares hit, you can expect that computers and wires in cars will fry, burn up. Cars won't work anymore because of electric damage from the solar flares.

Q: What is the best vehicle for people to have? A heavy-duty truck, or perhaps a small motorcycle?

DM: Motorcycles have gasoline issues. An alternative source will be needed for gasoline. A motorcycle is a good idea as long as it does not have a computer.

If you have a car, you will need to make sure that your car is rebuilt without the computer, and that the wires are properly covered so the electromagnetic pulses cannot go into the battery and the ignition. With that protection for your vehicle, you will need to consider an alternative fuel source. If they can pump the gasoline out of the tanks at gas stations, it will be prohibitively expensive. I recommend bicycles with big tires on them. You do not need to worry about bicycles at the beginning of the catastrophic changes. Later, you will be able to resurrect some of your vehicles. Human beings are ingenious. If your computer is fried in your car, it will not work. Unless you have another computer to install in your car, or another ignition, you will not be able to fix the car.

Resourcefulness

ॐ Human beings need to learn to be completely independent, free of any reliance on anything. You may be living off the grid from 2014 until approximately 2024. You know what, though? I think it's good, because when you look at situations, you ask, "What can we do? How can we best create this?" You are not looking at a situation and saying, "Oh my goodness, life is going to be miserable." Americans just forgot what it is like to come from a simpler place and time.

Each of you creates your reality. Whether it is fearful or joyful, you create this reality. As you're creating a reality, look at what you can do. Create, make things come together, and make something better. Ingenuity is the art of doing more with less, of making a needed item from simple materials. Miracles become realities. You have so much you can gain. If you do not know how to preserve your own vegetables, then you need to find somebody who does. What can you do to show others an easier way? Important people will be those who know how to knot and make a net, people who know how to use and make a rope, because a rope will be very good.

Cans of sardines and tuna fish may be worth more than the gold or silver coins you hide. Fish is food and can be traded for something you need a little bit more. Stock up. There are many nutrients in tuna and sardines. Fish is great protein for the human body. Stock up on honey. Salt is a necessity; it preserves meat and flavors food. Salt can be used in many ways, so start collecting salt. Go to the feed store and buy as many twenty-five-pound bags of salt as you can afford—some for you, and some to sell or trade.

Keep your survival needs stocked up to eliminate having to leave your home and stand in line for a handout that might not be available. Keep your fuel tanks full. This means gas, propane, or diesel. Buy a number of small propane tanks and attachments for a lantern, a stove, and a heater. Stay warm by sectioning off a well-ventilated area of your house.

Humans use plastic bags, many plastic things. You can use plastic bags to stay warm. Did you know that? Plastic can be cut, or you can glue plastic parts together, melt them together. Slippers and hats can be made of plastic. Plastic bottles that don't break down can be used to create resources like walls in a house, flower pots for plants, solar lights, and toys for children. Use your creativity on a practical level and integrate new ways for a new world. Reusing plastic will help by not leaving a footprint on the planet. In the winter, collect snow in a bucket and boil it. On days where there is plenty of rain, put out a rain barrel to collect water.

Q: What should be done with trash?

DM: You dig a hole deep and you bury it.

Resourcefulness is crucial and will require supplies you will not be able to get at your local hardware store any longer. Buy them now while you still can. Start collecting anything that is solar-powered or hand-cranked. Get the basics—an ax, handsaw, screwdriver. Learn basic repair skills.

Know how to lubricate or grease your tools and equipment. Collect fishing line, dental floss, chains, twine, and string. Buy nails, hammers, hand-powered tools, saws, clamps, vises, anvils, sewing needles, thread, scissors, razor blades, box cutters, crowbars, sledgehammers, hoes, rakes, syringes, safety pins, clothespins, paper, pencils, erasers, screws, bolts, and nuts. Buy an assortment of different adhesives such as duct tape, plumbing tape, masking tape, black electrical tape, super glue for the medicine kit (great for sealing cuts), basic glues, epoxy, and J-B Weld (cold welding compound).

Collect common ingredients you can use for many purposes. Buy twenty-five pounds of baking soda. It is very versatile for cooking, cleaning laundry, and medical use. Borax is good for all kinds of things as well—as a pain reliever for arthritis and as a laundry booster. Castile soap can be used for bathing and for laundry soap. Ammonia, bleach, iodine crystals, and salt are all useful. Activated carbon can be used for filtering water or air and to treat accidental poisoning. Metal clothes hangers, which are now somewhat difficult to find, make a good tool. Go to a drycleaners and see if you can buy a bunch from them. A metal clothes hanger can be used as a dowsing rod, a plant stake, and a lock pick for a car door. It is also strong enough to hold something in place. Metal hangers don't take up much room in the closet should you decide to use them to hang your clothes.

Can you change a bike tire or fix a flat tire? If not, learn how. Buy extra bicycle tubes and tires and find a way you can protect them. What would you need to make a tire patch? What can you use to line the inside of the tire so you won't puncture the tire? Sheets of plastic or bubble wrap placed on a slightly damp window with duct tape make good insulators for windows and effectively reduce your heating bill. Plastic can also be used to create a small greenhouse.

Faraday Cage

Q: I heard that an electronic device could be placed inside a trash can on top of a bathroom mat with a rubber bottom to protect electronics from EMP damage. Is this true?

DM: Well, maybe not, unless the trash is all metal. I recommend you wrap each item up in foil and then in plastic. Make sure all plugs are disconnected, and individually wrap the cords as well.

Keep everything wrapped and separate, and put them in your Faraday box. Take out the battery; you do not want a battery connected to your computer. If you have a computer, you will want to create a special environment for it so it cannot be hurt. But, yes, a rubber mat is not going to cause any harm because it is like a cushion. Get a laptop computer and put it in your little Faraday cage too. There is less of a chance that those energy pulses will affect a laptop.

ॐ∽

A Faraday box or cage can be built around your home or car using simple chicken wire. A Faraday cage is a metal box made out of chicken wire overlapped to make sure everything is covered.

This is probably the most economical way to turn your garage into a Faraday box. Go to Home Depot, buy a bunch of the small-mesh chicken wire fencing, and cover the whole garage—windows, walls, floors, and ceilings. Ask for metal fencing that comes in three feet by ten feet rolls.

Make sure there are no holes in the Faraday box. The doorway has to be covered by the wire mesh too, and the mesh needs to make good contact with all the surfaces. The wires on the side of the doorjamb and the doors need to come into solid contact with each other. Now you have a perfect Faraday box, as long as no electricity is coming into your garage. Keep your computers and delicate electronic equipment in your garage during bad solar days.

Vehicles

ॐ∽

Q: In preparation for the EMPs from solar flares affecting electrical systems in cars, some people have disconnected the electrical parts in their vehicles. The vehicles still run; they just take more gas. Is that something that people can consider who are stuck with vehicles with computers? Can they disconnect the computers and still have the cars work?

DM: Yes. It will be important to disconnect the computer. Use what you have. In a period of time when you cannot run to the store to buy the part you need, how can you use what you have and make that work for you? People do not realize they need to buy new computers for their cars and place them in Faraday cages to keep them safe.

❧◈☙

To avoid fried wires from a super solar flare, a vehicle needs to be turned off or parked in a Faraday cage. The bottom of the car is not solid, and the car's grill has more space than the radiator can fill. This allows EMP energy to travel behind the radiator to the lights, wires, and ignition.

Do not take your car out during solar flare activity. I suggest storing an extra car computer in a small Faraday box within your car at all times. Put all the things that are susceptible to an EMP in the box. You will need all of the different computers for your car, any of the electronic gadgets, and a new electronic ignition. When an EMP hits an older car, plan to replace condensers, coils, and fuses.

Airplanes

❧◈☙

Q: Will airplanes stop working when the super solar flare hits?

DM: Yes. Airplanes flying in the sky will stop working because the electrical systems cannot be turned off fast enough. Once a plane's electrical system is affected by the solar flare's radiation, it will not work right. The airplane could even crash.

Q: Will the super solar flares burn the electrical system of an airplane parked on the ground?

DM: Airplanes on the ground need protection. Electrical systems are more protected when turned off. It's better for your airplanes and cars to be protected in a garage so they can't be hurt by any of the flares. Solar flares create a magnetic energy that goes into any holes in the plane or car. The energy will go up inside and zap a computer. If the computer is turned on, the wires could fry. It's like ... hmm, you know when you have a lightning storm, you turn off your computer because you don't want the lightning to hit your computer? It's the same thing with a solar flare. The only problem is you will probably not know when one is going to hit unless you have warning that a flare is headed your way. The best and safest method of protection is placing the computer in a Faraday box.

ॐ

Lightning strikes have brought down planes. Airplanes are not Faraday boxes. They have antennae that stick out to receive and transmit information to those on the ground. Antennae are very susceptible to EMPs and lightning. When an EMP hits a commercial airplane, the pilots will lose all of their instrumentation—air speed, location, level altitude, wing flaps—all of which are electronically controlled.

Without computerized instrumentation, the plane will crash when hit by an EMP. In Cessnas and old-fashioned planes, pilots fly by looking around the area. If those planes are hit by an EMP and lose all instrumentation, they will be able to coast to the ground.

Trains

ॐ

Q: Will trains that are running stop immediately?

DM: They won't run very long if they are zapped. They will scoot along a little bit because of their momentum; they won't just go clunk. They'll scoot along and then they'll go clunk. Underground trains that do not have an energy source above the ground may be safe. So trains under the ground need to make sure that whatever is controlling them above the ground is protected.

ॐ

Electric trains both above and underground have electronic instrumentation. When an EMP hits, the instrumentation will go down and the train will lock up. Once the EMP hits, trains that are not moving will have their electronics fried. If the trains are moving when the EMP hits, they will lock up. An old steam locomotive will just keep on going. A train that runs on diesel will keep moving until it runs out of fuel or the engineer stops the train. Most likely a diesel train will not start again because its starter will burn out.

Dowsing in a Bug-Out Situation

Folklore is solidly based in fact. For thousands of years our ancestors have dowsed to hunt game and to find water. Dowsing is not rare skill—only an unusual one that gives information in an unconventional manner.

Can dowsing help in a bug-out situation? From a survivalist viewpoint, the answer is yes. Dowsing is the easiest way to find subterranean water. You can also tell how deep and how large the water area is below your feet.

If the system fell apart tomorrow and you needed to bug out, you probably would not be able to haul enough water in your pack. Keeping extra water in the car is a good idea. But what if you find yourself in an area you are unfamiliar with? How would you find water?

Dowsing is a genuine phenomenon and has been proven many times over. Our ancient ancestors would take a forked stick from a tree and would use that humble stick to lead them to water. What about that handy dandy fishing pole you have to catch fish? Will that work? Yes, it will.

When the forked stick starts moving in your hands, follow where it leads. You will know when you have found the spot when the tip of the stick or rod pulls down toward the earth. How deep under the surface of the earth will you have to dig to get to water? Mark your water spot, and from that point walk backward to discover the depth and how large an area the water covers under the ground.

Can you use a dowsing rod to lead you to a pond or creek? You can. Follow where the rod leads you. The rod works with your own gut survival mechanisms. Just as you use a compass for direction, a dowsing rod gives you a direction to take in finding a body of water.

What happens if you are lost and your compass is broken? How do you get back to your camp in the safest, fastest way? Can dowsing help you? Again, the answer is yes if you know how to use a dowsing rod or a simple pendulum.

Dowsing the ground and dowsing a map are closely related skills. You can find plants to eat and animals to hunt by using a dowsing rod or pendulum.

You can use dowsing to discover gold, gem veins, metals, and oil. After the earth changes, when America is rebuilding, it might be necessary to locate water, electric and telephone lines, buried treasure, dead bodies, and lost objects—including missing kids.

Dowsing is like any survival skill you can learn. You need to practice and use it before you need to put it in action. It takes practice, just as when a baby trying to walk falls, gets up, and tries again. My grandchildren love to dowse. In our house, it is like having an Easter egg hunt with money. I hide change and they find it using their dowsing rods. *Anyone* can learn the art of dowsing to find just about anything.

Preserve Your Digital Memories

For a Post-Collapsed Environment

A generation ago our ancestors saved special papers and drawings, edges curled from age. Letters, faded photos, and home movies were a vital link to the past. These personal links to our past created our personal histories. Today much of our personal information—the first pictures of the newest family member and other family news—is digital. In a post-collapsed environment, our lifestyle will not be like our lives today. Photos of today will create history for future generations.

It is hard to imagine a time when there may not be electricity, an active Internet, radio, or cable TV. Be sure to print some of those pictures and memories of your life. Print your documents and put it on a flash drive for those who may not have access to the information. Put your PDF files and e-books on a tablet or Kindle reader. It will not take much energy to recharge those devices in a post-collapsed world when, at least for a while, the Internet will be a thing of the past.

Another way to use digital technology in your favor would be to put all your important information, like bank account numbers, passports, drivers' licenses, medical information, and such, on a couple of small flash drives to keep in your "get out of Dodge" bag. Keep your computer, digital camera, and small, important electronics in a simple Faraday cage. Remove the batteries and wrap each item and its electrical cord separately.

Digital—Internet, GPS, and Smartphones

Be careful what you put on the Internet. Have you noticed that after searching the Internet, suddenly the items from your searches seem to pop up on all the pages you go to? Do not upload any of your personal information to "the cloud." The Internet is how the government will track you. Do not put information on the Web that is personal and can be scrutinized by the government. Yes, the government runs the Library of Congress. Use of this information helps to preserve your digital works, but keep your personal information secret.

Cooking in a Post-Collapsed Environment

The breakfast your farming ancestors ate consisted of bacon, eggs, potatoes, orange juice, milk, biscuits or dense bread, butter, and gravy.

Obesity in the new world will be rare. Imagine a life without a low-fat or low-carb diet. Your new life will be more physically oriented. You will get the exercise your body needs by moving your muscles to keep your body and hands limber. The good news is that physical labor means your body will need more calories.

Who knows? You may need to cut down small trees by whacking them with a knife, or by sticking your knife in the wood and pounding on it with a small log. Try it out. You will find you do not have to be like the mythical king of lumberjacks, Paul Bunyan, to cut trees.

By growing your gardens and hunting or raising your meat sources, you will no longer eat the added spice of toxins sprinkled liberally in your food today. Day by day, you and your family will become healthier and more physically fit during this period of your life.

Tip: Calories keep you warmer at night, so eat a high-calorie meal. Eating and cooking with coconut oil increases body temperature.

How would you cook if you did not have electricity, natural gas, or propane? Before a disaster hits, it might be a good idea to look at different ways to cook off the grid. Cooking off the grid can be a challenge if you have not prepared beforehand. For emergency cooking, heat food with candle warmers, chafing dishes, and fondue pots. Eat canned food out of the can. When heating in the can, be sure to open the can and remove the label first.

Cooking with a camp stove and barbecuing with propane require fuel. How much fuel would you need to store for each member in your household or community? How much can you carry for those who need to get out of Dodge?

Dutch Oven

Hundreds of years ago, pioneers cooked in a fireplace or in a lean-to behind the cabin. One of the most important pieces of equipment in the Lewis and Clark expedition was a large Dutch oven.

When cooking in your fireplace or, if you are camping, in a fire pit, it is best to use cast-iron cookware. A Dutch oven is a cast-iron pot with a flanged lid (to hold the hot coals) and a handle in the center of the lid. The pot itself had a flat bottom with three two-inch legs attached. Paul Revere, it is rumored, did the first and final design of the Dutch oven.

Stack a Turkey Dinner and Dessert

Build your fire. While waiting for the wood to burn hot, place a turkey in the largest pot, put the lid on, and place in the coals. Cover the lid with coals. Now prepare the dressing in the slightly smaller pot. Place this pot on top of the first, covering the lid with coals. The next item is the vegetable. Place in the pot with a bit of seasoning and place on the pots in the fireplace. Finally, prepare and place your dessert on the top of the stack, covering the top with plenty of coals. Add extra coals to the lids where needed, and let cook. Hours later, the entire meal will be cooked.

Solar Cooking

Take advantage of free solar energy whenever the sun is shining to create delicious, tender meals for you and your family. Buy a solar oven or make one of your own.

Basically all that is needed is a box with a hole cut out of the top. Paint the inside of the box black. Place a piece of glass covered with clear plastic wrap on top of the hole in the box. Cut a door flap. Close the door by propping a stick against it. This is your oven door. Inside of the oven, place a clear glass bowl flipped upside down. Set a black pot in a cooking bag on top of the bowl. This generates more heat.

Place the food in the solar oven early in the morning and enjoy your day. Later, when it is time to feed the family, the sun will have cooked your food. The longer your meal cooks, the more tender the food will be. Vegetables are cooked without water, and you can even bake cookies and bread! Use your favorite Crock-Pot or slow-cooker recipes in a solar oven. Placing water in the pot will allow you to measure the temperature. Try cooking your food in darkened canning jars with regular canning lids and rings tightened. The rubber seal allows excess pressure to be released, but a low increase in pressure is retained and speeds the cooking process. Use standard canning jars lids as they are designed for pressure. At 170–180 degrees Fahrenheit, a solar oven is hot enough to cook many foods, given a long enough cooking period.

In addition to cooking, a solar cooker can be used in a variety of other ways, including:

> » Naturally dehydrate fruits, vegetables, and meats

> » Heat water for a sponge bath

> » Kill infestations in grains or dried foods

- » Dry firewood

- » Sprout foods

- » Decrystallize honey or jams

Research instructions for pasteurizing, sprouting, dehydrating, sanitizing, and decrystallizing, and print hard copies of the instructions. Teach yourself these methods. Do not wait until an emergency or disaster situation to learn survival techniques.

Note: Solar cooking is most like baking or roasting.

Dehydrating

Did you know dehydration is one of the best ways you have to store foods when there is no electricity for refrigeration? A couple of generations ago, parents would have their children climb on a tin roof and lay sliced fruits and vegetables on the roof.

Have you ever wondered where the term "string bean" came from? Our ancestors used a needle and thread to string the beans for hanging to dry.

Summer in Southern California as well as states like Arizona and New Mexico is hot. When you get in the car, most of the time it is too hot to touch the steering wheel, even with a solar reflector to decrease the heat. Why waste this heat when you can use it to dehydrate your fruits and vegetables? In a post-collapsed world, your car can be used as a dehydrator by placing sliced vegetables and fruits on trays and covering them in clear plastic wrap.

In cooler climates, keep the windows rolled up. In hotter areas, turn the pieces over more often and crack the door for air if you can't roll down the window.

A solar food dehydrator and a solar oven are very much alike. In fact, you can use your solar oven to dehydrate your food. After your food is dried, put it into plastic bags or a container with a lid. Many of these will last for months, if not a year, or longer and will be a nice change in a new world.

Lighting

✺✺ Humans need a source of light to survive. Have candles because light will be important. You can sleep when the sun goes down, but you will still need candles, solar-powered batteries, and hand-cranked tools—any items that do not use electricity. Also, if you have a generator, hook up those teeny-tiny Christmas tree lights. Those would be good lights to light the room, and they don't use much power.

✺✺

What do you do for light during an emergency? Buy candles, solar flashlights, LCD lights, and hand cranked flashlights.

Make an oil lamp with a mason jar. Any oil works, but, I use olive oil because the oil does not smoke.

Buy some of the inexpensive, outdoor solar lights on a stick. The best part is the cost is only a few dollars. Take off the stick part of the light and put the lamp part into a clear glass jar. A jar with a glass lid and a metal seal is best. Put your new light out in the sun and bring it in at sundown to light up areas of your home. Another idea is to use the intact light. Put the sticks into a vase or pot filled with stone. Charge them in the sun during the day. Bring the lights in at night to place around your home. These lights will last for a season once opened. Stock up on this item.

Did you know a sawdust candle is easy to make to provide a large amount of heat for warmth and cooking?

Soap in a Post-Collapsed World

Having plenty of soap will save lives to clean wounds, for washing and to keep your environment healthy. Soap can be made inside on the stove or on a campfire if the need arises.

There are three things you need to make soap: fat or oil, lye, and water. The oil can be any kind you choose, even used oil. The hardest part of making soap is finding the 100 percent lye. Major hardware stores do not carry it, so try Ace Hardware. If you decide to make your own soap, buy the crystal type of lye and not the liquid. You can even make your own lye by collecting hardwood ash from your fireplace, wood-burning stove, or fire pit, putting water in it, and letting the mixture sit overnight.

Leave the soap plain or add honey, milk, oatmeal, or a bit essential oils for scent. Use your soap for all washing and cleaning. Soap is going to be a valuable item for barter.

Chapter 8

Medicine for a New Era

≈≈ It is better to take the medicine that heals than the poison that kills. ≈≈

≈≈ People think the medicines pharmaceutical companies make are going to increase their lifespans. That is not true. Taking these medicines creates more problems.

Amino acids are better than synthetic antibiotics because drug-resistant bacteria are not resistant to the amino acids. Superbugs, like some strains of E. coli, are resistant to all the antibiotics known to man. Amino acids come from nuts, beans, and red meat. If you are infected with a strain of E. coli that's resistant to antibiotics, increase your intake of amino acids. That will fight the E. coli.

Amino acids will also fight MRSA (methicillin-resistant *Staphylococcus aureus*) and other staph infections you may get at the hospital. Human beings sometimes go to the hospital and come out sicker than they went in. Take magnesium and eat onions, garlic, and ginger to maintain a healthy immune system.

Being healthy means eating foods that have not been genetically modified or altered in any way. Eating healthy means eating what was around a hundred years ago. You can bet there will be a new bug that comes out, and doctors will say, "Oh, you have to take this medicine to get better." There are many things your government is doing to eliminate high population—in many countries, not just in the United States. It is called population control. Eugenics is a reality, now and not in the future.

≈≈

Q: Didn't John Holdren write a book on genocide in the seventies?[24]

DM: Yes, He believes in population control and sterilization of women and men who are of lower social classes. Bill Gates of Microsoft[25] believes in this as well. He wants to experiment, and he has no problem putting faulty vaccines into the bodies of infants, the elderly, and Americans.

This is the beginning of manipulating the genetic code, known as eugenics.[26] Eugenics will be used in deciding which healthy child will go to a public school and which child will be banned due to the genetic code a child carries. Backed by government power, the eugenics phase will lead to secret, forced sterilizations of certain races.

Q: Are these viruses targeted by race, meaning everyone would get the virus but it will affect certain people, a certain genetic code? Like if Jill it was infected and someone else was infected, the virus would hit the other person but not Jill?

DM: Exactly. Genetic profiling is targeted toward a specific race to control or eliminate the population using eugenics.[27]

Black people and anybody with a dark brown skin are more likely to get cancer. Why do you think researchers go over to Africa to try all of those vaccines? It's because the dark skins of the people tend to create cancer. The darker the skin is, the more susceptible the person is to cancer.

Q: Oh, because it sucks in more of the sunlight and more of the radiation, is that what it is?

DM: Their bodies create protection from the sun and block vitamin D3, so people with dark skin should be taking a lot of the vitamin D3.

---

24   John Holdren, Ideological Environmentalist http://zombietime.com/john_holdren/

25   Jason Bermas Breaks Down Bill Gates's Eugenics Speech http://www.youtube.com/watch?v=5HdFkOlNAkM

26   Bill Gates Eugenics TED video http://www.youtube.com/watch?v=JaF-fq2Zn7I

27   Unjust and Criminal uses of Vaccines and Medical Experiments on Children, People of Color, Women, and Inmates (1845 - 2007) http://www.tumblr.com/tagged/medical-experiments

Q: If someone has light skin, they need to take 8, 000 IU of vitamin D3 a day. How much should someone with darker skin take?

DM: About 10,000 IU, depending on how large the person is. A child would not take this amount. If people were given vitamin D3, they would be able to fight off cancer.

Q: Oh, so not kill them off per se but sterilize them so they can't have any kids and produce offspring in the future? In other words, genocide through the bloodlines? This comes out to be the same thing in my eyes.

DM: To eliminate the population's growth over the years, vaccines will kill babies who are already born. Vaccines are extremely dangerous. All of them are bad; there are varying degrees of how bad. Most of the vaccines have viruses in them, some of which are cancer, such as leukemia. Some of them have HIV in them. This is what you need to know every time you take a vaccine of any kind, even if it's a flu shot.

Q: Some places made it mandatory that you must be vaccinated. There's an armed guard at the courthouse to make people get vaccinated. They had no choice.

DM: It shows how much your government is in control. This is how you know you do in fact live within with a corporation. Every American is a citizen of the corporation, and the government can demand whatever it wants to enforce.

Q: Newspaper articles warn of biological terrorism aimed at the animals we eat. Is this true?

DM: Animal food sources will probably not be a target. There will be attempts to poison water sources. Terrorists will attempt to knock out communication, like electricity and the Internet. Anthrax is one of the words.

Q: What will happen within the illegal drug trade?

DM: Drugs have a purpose, and the illegal drug trade will continue. Your government is deeply involved in illegal drug trading. Pharmaceutical drugs are manmade. The art of healing with plants and minerals is known by only a few. This is knowledge that will be needed. White willow bark and turmeric should be stored to use for medicinal purposes.

Alcohol will become scarce, yet needed to clean and prevent infections. Think of the cowboys and Indians. When a cowboy was hit by a bullet, alcohol was poured into the wound, and then poured onto the knife. The cowboy also drank some. The bullet was taken out, and the doctor took a swig for a job well done. Making a still is not difficult. Somebody will get rich making alcohol.

Q: After an earthquake destroyed so much of Haiti, four phases of chaos were experienced, including the spread of disease—a cholera outbreak in 2010. Will there be widespread disease during the years of solar flare activity and increased natural disasters?

DM: Yes, there will be numerous diseases and outbreaks. This is why living away from the population of people will help you survive. Referring to the solar flares, loss of electricity will cause failure of sewage collection.

Q: Will there be any cures with synthetic drugs?

DM: Pharmaceutical companies do not want anyone to get healthy because they won't make as much money. Your government creates diseases to scare the people.

ॐ

Recently HBO host Bill Maher on Star Talk Radio said,

"I'm consistently pro-death ... My motto is let's kill the right people."[28]

Did you know the United States is not developing new types of antibiotics? Pharmaceutical companies are not researching alternate ways to make new antibiotics for new infections. [29]Other drugs produce more money. It is not about the people they can save, it is about how much money the company can make. The old antibiotics are outdated and will be useless for the new superbugs. Unfortunately, the new drug-resistant superbugs have nature on

28   Bill Gates Eugenics TED video http://www.youtube.com/watch?v=JaF-fq2Zn7I

29   http://www.washingtonpost.com/national/health-science/nih-superbug-outbreak-highlights-lack-of-new-antibiotics/2012/08/24/ec33d0c8-ee24-11e1-b0eb-dac6b50187ad_story.html

their side and over the last ten years have become resistant to every antibiotic known to man. What does this mean to us and the future generation?

Dr. Margaret Chan, the Director-General of the World Health Organization, recently stated:

> "For patients infected with some drug- resistant pathogens, mortality has been shown to increase by around 50%. ...
>
> Many other pathogens are developing resistance to multiple drugs, some to nearly all. Hospitals have become hotbeds for highly resistant pathogens, like MRSA, ESBL, and CPE, increasing the risk that hospitalization kills instead of cures. These are end-of-the-road pathogens that are resistant to last-line antimicrobials.

If current trends continue unabated, the future is easy to predict. Some experts say we are moving back to the pre-antibiotic era. No. This will be a post-antibiotic era. In terms of new replacement antibiotics, the pipeline is virtually dry, especially for gram-negative bacteria. The cupboard is nearly bare.

Prospects for turning this situation around look dim. ...

A post-antibiotic era means, in effect, an end to modern medicine, as we know it. Things as common as strep throat or a child's scratched knee could once again kill."

DreamMyst has repeatedly stated the drugs we take have bad side effects, like autism, permanent brain damage, kidney damage, and many other life-threatening dangers.

Superbugs and Natural Health Solutions

Researching the information DreamMyst has provided, I have found oregano and garlic alone will kill any infection, including a superbug.

If you get E. coli, or a virus like West Nile, eat garlic and onions and use colloidal silver, which is an antibacterial agent. Take it internally for either prevention or treatment approaches. Use colloidal silver to clean surfaces in the area of the infected person to prevent further contamination. Devices can be bought on the Internet to make your own colloidal silver with distilled water.

Eat healthy. Take vitamins B3, D and C daily to build your immune system. Superbugs cannot thrive if your health is not compromised. If you do get sick, wash your hands often and demand that health care professionals wash their hands in front of you. If your doctor wears a tie, have him either remove it or throw it over his shoulder before he washes his hands. Wash the surfaces you touch with colloidal silver water. Eat superfoods like coconut oil, acai, honey, hemp seeds, and organic cacao butter, and don't forget amino acids.

Vaccines: the Good, the Bad, and the Ugly

The *good* part about vaccines is that you don't need them. Today's children will be healthy without them. There are natural ways to treat whooping cough, influenza, swine flu, and superbugs without nasty side effects.

Vaccines are the vehicle through which infectious diseases are introduced to the population. *All* vaccines use toxic ingredients like neurotoxic aluminum, thimerosal, and polysorbate, and carry live viruses that cause the infectious diseases they claim to prevent. For example the MMR (measles, mumps, and rubella) vaccine causes measles. The majority of the children who catch measles have been vaccinated.[30] Increasingly parents are experiencing the heartrending consequences of MMR and other vaccines, which include neurological damage, autism, paralysis, chronic illness, extreme colitis, skin lesions, difficulty breathing, and death occurring shortly after or during a scheduled series of inoculations.

---

30   http://www.cdc.gov/mmwr/preview/mmwrhtml/00000359.htm http://www.ncbi.nlm.nih.gov/pmc/articles/PMC1646939/

http://www.vaccines.me/articles/jfdlf-explosive-school-based-measles-outbreak-in-vaccinated-students---finland.cfm

Babies between the ages two and four months old receive the DPT injection (a combination of diphtheria, pertussis and tetanus vaccine). This shot is known to cause severe and permanent brain damage in some children.

Flu shots increase your vulnerability to the flu. The swine flu vaccine has some bad side effects. Finnish researchers have concluded[31] that the swine flu vaccination causes a chronic nervous system disorder that makes people fall asleep wherever they happen to be. This disorder is known as narcolepsy. In addition, other documented side effects are paralyzing physical collapses and hallucinations. The Finnish government has acknowledged this[32] and is paying for lifetime medical care for seventy-nine children who were affected by this vaccine.

Most outbreaks of infectious disease, like the recent whooping cough outbreaks, happen among children who are already vaccinated. These children are *more* vulnerable to infection than unvaccinated children are. The whooping cough vaccine has *not* been tested for long-term effectiveness or protection. Merck vaccine scientist Dr. Maurice Hilleman [33]admits that vaccines given to Americans were contaminated with cancer viruses, SV40, and HIV. The yellow fever vaccine had leukemia virus in it. AIDS and leukemia suddenly became pandemic from wild viruses.

The Institute of Medicine has openly admitted that[34] the influenza vaccine is convincingly linked to causing anaphylaxis, a serious allergic reaction that is rapid in onset and may cause death. It typically results in a number of symptoms including an itchy rash, throat swelling, and low blood pressure.

The TT (tetanus toxoid) vaccine is also likely linked to causing anaphylaxis. Vaccine injections of all kinds are convincingly linked to causing deltoid bursitis (severe pain and swelling at the injection site) and syncope (loss of consciousness).

---

31 http://www.google.com/hostednews/afp/article/ ALeqM5g1doyMOnXuq77VZHACz_rcbX99BA

32 http://www.herbalhealer.com/breakingnews.shtml

33 http://tv.naturalnews.com/v.asp?v=13EAAF22CDA367BB3C2F94D2CD9 0EF7B

34 http://www.vaccineinjuryhelpcenter.com/iom-report-admits-vaccines-cause-measles-seizures-anaphylaxis-etc/

In addition, the Institute of Medicine admits that vaccines cause measles, anaphylactic shock, febrile seizures, and possibly other fatal side effects. Also it was the Institute of Medicine that declared Agent Orange was safe for the US veterans who fought in Vietnam.

Funding for the Institute of Medicine comes mostly from the military, government, pharmaceutical companies, and special interest groups. Bill Gates of Microsoft has a love for vaccinations and is a supporter of global population reduction through vaccines. In 2009, he collaborated with Merck[35], the world's largest maker of vaccines, to develop a technology that allegedly can be used to develop eugenics vaccines. These vaccines target specific races and nationalities with infertility-inducing pharmaceuticals.

Did you know that in 1950, the navy sprayed a cloud of bacteria from ships into San Francisco?[36]

In order to determine how susceptible an American city could be to biological attack, the US Navy sprayed a cloud of *Bacillus globigii* bacteria from ships over the San Francisco shoreline. According to monitoring devices situated throughout the city to test the extent of infection, the eight thousand residents of San Francisco inhaled five thousand or more bacteria particles, many becoming sick with pneumonia-like symptoms

In 2007, Maryland's governor and public health officials, threatened two thousand parents with arrest and thirty days' imprisonment if they did *not* submit their children to state mandated vaccinations.[37] The children and their parents was herded into the county courthouse and guarded by security guards and attack dogs as a district judge oversaw the mass injection of schoolchildren with vaccines containing toxic mercury.

---

35   http://www.youtube.com/watch?v=JaF-fq2Zn7I&feature=youtu.be

36   http://www.sfgate.com/news/article/When-U-S-attacked-itself-Government-tested-2864377.php

37   http://www.huffingtonpost.com/scott-kahan-md/rick-perry-health_b_932924.html

http://articles.mercola.com/sites/articles/archive/2011/11/05/health-liberty-and-forced-vaccination.aspx

New Jersey mandates the mass vaccination of all children with four different vaccines, stripping away the health freedoms and criminalizing parents who refuse to participate.

Medicine for Mother Earth and Her People

Put these items in your herbal medicine bag: vitamin D, vitamin C, and vitamin B3. Be sure to include herbs that fight contagious bacteria and cancer: turmeric, garlic, oregano extract, ginger, colloidal silver, honey, cinnamon, cloves, and green tea.

Mixing our medical resources of both traditional and alternative therapies, which include the use of honey, essential oils, colloidal silver, tea tree (melaleuca) oil, and herbs and barks such as white willow bark, will help keep us healthy and relieve pain. The active ingredient in aspirin can be obtained by chewing on a cut strip of the underbark of a willow, aspen, or poplar tree.

The most effective herbs are echinacea, goldenseal, sage, peppermint, thyme, calendula, cayenne (improves circulation for better absorption of antibacterial herbs), ginger, and garlic. Garlic is known for its antibacterial, antifungal, and antiviral actions. Lucky for us, Mother Nature has provided plants that heal.

The antibacterial effect of colloidal silver was used before antibiotics. Today it is used in topical creams to prevent infection.

Unfortunately, herbs do not contain megadoses of any one naturally occurring antibiotic, making their effects mild and slower to take effect. Taking the above-mentioned herbs at the first signs of sickness will shorten the duration of the sickness and allow the body to heal itself.

Putting together an herbal medicine bag is easy. Include Ace bandages, Band-Aids, gauze, tapes, topical disinfectants for wounds, splints, and slings. Other items to add are cold packs, heat packs, alcohol, iodine, baking soda (sodium bicarbonate), magnesium oil for pain relief. Include borax and sulfur) to use as an antidote for acute exposure to radiation.

Amino Acids

࿊ Eat amino acids. People who are allergic to iodine can try liquid amino acids in foods. Amino acids cure and prevent infections from E. coli, MRSA, swine flu, and all of those bugs that have been engineered.

Eat raw garlic. Cut a garlic clove really, really small, pick the pieces up, put them in your mouth, and swallow them down with water really fast. It is better than the garlic in the capsules, and any garlic will work. Take lots of it.

Eat any kind of onions, and eat lots of onions in your food. Take magnesium to keep your immune system healthy. These natural supplements work. You can also take colloidal silver both as a preventative medicine and as an antibiotic. Have some colloidal silver stored in case you get sick.

࿊

Medicinal Herbs

Learn wild food skills and gather wild foods in your area. Use the herbs to trade and to supplement your food stores. Go on an herb walk in your area and learn to recognize five or six plants you can use for medicine or food.

Thyme essential oil is antibacterial. It can be put into water and used as a hand sanitizer.

Keep either dried herbs or their tinctures. Dried herbs should be kept for a year, at the longest, before being replaced. Keep them in clean, screw-top glass jars and be sure to label them with the date and contents. Store a tincture in a dark glass bottle for up to three years.

Homeopathic Medicine First Aid Kit

- » Silver hydrosol
- » Colloidal silver generator

» Distilled water maker

» Silver gel

» Silver bandages

» Shelf-stable probiotics

» Aloe

» Arnica ointment

» Calendula: Provides an excellent home cure for cuts, grazes, minor skin complaints, bruises, blisters, diaper rash, and other ailments such as athlete's foot

» Echinacea: Especially useful as an immune booster

» White willow bark: As powerful as taking an aspirin

» Slippery elm

» Oil of oregano

» Rescue remedy

» Stabilized-allicin garlic

» Yarrow

» Marijuana

» Iodine

Poppy Seeds

Q: Can poppy flowers be boiled to make a tea or does tea have to be made from the crushed seeds?

DM: Use whole seeds. You can use the raw pods, but don't boil them.

Poppy seeds are legal in every state. They can be made into poppy juice and used as an opiate narcotic, which can help people who need it for severe pain or to transition out of this life. Poppy-seed tea is gentle and has an all-over effect on the body, relaxing muscles and bringing about a quiet, peaceful, contemplative state of mind.

When making poppy-seed tea, do not boil the seeds, only the water. Let the water cool to very warm. Pour the poppy seeds and about two tablespoons of blackberry vinegar or lemon juice into a liter-size bottle and add hot water. Shake the seeds in a jar for about twenty minutes and let sit several hours or days, shaking a few times a day.

You will need at least two hundred milligrams of unwashed seed for one small cup of tea. Add juice and a little of the tea and drink. Start with small doses until you know the quality of the seeds. Reuse three or four times. Health food stores carry bulk amounts of poppy seeds.

Herbs for West Nile Virus (WNV)

West Nile virus is expected to hit all fifty states within two years. There is no vaccine for the virus. People with low immune systems are the ones who are vulnerable to this disease. Catnip oils are up to ten times more effective than DEET at repelling mosquitoes, flies, bees, and some kinds of cockroaches. Use mint, citronella oil, rosemary, lavender and cypress oil.

Herbs for cancer

Turmeric, garlic, ginger, poke root, dandelion root, echinacea, chaparral, cat's claw, mistletoe, maitake mushrooms, kelp, burdock root, green tea, cinnamon, clove.

Herbs for headaches, coughs, colds, and fevers

Angelica, garlic, ginger, lavender, and echinacea are excellent herbs to keep on hand for fever, sore throats, and cold symptoms.

Lime flowers and rosemary are useful herbs for tension headaches. Store dried mint, parsley, and thyme to help alleviate coughs.

Herbs for rheumatic pain

Angelica, bay, and parsley, taken regularly, offer relief from rheumatic pain. Lemongrass treats arthritic conditions and rheumatism because it possesses anti-inflammatory and antispasmodic properties. Oil obtained from lemongrass is great when applied to painful joints.

Herbs for insect bites, skin rashes, cuts, bruises, blisters, and other skin complaints

Keep basil and parsley for insect bites and stings. Skin rashes and diaper rash respond to bay. Comfrey soothes bites and sores.

Herbs for digestive complaints, stomachaches, and diarrhea

Marjoram is useful for diarrhea. Both marjoram and thyme help with flatulence. Sage is superb to use for gastritis and diarrhea. Keep ginger for acid indigestion, travel sickness, and morning sickness. Mix with peppermint and fennel for moderate to severe nausea. Mint is good for abdominal aches and pains.

Herbs for insomnia and fatigue

Valerian, mint, lime flower, and lavender are herbs for insomnia.

Chamomile helps fight fatigue, and kava is an herb that serves to calm and soothe anxiety at night.

Hemp

❧❧

Q: Can you explain to parents how marijuana would be safely administered to their children for the removal of radiation?

DM: Make an ointment and rub it on their skin. Eat the raw leaf. It has a different effect on the physical body, not the same as smoking it. The effects are not the same. Rubbed into the body, marijuana heals pain, plus the raw plant itself is filled with nutrients and is good in a salad. Used as a tea, it is a powerful pain reliever, helps nausea, and builds appetite.

As you feed your body, keep the thyroid filled with seaweed and blue-green algae. Take herbs and minerals that block radiation. Do this on a regular basis, starting now. If you start now, you are feeding the thyroid. When the thyroid and parathyroid are filled with healthy iodine, they will be protected from solar flare radiation or from a leak in a nuclear power plant. When the thyroid is not filled with healthy iodine and good stuff, it will fill with radiation.

Q: Will the marijuana plant be beneficial in the future by absorbing toxins within the earth?

DM: Wherever there is radiation, you want marijuana plants because they cleanse the radiation in the soil, water, and air. Sunflower plants and mushrooms work as well. This is a safe way to clear up radiation on the property, so that is good.

Q: DreamMyst, how much packaged seaweed should be eaten in order for it to be beneficial?

DM: You have to eat buckets of that kind of seaweed to get enough to protect your body. You can buy capsules and take these capsules two or three times a day.

Q: Is taking liquid sulfur as effective as eating food that has sulfur in it?

DM: Using both is a good idea. If you don't have one, at least you have the other.

Q: Will life spans increase, decrease, or remain the same during the economic depression and earth changes?

DM: Well, right now they're on the increase. Life spans will increase. Then over time, depending on how long it takes to rebuild your global community or planet, many people will have shortened life spans. This is because it will take time to rebuild and create the plants and foods that are going to keep you healthy and give you a long life span.

Q: Is it important to take colloidal silver to stay healthy?

DM: Colloidal silver has other benefits, which is why it is good to have on hand. It purifies your water. It works as an antibiotic. It is great for sanitizing an area.

Q: Will healing in the future be done with energy work and herbs?

DM: Yes, and acupuncture as well because acupuncture will help the physical as well as the energetic body. Learning and knowing the different herbs that are indigenous to the area where you live is very important. It will be a very wise person who learns, memorizes, and uses local herbs.

❧☙

There will be a time when pharmaceutical drugs will no longer be available. Cannabis works as well as ibuprofen, without the upset stomach many people get from taking over-the-counter medications. Cannabis, commonly known as marijuana or hemp, grows easily, has beneficial medicinal uses, and is an excellent treatment for radiation sickness and exposure.

Radiation Symptoms

» Nausea

» Diarrhea

» Loss of appetite

» Red, itchy skin

» Hair loss

» Bleeding

» Vomiting

» Weight loss

» Weakness

» Sore throat

» Recurrent infections

» Anemia

In addition, it has incredible nutritional and healing benefits—much like wheatgrass juice. It works for people and animals. It may be the cure for cancers, and relieves migraines, nausea, and vomiting.

Cannabis increases appetite, relaxes the body, is antidepressive, regulates hormones, cleanses the colon, and is helpful for degenerative conditions, inflammatory diseases, and physical pain. Raw cannabis is a superfood containing all the essential amino acids and everything the body needs. It is high in tryptophan, which is extremely lacking in most diets but is essential for the production of serotonin in the brain. Marijuana is one of the most nutritious leafy greens you can eat, with the largest chlorophyll content and the highest amount of antioxidants, including THC.

There is a substance called anandamide in both raw chocolate and raw cannabis. It makes you feel good and happy, but not drugged. Consuming one leaf daily keeps up a level of the cannabinoids, which are regulators. Cannabinoids can *up*-regulate, or *down*-regulate depending upon what the body needs. In other words, if your body needs to clot blood, the presence of cannabinoids helps. If the body is beginning to form a clot in response to irritation inside the arteries, which could travel to your heart and kill you, the cannabinoids will likely stop the clot from forming. The cannabinoids must already be present in the body from daily consumption.

You will not get high from eating the raw plant if you do not dry or heat it in any way. *Any* heating, even drying, starts the decarboxylation, the removal of the A from THC-A. You end up with THC. THC gets you high; THC-A does not. Use the fresh, green, undried, raw leaf— right off the plant shade leaves (like kale or spinach) or fan leaves. Wash the leaf well and soak for five minutes.

Ten leaves is a daily dose for an adult. Split the juice into five parts or take sips five times a day. The juice only keeps for one day. Mix it with other juices to improve the flavor or use raw, unheated honey to preserve the juice for up to three days in a glass jar with less than a tablespoon of air. It is preferable to juice daily. Make green smoothies by using a wheatgrass juicer or chop finely in a food processor. Add carrots and honey to your juice or consume in other raw foods and salad. Fresh, raw cannabis, consumed daily, might be just the ticket for excellent, vibrant health.

Growing cannabis can improve the soil when it is grown as a break crop to relieve and revitalize the soil between crops. Marijuana puts nitrogen back into the soil, suppresses weeds and diseases, and cleans contaminants out of the planet.

The cannabis plant has amazing healing powers. However, the same plant eats away nuclear waste and contamination. Sunflower and marijuana plants thrive in radioactive environments. They have the property of absorbing metals through their roots, and catch uranium or the ranelate 90, which are particularly harmful to humans once absorbed. Such elements accumulate in the leaves. Marijuana and the sunflower have the power to absorb radioactive metals and help decontaminate areas affected by radioactivity. After completing the process of absorption, incinerate the plants. The ashes will need to be treated as radioactive waste.

This multipurpose plant could significantly reduce high levels of radiation with minimal environmental disturbance and minimization of secondary air and waterborne wastes. The US Environmental Protection Agency has estimated that more than thirty thousand sites in the United States alone require hazardous waste treatment.

Pine Needles for Health

Pine needles helped our ancestors survive during their first winter in the Americas. Native Americans still use pine needles, which are high in vitamin C and vitamin A. Pine-needle tea is high in fat-soluble vitamin A, an antioxidant beta-carotene, which is needed for radiation therapy, healthy vision (especially in low light situations), skin and hair regeneration, and red blood cell production.

The amount of vitamin C in pine needles is reported to be five times the amount found in a lemon, which is 83.2 mg. This means pine needles yield more than 400 mg per cup of brew. Vitamin C is an antioxidant and an immune-system booster.

A batch of pine-needle tea yields shikimic acid, which is the basis for Tamiflu, one of the drugs recommended by the CDC to fight the flu.

Use the inner bark to treat wounds and insect bites. Apply as a bandage, tied in place with string, and kept moist—or place directly on the wound after the bark is ground up and soaked in liquor. Make cough syrup by steeping the bark in a jar of hot water. Add brandy and honey to flavor and preserve the syrup.

Use the needles to make tea, soups, and food recipes. Pine-tar soap is helpful for topically treating skin conditions such as psoriasis and extreme eczema. Made into massage oil, pine tar is effective for painful muscles and arthritis. Pine needles and a steamy room will help with breathing problems. Native Americans filled mattresses with pine needles to repel fleas and lice, and wove needles into baskets.

Pine Needle Recipes

Select the newest needles, at the end of a branch. Chop the needles into small bits, about one-quarter to one-half inch long. Add some orange peel.

Heat about a cup of water to almost boiling. Pour the hot water over about a tablespoon of the chopped needles. Allow to steep (covered) for five to ten minutes, until the needles have settled to the bottom of the cup.

Medicinal Tea:

This process releases more of the oils and resins that contain the medicinal compounds, and tastes a little like turpentine.

Recipe:

One ounce baby pine needles

One and a half pints water

Put the herbs into an enamel, glass, or stainless steel pan (do not use aluminum). Bring to a boil and simmer for ten minutes or until the liquid is reduced by one third.

Place the water and needles in a Thermos. Let sit overnight for twelve hours. Strain and remove the needles. Drink throughout the day.

Continue to drink one pint of pine-needle tea every day for one month, several times a day, for maximum medicinal effect.

Pine-Needle Vinegar is deeply scented and is an alternative to balsamic vinegar. Use pine vinegar in salad dressings or as a hot drink to help ward off seasonal colds.

Recipe: Take a clean, sterile glass jar and add enough pine needles to pack the jar.

Bring sixteen ounces of cider vinegar to a rolling boil and remove from the heat. Cool to room temperature. Pour the cooled vinegar over your jar of pine needles and fill to the top. Screw on the cap. Leave in a darkened cupboard for six weeks. Makes sixteen ounces.

Massage Oil and Room Freshener: Gather a handful of pine needles, lavender, and orange peel in oil. Pour into a jar and add enough oil to cover the herbs. Heat in the hot sun for the day, and let sit for a week in the dark. Put some pine oil in a jar on a candle warmer; add it to baths; or use for massage after filtering it. Pine oil added to your household cleaner will disinfect surfaces and help to purify the air. Edgar Casey said that a mixture of pine-needle oil massaged into the skin, especially along the spine, was an effective treatment for Parkinson's disease.

Pine tea Do not drink this tea if you are pregnant, as it may bring on a miscarriage.

Minerals of the Earth

Magnesium

☜☞ I recommend humans take magnesium every day. If I could only recommend one life-enhancing supplement to take with you into the new world, it would be magnesium. Humans are deficient in magnesium, and it is this mineral that builds the immune system, helps to prevent and heal cancer, and rebuilds healthy muscles. People who live in this toxic age need to stay healthy.

Magnesium can be difficult for some to take internally, but it is effective when rubbed into the body. Magnesium oil is not oil; it feels kind of oily, which is great if you are massaging it into the skin. It dries quickly. You can even use it to make your body smell better—you know, like a deodorant.

To find magnesium flakes, go to an aquarium store and ask for magnesium flakes like the brands Mag-Chlor or Magflakes.

Recipe for Magnesium Oil

Magnesium oil to spray on the skin

1. Boil one cup pure water, pour into a container with a lid, then mix one cup magnesium-chloride flakes. Shake until dissolved.

2. Feel free to use more or less of the magnesium flakes.

3. Store at room temperature and use as needed.

4. This mixture can be used as a foot soak or in a spray bottle as a body spray.

5. Apply magnesium oil directly to the skin.

Note: Do not put on cuts. It stings!

Clay is fine and smooth like flour, and binds to toxic substances. Taking clay internally and externally will remove radioactive toxins from your body. Taken internally, clay naturalizes and removes toxins through your feces. Make a paste of the clay and apply it to your body.

Use bentonite clay and put it in your kit.

Zeolite is a mineral. The positively charged, radioactive toxins and heavy metals bind to it. Zeolite is sprayed around areas of radiation fallout and is used on and around containers of radioactive waste to protect the environment if any should open.

Clay and zeolite, taken internally, will be particularly important in the new world until the earth has detoxified.

Tip: Baking soda, combined with other strong, natural substances like magnesium chloride, selenium, and iodine, has the best chance of weathering a toxic storm like radiation fallout.

Stockpile Eleven Over-the-Counter Medications

In a post-collapsed situation, over-the-counter (OTC) medications, along with a supply of antibiotics, will keep you, your family, and your community healthy. These medicines are safe for both adults and children. Buy the pill or capsule forms of these products because they retain their potency longer. Store them in a cool, dark place.

When used alone or in combination, these medications treat many conditions, including headache, fever, sore throat, earache, menstrual cramps, heartburn, arthritis, ulcer, diarrhea, allergies, hives, congestion, dizziness, mild anxiety, nausea, vomiting, poison ivy, athlete's foot, ringworm, eczema, insomnia, backache, gout, diaper rash, yeast infections, and many more.

1. Ibuprofen (Motrin, Advil) 200 mg can be taken in a dosage of one or two pills every four hours, three pills every six hours, or four pills every eight hours. Ibuprofen is the most versatile treatment for pain and inflammation. Use this to relieve headache, earache, sore throat, sinus pain, stiff neck, muscle strain, menstrual cramps, arthritis, gout, and back pain. It is effective at reducing fever and is safe for children. Do not use for most stomach-related pain. Ibuprofen may decrease the pain of kidney stones, kidney infections, and bladder infections. Common side effects include stomach irritation or heartburn.

    Combined with acetaminophen, ibuprofen is nearly as effective as codeine, tramadol, or hydrocodone in relieving more severe pain.

2. Acetaminophen (Tylenol) in 325 mg and extra strength 650 mg in dosages of one to two pills every four hours. It is the only pain reliever that is not an anti-inflammatory drug, but is used for the same conditions as ibuprofen. Acetaminophen is an effective pain reliever when combined with ibuprofen in full doses for severe pain. It does not thin the blood or cause stomach irritation. Acetaminophen is available in pediatric dosages, both for pain relief and fever reduction. Acetaminophen has few side effects but, high doses with alcohol can lead to liver failure.

3. Diphenhydramine (Benadryl) is available in 25 mg and 50 mg and is an inexpensive antihistamine. Diphenhydramine is used for drainage due to respiratory infections and nasal allergies in both adults and children. It relieves rashes, hives, and itching, including poison ivy. The 25 mg dose can be used every six hours for mild reactions and the 50 mg dose can be used every six hours for severe reactions. At the 50 mg dose, this medication is useful in relieving insomnia, nausea, and mild anxiety.

4. Loperamide (Imodium) is the most effective medication for diarrhea and is available in both tablet and liquid form. Loperamide relievies intestinal cramping in children.

5. Pseudoephedrine (Sudafed) relieves congestion of both the upper and lower respiratory tract caused by infection, allergy, chemical irritation, mild asthma, or bronchitis. It can have a stimulative effect like to caffeine. Side effects of pseudoephedrine are rapid heart rate, palpitations, and increased blood pressure. Doctors do not recommend this for children under six years old.

6. Meclizine (Bonine, Dramamine) is an anti-emetic drug that is available over the counter. Use for nausea, vomiting, motion sickness, and dizziness. Can cause drowsiness and acts as an anti-anxiety medication. Take one 25 mg tablet one hour for motion sickness and 50–100 mg daily in divided doses for dizziness, anxiety, or sleep.

7. Ranitidine 75–100 mg (Zantac); omeprazole 20–40 mg (Prilosec); and cimetidine 200–800 mg (Tagamet). Ranitidine is best for the treatment of heartburn, ulcers, and other acid-reducing conditions. Ranitidine is inexpensive, and is useful for relieving hives.

   Tums or Maalox is okay to use in solid form and are useful for ulcer disease and acid reflux.

8. Hydrocortisone cream in the 1% version is the strongest over-the-counter steroid cream. Both adults and children can use this cream to treat inflamed and/or itchy rashes like eczema, poison ivy, diaper rash, and minor genital irritations. It reduces inflammation such as allergic dermatitis. Apply three to four times a day to affected area help prevent infections.

9. Triple antibiotic ointment (Bacitracin, Neosporin, Bactroban), when used on an abrasion, laceration, insect bite, or sting, prevents skin infections. Use to treat superficial skin infections.

10. Clotrimazole miconazole (Lotrimin/Monistat) is in both Lotrimin and Gyne-Lotrimin. Gyne-Lotrimin is used to treat female yeast infections and any fungal or yeast infections such as athlete's foot, jock itch, ringworm, diaper rash, and skin fold irritations. Depending on the strength, you may need to apply twice a day externally, or once daily intravaginally for three days—if needed, up to one week.

11. Aspirin, 325 mg, thins the blood, is important as an anticoagulant and for coronary artery disease. For heart attack, give one adult aspirin immediately to chew. Two adult aspirins relieve pain, fever, and inflammation. A baby aspirin (81 mg) taken daily will help with coronary artery disease and serves as an anticoagulant. A higher dose is necessary to replace medicines like Coumadin. In a collapsed environment, this over-the-counter medicine will be a lifesaver.

Multivitamins

In addition to the eleven over-the-counter drugs, it is beneficial to stockpile multivitamins.

Take once a week, as most commercial vitamins have more nutrients than your body can absorb daily. In a post-collapsed environment, taking a multivitamin will prevent most problems caused by dietary deficiencies of vitamins and minerals. Stock up on vitamin C D and E.

Antibiotics

ॐ∽

Q: During the period of collapse, will medicine go away completely with regard to buying it in a store?

DM: Yes, pharmaceutical medicine will go away as far as buying it in a store. There will be enough people putting it away and hoarding it that it will be available. Those with enough money to barter will be able to connect with medicine, at least early in the transitional stages. Later medicine and medical care will be a blend of pharmaceutical medicines and the natural medicines and herbs.

Q: Will one pharmaceutical drug manufacturer survive the collapse?

DM: No. There will be supplies available in their warehouses that they put away as investments. Those pharmaceuticals will be used. Pharmacists will also have some of the supplies to make some of the remedies, or have pills stored away. The smart pharmacists will have enough, just as the smart survivalists will have items for barter.

Q: I have heard there is a shortage of lifesaving pharmaceutical drugs for cancer and other illnesses. Is the shortage manmade?

DM: Yes, the shortage is manmade because there is not very much profit in these types of drugs. There is no reason there should be a shortage except that American people rely on pharmaceutical drugs. They do not eat healthy. They take manmade drugs to maintain health. They rely very much on pharmaceutical drugs and processed foods.

ॐ∽

In a post- collapsed world, a trip to the neighborhood pharmacy to fill your prescription will not be an option. Even aspirin will be unavailable. Without lifesaving antibiotics, many people will die from infections. Antibiotics will be an exceptional barter item.

There is a simple and inexpensive way to stockpile antibiotics.

DreamMyst advises that you buy bird or fish (aquarium) antibiotics.

The only ingredient in bird and fish antibiotics is the antibiotic, unlike many of the pet antibiotics that have fillers or added ingredients. Be sure to verify that the only ingredient on the bottle is the antibiotic itself. Bird and fish antibiotics can be purchased without a prescription. They are the same antibiotics doctors prescribe. Dosages are *exactly* the same for humans.

The antibiotics mentioned will treat 90 percent of the bacterial diseases and even some forms of anthrax. Antibiotics do not work for viruses like influenza, the common cold, and other infections; antibiotics only work against bacteria. The overuse of antibiotics creates resistant bacteria, and can hide a symptom. Do not end treatment early you may become re-infected. Allergic reactions to antibiotic drugs can lead to anaphylactic shock. Tetracycline (Fish-Cycline), once expired, may cause kidney damage, so of it after its expiration date. Most of these medicines have a long shelf life even if past the expiration date.

» Amoxicillin 250 mg *and* 500 mg (Fish-Mox, Fish-Mox Forte)

» Ampicillin 250 mg and 500 mg (Fish-Cillin, Fish-Cillin Forte)

» Azithromycin 250 mg (Zithromax-Fish)

» Cephalexin (Keflex) 250 mg and 500 mg (Fish-Flex, Fish-Flex Forte)

» Ciprofloxacin (Cipro) 250 mg and 500 mg (Fish-Flox, Fish-Flox Forte)

» Clindamycin 150 mg (Fishcin)

» Doxycycline 100 mg (Bird-Biotic)

» Metronidazole 250 mg (Fish-Zole)

» Penicillin 250 mg and 500 mg (Fish-Pen, Fish-Pen Forte)

» Sulfamethoxazole 400 mg/Trimethoprin 80 mg (Bird-Sulfa)

» Tetracycline (Fish-Cycline) Once expired, tetracycline may cause kidney damage. Throw it away after its expiration date.

Most of these medicines have a long shelf life, even past the expiration date. People who are allergic to penicillin should be able to take doxycycline, ciprofloxacin, tetracycline, erythromycin, sulfa drugs, and metronidazole. If you are allergic to penicillin, you may also be allergic to Keflex. With the exception, of amoxicillin and ampicillin, the medicines listed below are suitable for people with penicillin allergies.

Antibiotics are used for specific illnesses. Penicillin and cephalosporin medications require 500 mg dosage for adults, 250 mg dosage for children, three to four times and a day. For Metronidazole 250 mg dosage and doxycycline 100 mg dosage, take twice a day.

Amoxicillin (Fish-Mox, Fish-Mox Forte, Aqua-Mox) 250 mg and 500 mg Take three times a day. Children are usually prescribed Amoxicillin in liquid form because it is better absorbed and more versatile. Amoxicillin is for the following conditions:

» Actinomycosis (causes abscesses in humans and livestock)

» Anthrax (prevention or treatment of cutaneous transmission)

» Bronchitis

» Chlamydia (sexually transmitted)

» Helicobacter pylori (causes peptic ulcer)

» Lyme disease (transmitted by ticks)

» Otitis media (middle ear infection)

» Pneumonia (lung infection)

» Sinusitis

» Skin or soft tissue infection (cellulitis, boils)

> » Tonsillitis or pharyngitis (strep throat)

> » Urinary tract infection (bladder and kidney)

Warnings: A common form of allergic reaction to amoxicillin appears as a rash, diarrhea, itchiness, and respiratory issues. If there is an allergy to amoxicillin, use another antibiotic such as cephalexin or sulfamethoxazole/trimethoprin.

Adult dosage: maximum is 500 mg. Take orally three times a day for ten to fourteen days.

Children's dosage: 250 mg. Take orally three times a day for ten to fourteen days.

Infant dosage: Administer 20–50 mg per kilogram of body weight twice per day (20-30 mg/kg for infants less than four months old). Break a tablet in half or open the capsule to dispense an appropriate dose. For children too small to swallow a pill whole, crush a tablet or empty a capsule into a small glass of water or juice. Have the child drink it; then, refill the glass, swirl the liquid a bit and have the child drink again.

Azithromycin (Zithromax-Fish) 250 mg part of the erythromycin family.

Azithromycin is for the following conditions:

> » Bronchitis

> » Chlamydia and gonorrhea

> » Ear infections

> » Lyme disease (early)

> » Pneumonia

> » Skin infections

> » Some throat infections

> » Sinusitis

> » Tonsillitis

» Typhoid fever

» Whooping cough

Adult Dosage: Take a double dose the first day and then take once a day (250 mg or 500 mg) for five days. For acute bacterial sinusitis, take once daily for three days. If the 500 mg dosage causes side effects of nausea, vomiting, diarrhea, or dizziness, take the lower dosage. Pregnant women can take azithromycin. People who have penicillin allergies can take azithromycin.

Ciprofloxacin Cipro (Fish-Flox, Fish-Flox Forte) should be taken with eight ounces of water.

Ciprofloxacin is for the following conditions:

» Acute sinusitis

» Bladder or other urinary infections, especially in females

» Bone and joint infections

» Infectious diarrhea

» Inhalational anthrax

» Lower respiratory infections such as pneumonia

» Prostate infections

» Skin infections such as cellulitis

» Typhoid fever caused by salmonella

Warnings: Do not use this during pregnancy. Among other side effects, Cipro has been reported to occasionally cause weakness in muscles and tendons. In children, ciprofloxacin may also cause joint and muscle complications, so it is restricted in pediatric use for:

» Urinary tract infections and pyelonephritis due to E. coli (the most common type)

» Inhalational anthrax

Adult Dosage: Take 500 mg twice a day for seven to fourteen days. In the case of bone and joint infection, take the antibiotic for four to six weeks. If you have anthrax, take for sixty days. For mild urinary infections, 250 mg doses for three days are usually sufficient, although it is usually best to continue the medication for two days after improvement is noted. 250 mg and 500 mg dosages are for someone who is allergic to penicillin.

Children's Dosage: This is measured by multiplying 10 mg by body weight in kilograms (1 kilogram equals 2.2 pounds). The maximum dose should not exceed 400 mg total twice a day, even if the child weighs more than one hundred pounds.

Clindamycin (Fishcin) 150 mg

Clindamycin is for the following conditions:

» Acne

» Dental infections

» Soft tissue infection

» Peritonitis (inflammation of the abdomen)

» Pneumonia and lung abscesses

» Uterine infections (such as after miscarriage or childbirth)

» Blood infections

» Pelvic infections

» MRSA

» Parasitic infections (malaria, toxoplasmosis)

» Anthrax

Warnings: Use caution in individuals with a history of gastrointestinal disease, particularly colitis. Discontinue the medication if you develop diarrhea during treatment, as a serious colitis (infection of the intestine) can develop. This drug has had no ill effects in animal testing, may be safe during pregnancy, and okay for people with penicillin allergies.

Adult Dosage: Take 150 mg or 300 mg doses every six hours with a glass of water.

Children's Dosage:

Babesiosis 5 mg/kg (maximum dose 600 mg) every 6 hours plus quinine 8.3 mg/kg (maximum dose 650 mg) every 8 hours for 7 to 10 days.

Bacterial Endocarditis Prophylaxis 1 year or older: As an alternative in penicillin-allergic patients, 20 mg/kg (maximum 600 mg) orally within 1 hour before procedure.

Surgical Prophylaxis 1 year or older: As an alternative in penicillin-allergic patients, 20 mg/kg (maximum 600 mg) orally within 1 hour before procedure.

Doxycycline Vibramycin and Vibra-Tabs (Bird-Biotic) Doxycycline is for the following conditions:

» E. coli, shigella, and enterobacter infections (diarrheal disease)

» Chlamydia (sexually transmitted disease)

» Lyme disease

» Rocky Mountain spotted fever

» Anthrax

» Cholera

» Plague (*Yersinia pestis*)

» Gum disease (severe gingivitis, periodontitis)

» Folliculitis (boils)

» Acne and other inflammatory skin diseases

» Some lower respiratory tract (pneumonia) and urinary tract infections

» Upper respiratory infections caused by strep

» Methicillin-resistant *Staphylococcus aureus* (MRSA) infections

» Malaria (prevention)

» Some parasitic worm infections (kills bacteria in their gut needed to survive)

Warnings: While doxycycline is not generally recommended for use in children under the age of eight, it is indicated for Rocky Mountain spotted fever. Do not use during pregnancy. One of the side effects of antibiotics is antibiotic-associated diarrhea, so only use an antibiotic if there is no prolonged diarrhea, high fevers, and bleeding.

Adult Dosage: For most types of bacterial infections, take 100–200 mg per day for seven to fourteen days. To prevent malaria, adults should use 100 mg per day.

Children Dosage: Administer 1–2 mg per pound of body weight, per day, for seven to fourteen days. The exception would be for anthrax, which should be taken for sixty days.

Metronidazole Flagyl (Fish-Zole) 250 mg is for the following conditions:

» Bacterial vaginosis (common vaginal infection)

» Bacterial vaginosis

» Bone and joint infections

» Colitis due to clostridia bacterial species (also caused by taking clindamycin)

» Dental infections (sometimes in combination with amoxicillin)

» Diabetic foot ulcer infections

» Diverticulitis (intestinal infection in older individuals)

» Endocarditis (heart infection)

» *Helicobacter pylori* infections (peptic ulcers)

» Meningitis (infection of the central nervous system)

» Pelvic inflammatory disease (a female infection, which can lead to abscesses—used in combination with other antibiotics)

- » Peritonitis (abdominal infection due to ruptured appendix, etc.)

- » Some skin infections.

- » Some pneumonia

- » Uterine infections (especially after childbirth and miscarriage)

- » Protozoal infections

- » Amoebiasis (dysentery caused by contaminated water or food)

- » Giardiasis (infection of the small intestine caused by contaminated food or water)

- » Trichomoniasis (vaginal infection that can be sexually transmitted)

Always sterilize your water before drinking it. The purest mountain stream water may have amoebiasis and giardiasis.

Warnings: Drinking alcohol while on metronidazole will probably make you vomit. Do not use metronidazole during pregnancy

Adult Dosage: Amoebic dysentery: 750 mg orally three times daily for five to ten days.

Pelvic inflammatory disease (PID): 500 mg orally twice daily for fourteen days, in combination with other drugs such as doxycycline or azithromycin.

Bacterial vaginosis: 500 mg twice daily for seven days.

Trichomoniasis: single dose of 2 g (four 500 mg tablets at once, or, two 1 g tablets).

Giardiasis: 250 mg orally three times daily for five days.

Helicobacter pylori: 500–750 mg twice daily for several days, taken in combination with other drugs like Prilosec.

Clostridia infections: 250–500 mg orally four times daily, or 500-750 orally three times daily.

Children Dosage: Normal dosage is 35 to 50 mg per kilogram of body weight per day, orally in three divided doses for ten days, maximum 750 mg, regardless of weight. Here are specific children's dosages for each condition:

Anaerobic infections: Take 7.5 mg per kilogram of body weight orally every six hours, not to exceed 4 grams daily.

Giardiasis: Children: 15 mg per kilogram of body weight per day, orally in three divided doses (no more than adult dosage regardless of weight).

Sulfamethoxazole 400 mg and Trimethoprim 80 mg (Bactrim and Septra) are two antibiotics taken together because the combination is stronger than one drug taken alone. Sulfamethoxazole and Trimethoprim are for the following conditions:

- » Acne

- » Chronic bronchitis and pneumonia

- » Ear infections

- » Kidney and bladder infections

- » Intestinal infections caused by E.coli, Salmonella, Shigella Skin and wound infections

- » Traveler's diarrhea

Warnings: Sulfamethoxazole 400 mg /trimethoprim 80 mg can cause allergic reactions. These reactions are almost as common as penicillin allergies.

Adult dosage: One tablet every twelve hours for ten days for most of the above conditions in adults. For traveler's diarrhea, take one double-strength dose daily or three times per week, depending on severity.

Children's dosage: For urinary tract infections or acute otitis media, administer 8 mg per kilogram of body weight of trimethoprim and 40 mg/kg sulfamethoxazole per day, given in two divided doses every twelve hours for ten days.

Infants dosage: Do not give to infants two months old or younger because it may cause cleft palate anomalies.

Take Probiotics after Antibiotics

Natural antibiotics can treat most bacterial infections without killing the good bacteria, or worry about side effects. Sometimes there is a need for antibiotics, and they are great at what they do: they kill bacteria, both good and bad. Replenish your gut with good bacteria by taking supplements containing live bacteria and probiotic foods like yogurt, kefir, kombucha tea, fermented sauerkraut, and fermented pickles.

Buy the *Physician's Desk Reference* or go to www.drugs.comorrxlist. com for more information.

Your Shiny Brights
Oral Health Care and Dental
Supplies for the New World

What will you do when someone you love has a toothache, broken denture, or cavity and there is not a dentist to take care those teeth? During the transition of a collapsed economy and earth changes, eventually a traveling dentist may stop to see if you need help, but in between, a wise person will use good dental hygiene to prevent dental issues.

As dentists like to say, you do not have to floss all your teeth, only the ones you want to keep. Do you have a one-year supply of dental floss and new toothbrushes stockpiled? Do it. The supply won't expire and prices are bound to go up, so you will be glad you did. If not, you may have to substitute by chewing on twigs, bird feathers, animal bones, and porcupine quills. Toothpaste is important to stock. You can also use baking soda or chalk as a toothpaste, though these are abrasive. If you forgot to pack a new toothbrush and your old one bites the dust, you can always rub baking soda or chalk against the teeth to clean them.

Fresh water and salt water are okay for brushing your teeth, except you do not get that just-washed toothpaste taste. Coconut oil can be used to brush your teeth, as can honey. Mouthwash is not necessary. Use salt water, peroxide, or colloidal silver to keep your gums and teeth healthy and free from infection.

Pack These Items in Your Basic Dental/Medical Survival Bag

- » Aspirin (very long shelf life) or ibuprofen (Motrin or Advil)
- » Tea bags (The tannic acid in tea acts as a blood-clotting agent for bleeding lips, gums, and tongue.)
- » Toothbrush, toothpaste, dental floss
- » Sensitive toothpaste
- » Toothpicks with a rounded edge
- » Small mirror with a handle
- » Vaseline (Can be used to hold a crown in place until it can get fixed.)
- » Q-tips
- » Crème Benzocaine for pain relief
- » Hot and cold packs for swelling
- » Dental fix kits (These have Eugenol pellets, Eugenol liquid, and a kit with the adhesive sealant. Dental fix kits can be purchased at Rite-Aid or Wal-Mart.)
- » Canka (Comes in a tube and has benzocaine to coat a canker sore or gum.)

When help is not going to arrive, then knowing how to fix teeth is a priority. The ability to repair or remove a tooth during an emergency or for long-term care in a degraded environment will be an extremely valuable skill.

Infections and Abscesses

Infections or abscesses are painful and dangerous. Knowing what to do will ease the pain from the pressure. Warm salt water (one teaspoon of salt in six ounces of water) may help draw the infection or pus out of the gum tissue. If there is something that looks like a pimple on the gums, puncture it and drain the pus for pressure relief.

Dental Antibiotics for Adults

» Penicillin (Fish-Pen Forte): 500 mg every eight hours

» Clindamycin (Fishcin): Two or three 150 mg tablets a day taken with food

Dental Antibiotics for Children

» Amoxicillin (Fish-Mox): 20–50 mg per kilogram of body weight

» Amoxicillin for infants less than four months old: 20–30 mg per kilogram every twelve hours

» Clindamycin (Fishcin): 8 mg per kilogram of body weight, three times a day with food

Pain Relief for Adults

For severe pain, alternate 800 mg ibuprofen (Motrin, Advil) every three hours with 1000 mg acetaminophen (Tylenol). Do *not* take both at the same time. Every three hours, take first one and then the other. This combination is a powerful pain reliever and is almost as effective as codeine, tramadol, or hydrocodone. They can be used around the clock for a number of days when taken with food. Acetaminophen does not irritate the stomach and does not thin the blood.

Pain Relief for Children

Acetaminophen (Tylenol): 20 mg per kilogram of body weight every four hours.

Ibuprofen (Motrin, Advil): 10 mg per kilogram of weight every six hours.

Tooth Trauma

When a permanent tooth falls out due to a fall or a hit to the face, pick it up, wash it off, and put it back in. There is a very good chance the tooth will survive. If the tooth is dirty and you do not have water, brush it off, hold it in your mouth, spit out the debris, and put the tooth back in its socket. The sooner the tooth is placed back into the mouth, the better the chance of it staying in place. If the tooth has been out for more than an hour, it will probably not adhere to the gums. If a child loses a baby tooth, leave the tooth out.

Cavities and Broken or Fractured Teeth

Lost crowns or lost fillings can be reapplied or replaced using dental cement. These fixes will not be permanent but can last until a permanent repair can be made. Dentemp One Step Dental Cement is available at discount outlets.

When the cavity is painful and there is a hole, here is a safe remedy for an on-the-spot painkiller. Dental clinics use Eugenol clove oil to pack a cavity or a painful, dry socket. The Eugenol kills bacteria in the tooth, taking away the pain. Tea tree oil and oil of oregano will cut the infection as well. The clove oil is what will relieve the pain. Clove oil's painkilling effect closes the open microtubules in the teeth caused by decay as it kills the bacteria. Clean the tooth with hydrogen peroxide diluted in water and Eugenol (clove oil). Soak a little pellet of cotton with the Eugenol and use tweezers to completely pack it as deep in the hole as possible. Fill the hole. Then use zinc oxide paste to cover to the hole and seal the cavity. Take acetaminophen for pain.

If you break or fracture a tooth that does not hurt, use care when biting down. Be careful with hot and cold liquids due to sensitivity of the tooth and nerve. If there is a hole but no pain, use zinc oxide Eugenol paste. Smear it on and let it set.

An organic, nontoxic medicine either for a cavity or to replace a filling is lime powder. Wash the area first with a little cotton pellet soaked with hydrogen peroxide. Mix lime powder or powered seashell with a fifty-fifty solution of hydrogen peroxide and boiled water. Place on the tooth. In six minutes, this mixture will start to set and the cavity will heal.

Four fluid ounces of Eugenol and a pound of zinc oxide powder will cost about twenty dollars.

To Make Temporary Dental Cement

Mix the following:

» Three to five drops of liquid Eugenol

» One to two scoops of the powdered zinc oxide

Place each of the above amounts on a tile or flat surface. Drag some of the powder over to the liquid, using a scraping and pressing motion. Work the powder into the liquid, cutting in more powder as you blend. When the mixture is no longer shiny, it is ready to use.

Supplies a Survival Dentist Will Need

» Rubbing alcohol, boiling water, or bleach to sterilize the instruments

» Hydrogen peroxide

» Nitrile gloves (Never stick your hands in someone's mouth without gloves.)

» Several large pink erasers to prevent being bitten.

» Oil of cloves (Eugenol)

» Oil of oregano

» Antibiotics and pain medication

» Dental mirror, pick, and long, sharp, pointed tweezers

» Plaque scraper or dental scaler

» Cotton pellets, Q-tips, gauze sponges

» Temporary filling material like Tempanol, Cavit, or Dentemp

» Candle or orthodontic wax for braces (Covering a tooth with dental wax is an effective way to fill a tooth until it can be fixed.)

Pulling Teeth

Teeth will need to be pulled and the correct equipment will make a painful job easier for both everyone concerned.

You will need:

» Curved needle-nose pliers or extraction forceps

Extraction forceps are much like pliers, but with curved ends, and come in both a lower and upper version. Extraction forceps are specific to the type of tooth, and have even ID numbers for upper teeth and odd ID numbers for the lower teeth.

The most commonly used are:

* 150 Upper Pre-Molars

* 151 Lower Pre-Molars

* 88R Upper Right Molars

* 88L Upper Left Molars

* 23 Lower Molars (referred to as a cow horn)

» Elevators (one medium and one small) are a thin, solid, chisel-like instrument used to help with extractions.

Get the free PDF download of *Where There Is No Dentist* by Murray Dickson at www.DreamMyst.com.

Tooth Powder Recipe

Add four parts baking soda to one part sea salt in a glass dish with lid. To flavor, add essential oil of lemon, thyme, or peppermint and a few drops of tea tree oil. Mix well and cover. To use, dampen toothbrush and dip into your powered toothpaste mix. Soak your toothbrush in baking soda and water.

Honey Remedies

⮫⮬ Honey from your own neighborhood is better than honey from China or from a different country because that honey may not be real honey. The honey you get in your own neighborhood has all of the same pollens that are in your neighborhood. If you have allergies, take honey. It will help you to heal from those allergies. This is why honey is one of those very important items to have. I suggest buying as many jars as you can because honey will last for many, many years.

⮫⮬

Bees make honey and pollinate plants. Without them, life goes away. Some of you may want to take up beekeeping as a way to produce your own pure honey. Eating local honey may relieve allergies and keeps the local beekeepers in business. Honey is a tasty and healthy gift from the universe, and its diversity for both cooking and medicinal purposes place it high on the list for survival food stockpiling.

Honey does not need to be refrigerated and if unopened has a storage life of hundreds of years. Honey has benefits besides that of a sweetener. It contains a wide complement of essential vitamins and minerals. It is safe for pregnant and nursing moms. It is a safe and wholesome food for older children and adults. Honey may be fatal for babies and infants under a year old as their digestive tracts are undeveloped.

Honey Storage

For best results, store honey away from direct sunlight in a cupboard. Make sure the cap is closed tightly. Honey absorbs moisture from the environment, which can lower its quality. To restore granulated honey to its natural state, place a granulated jar in hot water. When the granules are dissolved, remove the honey from the heat and cool as quickly as possible.

Remedies

Ear, nose, and throat infections: Thanks to its antimicrobial properties, honey not only soothes throats but also kills bacteria. Try a gargle with a mixture of two tablespoons of honey, four tablespoons of lemon juice, and a pinch of salt. Stir a bit of honey in tea or hot water. Do a honey rinse to flush out sinus cavities.

Insomnia: Drink a cup of honey water before bed as a sedative. Mix a teaspoon of honey into a glass of herbal tea or warm milk before bedtime.

Gum disease: Rub honey on gums after you brush your teeth.

Athlete's foot: Rub honey on the infected areas before bedtime, leaving it to dry overnight. Cover the treated foot with an old sock. In the morning, wash with water and dry thoroughly.

Burn treatment: Slather burned area with honey. Wait thirty minutes or longer. Rinse off.

Coughs: Boil some water with two garlic cloves and one tablespoon of oregano. Pour into a cup. Add one tablespoon of honey and drink. Mix equal amounts of honey and lemongrass juice, then drink to reduce coughs.

Or: Mix a syrup consisting of one-quarter teaspoon cayenne pepper, one-quarter teaspoon ground ginger, one tablespoon honey, one tablespoon apple cider vinegar, and two tablespoons water, then drink.

Honey and Lemon

Weight loss, digestive aid, and detox: Mix one teaspoon of raw honey (unheated) with two teaspoons of lime or lemon juice in a glass of room-temperature or lukewarm water. Take this remedy as a wake-up drink in the morning on an empty stomach. Take after an oily meal.

Cinnamon and Honey

Cinnamon's essential oils and honey's special enzyme makes these two antimicrobial foods which stop the growth of bacteria as well as fungi.

Arthritis, gout and fibromyalgia: Apply a paste made of the two ingredients on the affected part of the body and massage slowly.

Mix two tablespoons honey and one teaspoon of cinnamon powder into one cup of warm green tea. Drink this honey-cinnamon concoction daily—morning and evening.

Heart diseases, bladder infections, asthma, high cholesterol, and colds: Mix one teaspoon of honey with a half teaspoon of cinnamon powder. Take before going to sleep at night and first thing in the morning.

Indigestion: Cinnamon powder sprinkled on a spoonful of honey taken before food relieves acidity.

Eczema: Apply honey and cinnamon powder in equal parts on the affected area. Squeeze half a lime and mix with a teaspoon of honey in a glass of lukewarm water. Drink first thing in the morning for a few weeks or until the symptoms cease.

Natural Cough Expectorant:

Dice orange peel, onion, garlic, and ginger and place in a jar. Pour honey over the mixture until it is double the amount of the diced ingredients. Take every couple of hours or as necessary. When refrigerated this cough expectorant lasts for months.

Radiation Poisoning

Fukushima suffered core fuel nuclear meltdowns, which were worse than Chernobyl. This explains why radiation escaped into the air and ocean.

After the atomic bombing of Nagasaki in 1945, many people came down with symptoms of radiation poisoning. A young medical director trained in the art of benevolence, Dr. Akizuki, worked at a hospital in Nagasaki during World War II. With no medicine or equipment, he fed his staff and patients a macrobiotic diet of brown rice, miso, tamari (soy sauce) soup, wakame and other sea vegetables.[38] As a result, he saved everyone in his hospital while many other survivors in the city perished from radiation sickness.

Radiation Poison Prevention

Japan has seen more than its fair share of nuclear devastation. Currently, Japan is dealing with the leaking nuclear reactors in Fukushima province and the fallout of radiation.

Americans receive radiation poisoning from airport security scanners, x-rays, CT scans, nuclear medicine tests (such as PET scans and bone scans), injected radioisotopes, radiation therapy, and food irradiation. Unbelievably, tobacco products contain low levels of radiation. Any amount of radiation can be dangerous because of the potential effect it has on living cells. Radiation exposure from our environment can add up over a lifetime. How do we prevent radiation poisoning from harming children, pets, and ourselves? What do we take to combat the effects of radiation both before and after exposure?

Iodine supplements and natural algae will fill the thyroid preventing radiation from being absorbed by the thyroid. Detoxify radioactivity out of your body. This will protect you from environmental radiation poisoning in the future. The average recommended dosage for taking iodine supplements is between 12 and 50 mg per day for most adults.

---

38   http://www2.nbc-nagasaki.co.jp/peace/voice_en/en-no11.php

Radiation Vegetables

DreamMyst has strongly suggested planting root vegetables, such as yams, potatoes, and carrots that grow under the ground. Growing vegetables under the ground will produce healthy food that is not as contaminated by radiation.

Vegetables that will help to remove the effects of radiation are sulfur-rich vegetables, including broccoli, cabbage, and mustard greens. Apple pectin protects you from long-term effects of radiation. It draws radioactive waste from your body and passes it out through your colon. Apple pectin was used in the aftermath of Chernobyl to reduce the load of radioactive cesium in children. High-pectin foods include carrots, sunflower seeds, and apples.

Foods that cleanse the liver are artichokes, beets, and radishes. Fermented food can help to reduce high cholesterol levels in the blood. They strengthen and support the digestive and immune systems, which help fight and prevent diseases such as cancer. Examples of fermented food are miso and unpasteurized sauerkraut.

Kombucha is a fermented or brewed beverage that is cultured for a number of days. Use green tea in your kombucha brew for the added health benefits of active enzymes, probiotics, amino acids, antioxidants, polyphenols and *Saccharomyces boulardii*. Ordinary sugar can be used to ferment kombucha tea. For less sweetness, brew for a longer period—six to eight days.

As the radiation from Japan spreads, we will see more and more radiation in our food and the ocean. It is already in milk from cows that feed on grass. DreamMyst has said many times that in 2011 radiation traveled from Japan around the world. It settled everywhere, including grass and vegetable gardens. Radiation settles in the muscles of the cows that eat grass. Organic beef and free-range chicken may contain radiation.

When There Is Radiation Fallout

1. Protect your thyroid.

2. Protect your DNA from genetic mutation.

3. Remove as much of the radiation from your body as humanly possible.

The thyroid loves iodine, radioactive or not, and it quickly absorbs either one. If you take iodine before or immediately after exposure, it will fill up the thyroid, leaving no room for radioactive iodine to enter. Iodine usually leaves your thyroid in about twenty-four hours, but liquid iodine will work almost immediately once ingested. Potassium iodide, also known as KI, is a salt of iodine that is stable. Nascent iodine and all food-grade iodine may be used. Do *not* drink iodine products such as Betadine, which is not for human consumption.

How Much Iodine Do I Need?

According to the CDC and FDA, the following doses are appropriate to take after internal contamination with radioactive iodine.

Older adults over the age of forty should only take supplemental iodine when exposed to a large dose of radiation. This is because they tend to have an allergic reaction to iodine and are least likely to develop thyroid cancer. However, they will need to protect their cells from genetic damage.

> »   Adults up to age forty should take 130 mg of iodine. This is about 700 times the normal daily dose of 150 mcg (micrograms).

> »   Women who are breast-feeding should take 130 mg. Stop breast-feeding and use formula. Pregnant women need to take one dose.

> »   Children between the ages of three and eighteen should take 65 mg. (Children who weigh one hundred and fifty pounds or more should take 130 mg.)

> »   Newborns from birth to one month (both nursing and non-nursing) should be given 16 mg.

Important Note 1: Newborns less than one month old who receive more than one dose of iodine are at particular risk for developing hypothyroidism. If not treated, hypothyroidism can cause brain damage. Infants who receive supplemental iodine should have their thyroid hormone levels checked and monitored by a doctor. Avoid repeat dosing.

Important Note 2: The thyroid glands of a fetus and an infant are most at risk of injury from radioactive iodine. Young children and people with low stores of iodine in their thyroid are also at risk for thyroid injury.

Do Not Take Iodine:

» If you are already taking medication with high levels of iodine.

» If you are allergic to iodine.

» If you have an iodine-sensitive thyroid or condition, such as Grave's disease. Do not take supplemental iodine without your doctor's permission and guidance.

Natural Alternatives to Iodine

Potassium iodide will fly off the shelves in the feverish rush to buy iodine. Overdosing is a concern. Some of the signs of overdose are burning of the mouth, esophagus, or stomach, fever, nausea, vomiting, diarrhea, and/or a weak pulse.

According to iodine research by Dr. Guy Abraham and Dr. David Brownstein[39], as many as 96 percent of Americans are extremely deficient in iodine. The body does not produce iodine. Table salt with iodine does *not* have enough iodine to be effective, but the ocean is a rich source of foods filled with iodine.

---

39   http://www.vrp.com/test-kits/iodines-crucial-role-in-health-a-review-of-an-unforgettable-gathering-of-experts

For older adults, a superdose of iodine is not recommended as an alternative for counteracting radiation exposure. One-quarter teaspoon of organic kelp granules can provide 3 mg of iodine. To use this, all you need to do is sprinkle it on your food. It is actually a natural alternative to salt and is a superfood source very high in many other trace minerals. Try it on soups, salads, rice, stir-fry, and popcorn.

DreamMyst advises preventive action because you don't want to be caught with your pants down in case something does happen in our world of nuclear power. People can protect themselves from radiation through food and nutritional supplements, by storing water, and by using plastic and duct tape on windows and air vents in the event of nuclear fallout. Do not wait until the last minute to stock up on your food storage supplies, water, and emergency bag for each person in your family, including your pets. Who knows when a disaster is going to hit? Be prepared. Have an emergency bag for each car and one in the house.

"Do Not" List for the Health of Your Thyroid

» Do not eat meat, eggs, or poultry, or drink milk. If any of these are contaminated, you cannot wash the radiation off as you can with vegetables. Remember, radiation will work its way into the muscles of the meat you eat.

» Do not take iodine supplements unless you are exposed to radiation.

» Do not drink fluoridated city water.

» Do not brush teeth with fluoride toothpaste.

» Do not drink water with chlorine (city water and unfiltered bottled water).

» Do not eat breads, pastries, or baked goods with bromide. Bromide is an aluminum contained in most baking sodas. An aluminum-free baking soda can be purchased at a local health store.

"Do" List for the Health of Your Thyroid

>> Do take baths that remove radioactive toxins from your body. Here is the recipe for a twenty-minute sea salt and baking soda soak: mix half a pound of salt and half a pound of baking soda. Add to a very hot bath.

>> Do a heavy metal detox cleanse.

>> Do put one teaspoon of colloidal silver in your drinking water daily. DreamMyst suggests placing a pre-1964 silver coin, a silver spoon, or colloidal silver in your drinking water to keep it pure.

>> Do use a good antioxidant.

Algae: Chlorella and Spirulina

Chlorella improves the immune system, detoxifies the body, and protects against radiation. Chlorella algae is a known immune-system builder and heavy metal detoxifier. It binds heavy metals and transports them out of your body. Therefore, algae should be consumed after exposure to any type of radioactive contamination. Algae fills the thyroid, preventing radiation from being absorbed by the thyroid. The people of Japan have fared better than Americans would have with the radiation leaks from nuclear reactors. With a regular diet rich in seaweed, their thyroids are protected from absorbing large amounts of radiation.

Spirulina has helped to save many children from radiation poisoning. Given a protocol of 5 grams of spirulina a day for forty-five days, the Institute of Radiation Medicine in Minsk proved that children experienced enhanced immune systems, improved T-cell counts, and reduced radioactivity.

A megadose of vitamin C and D alleviates most of the horrible side effects of radiation therapy and is an effective help with chemotherapy treatment.[40]

---

40   http://www.cs.utah.edu/~spiegel/kabbalah/jkm021.htm
http://meditationexpert.com/RadiationDetox/

Chapter 9

Sustenance for Spirit and Divine Intervention

࿐ Discovering your truth is a lot like playing hide and seek. *You* seek your truth, and find it there waiting for you. ࿐

࿐ Universal light beings do not have emotions. We are not emotionally attached to human life experiences nor to the outcome of those experiences. Everything is Spirit and eventually all goes back to source. It is not that we do not care. We do, and so we discern and share with you the information we observe. Your transformations and the journey of discovery, as you and future generations experience a shift of physical and spiritual consciousness that has not occurred in over ten thousand years.

The universe is infinite. The universe has no beginning and no end. It is not filled with emptiness or nothingness, but rather is absolutely filled with "somethingness."

The phrase "As above, so below" means that all people from the inside out are a part of this somethingness. This explains how spirituality and metaphysical belief blur the sharp edges of earthly reality. Somethingness allows me to communicate through Susan without clutter. It is why more of you will experience seeing things or hearing things you have not seen or heard before. You will feel the connection. During a time of chaos, tyranny, and fear, it's easy for a universal light being to come and share insights. Even your first president was in communication with us.

Many of you beautiful people with your big, optimistic eyes and your bodies buried up to your necks in spiritual sand are doing your best to believe your government does not control with fear, and that truth is not an enemy of the state. You prefer to hope and believe the happy talk. It makes you feel better and gives you the fairy tale story that everything in your personal world is going to be okay. If you only think hard enough, somehow all of this can be avoided.

What you are expressing in this manner is fear. To deny or to attack a person is an act of fear: you think what that person is saying might be true. Your government uses fear mongering very well. Fear is a perception. It is not the truth. It is hard to hear the truth of the words I share with you.

৵৵৾

Denial Is the Lie You Tell Yourself.

৵৵৾ In a response that is dripping with resentment and contempt, a person often says, "Oh, that is fear-based information." Discomfort and fear brings all of your existing assumptions and beliefs to the forefront and disables critical thinking. You call something "fear-based" when you want to deny it because it might be true. Ignoring information is denial based on fear.

Others may manipulate and control you, using your fears against you so they can make you take an action of their choosing. This is fear-based. This is the only way you can say information is coming from a fear-based source. The idea of a terrorist on every street corner is deliberately fear-based because the government wants you to fear for your safety. As a citizen, you may become more obedient, more amenable to surrendering your rights for vague promises of security.

Information is power and enlightenment. Information cannot be fear-based because it is a tool. It is how you respond to information that makes it good or bad. It is what you do with the information that counts. If someone yells, "The sky is falling! The sky is falling!" and you look up to see what is occurring, is that fear-based? No. Taking action based on the information you receive is good. The action might only be to examine and determine if the information is true or false. Taking action that is appropriate to protect yourself and family is empowerment.

Living in a fear-based culture affects your state of mind and the decisions you make. New York City has set up surveillance systems throughout the city. The government is *spying* on you. They can *see* you. Is this fear-based information? *No*; not if it is true information. To deny information before examining it is fear-based behavior.

Fear itself is not a bad thing and has many uses. As an alarm, fear turns you away from entering a dangerous situation or calls you to action. As a distress signal, fear pumps adrenaline and other chemicals into your body that trigger fight or flight. Under the guise of foreboding, it is your intuition reminding you to be cautious and calling for reflection.

Fear is not negative. It is an emotional response. What you do with fear either empowers your life or destroys it. As always, the choice is yours to live in fear or to live in faith.

The universe will use your understanding, made from the choices you make. For example, if you are in the direct path of a volcano and have a warning that the volcano is going to blow, do you make the choice to stay exactly where you are or do you get out of the way? When children are not taught to look both ways before running into the street, they may be hit by a car. This in turn will set up another very different set of learning experiences for those involved. The universe will use these experiences for the divine good of all. The divine expects you to take responsibility for *all* actions. You pay the consequences of your choices, both here on earth and on the other side. Use discernment to take the easiest path to get to the end. Easy or hard, the choice is yours.

❧❦

Q: It is said by some, "We are creators of our own reality, and if we are to train ourselves for doomsday, we are contributing to that." What can you say to that?

DM: No. You are not contributing to doomsday because you are not putting energy into, "Wow, the sky is falling." You are not putting energy into it. You are taking actions to become prepared for any emergency.

Just like when you learn how to drive, you take a test that says you can drive, correct? When you plant a garden, you buy all the supplies you need so your food can grow, correct? That is all you are doing now. You are making preparations. You are not focusing on the world ending. You are not focusing on the sky falling down and hitting you in the head. What you are doing is taking care of yourself and your loved ones in the event everything happens, and that is not negative. If you focus on the thought, "Oh, this is the end," that does create the negative energy that creates the problems. When you understand and accept this is the cycle now, you then work on lifting it up. Pray it healthy. Think positive thoughts. Do whatever it takes. *Prepare.*

Humans are ingenious. You will be able to figure things out. At that point, it will take good can-do-it and get-it-done attitudes. There is always promising possibility. In times of hitting rock bottom, people roll up their sleeves and get busy.

How many times have you had a bad habit, and it took you too long to do something about it? Human beings don't want to change until they absolutely have to, when they hurt too badly stuck in the old tar pit. If there are no changes, more and more of your country will rely on nuclear power. Either way, change is coming. Why not make changes that are healthy for humanity?

Q: Some spiritual people think that if they bless the air, none of the poisons, toxins, and chemicals ever get into them. Is this true?

DM: Not true. Human beings have to believe with every ounce of their beings that they are healed. Very few humans have that power of focus, have the time to know it. They have not been trained to extend and use this information. Yes, you are all energy beings, but most of you do not know how to use the energy of who you are to remain healthy or eliminate physical pain. Taking care of your health, building your immune system, and, if you do get sick, taking vitamins B and D3 and eating healthy will prevent diseases from entering your physical body. Start working at both the physical and energetic level now. Make your own healthy food and get out of the city as soon as possible.

Q: Many people thought we were moving into a period of "a thousand years of peace," a more enlightened and peaceful state on our planet. It seems that Americans are going to face martial law, loss of electricity, natural disasters, nuclear bombs, and war on United States soil. How will this contribute toward peace?

DM: It could. After the solar flares, natural disasters and chaos, there won't be as many people on earth. There will be a thousand years of peace because there is going to be a much simpler way of life.

Do you know that in less than two and a half years when people who work for state governments will get laid off and the 401ks come due, there will not be enough funds? There isn't funding now, and there won't be in two years or less. That alone will crash your economy. This is why actions through your efforts are necessary. Do not think your economy will improve and that your government is going to change.

Q: Why do we need to experience the collapse of our government and economy and the hardships that result from the solar flare activity? Is there any way to prevent these events?

DM: Much of it is Mother Earth going through her birth and rebirth.

So much of it is the way the planets are lining up. Human beings will experience this event, which has never happened in the history of people existing on your planet. It has happened before, but there were not humans to record it.

Your economy cannot be changed either, being the way it is because of the decisions of government and the big banks. One president in particular sold your gold to other countries, which took gold out of the United States monetary system. Selling your gold to other countries is what brought Americans into their present economic condition. No president has fixed the problem by getting back the gold.

Politicians keep putting a Band-Aid on the economy, yet nothing has really changed for the better. It appears at times to get better, but the debt continues to grow because of mismanagement. It is too late now to change the economic decline. Your government would need to decide to close the borders, keep American money in the country, and change things in the United States that will save a lot of money.

꙳

Susan Norgren

DreamMyst teaches a limitless amount of subjects in regard to personal relationships with others, the soul, life after death, destiny, good and evil, the astral realms, time, space, the nature of reality here on earth, and those dimensions beyond physical existence.

The teachings of DreamMyst are not what most people might expect from a universal light being who makes known the unknown. She teaches that humans are more than the physical body, and that every person is a combination of energy and consciousness, creating the nature of reality. Many believe it doesn't much matter what we do because the god/goddess, the universe, the creator, or the infinite divine, everything gets absolved in the light of the divine and is used for the good. The divine will use everything for the best outcome. From that universal, spiritual level, yes, any life experience is perfect there. But as people living here on our planet, this should not be our concern. Our concern is how to live the best we can here on earth. We are the cocreators of our lives.

We do not have much control over the weather and many other things, but we do have choices we can make. When you prepare, you make a choice to walk a better path at both a physical and spiritual level. There is a price to pay for every action. What price do you want to pay?

In the physical world, the earth is going through earth changes. The government has created and uses HAARP (High Frequency Active Auroral Research Program) to modify the weather. The government uses fracking to create earthquakes. The government is not concerned about global warming, or about the adverse effects of chemtrails. Couple this with the thinning of the earth's aura (magnetic field) from solar storms and other cosmic activity, which increases the possibility of an electrical power grid "down" scenario, as happened in India. Today the weather we are experiencing will be the weather for a new generation. With drought in forty-eight states, the roads are deteriorating, and there are issues with the cooling ponds at the nuclear power plants. Living with radiation will become the lifestyle of our children and grandchildren. It will not go away; there isn't a cure for these changes.

The universe uses every experience and transforms the energy into good. It is too bad these experiences will not be transformed here on earth for many generations.

Ground with Nature and Your Environment

❧❦

Q: Why did the Mayans end their calendar on December 21, 2012?

DM: The Mayan calendar doesn't end. It's a circle.

Q: DreamMyst, on December 21, 2012, planets will align and the sun will travel through the Disc of the Plane, just as it did 26,000 years ago. Many humans wonder if something catastrophic and life-ending will happen on December 21, 2012.

DM: No. It is only the planetary alignment and the beginning point where everything comes into perfect alignment. You will get more and more activity after December 21, 2012.

Q: Did you exist 26,000 years ago?

DM: Yes; I existed even then. I have always been, and I will always be.

Q: What happened to life that existed on earth 26,000 years ago when the aligned planets passed through the Disc of the Plane?

DM: The effects of the planetary event 26,000 years ago changed what existed on earth. The problem with this earth's cycle of aligning with the Disc of the Plane is that there are human beings in the mix. That is all. Human beings are on this planet. In other aspects, your planet will continue to do what it needs to do to evolve, whether human beings are on it or not. When the dinosaurs were around, they experienced extinction. They were created and then they went away.

Human beings and the wild animals on the planet today were created from a cycle very similar to this one in many ways. Maybe creation was an asteroid. Maybe it was a huge solar flare. It wasn't the sun burning out.

The sun, your sun, continues to warm up. As that sun warms up, more and more solar flares will be ejected off the sun. Whether that solar flare will hit the earth depends on where the solar flare comes from. If the super solar flare explodes in a direction away from earth, then you don't have anything to worry about. But if a big solar flare jumps off the sun and shoots its way to the earth, then there is something to be concerned about.

Q: Is it possible there will be human life on another planet in the future?

DM: No, not yet. Human beings came onto this planet because of very special earth changes that happened to create humans and make it possible to live on this planet. There is not another that has what your planet offers. You know how your planet has ants? Ants and human beings and everything that is on your planet create balance. Like the Ice Age and other ages—all those ages helped create the ability for human life to be on the planet.

Earthing

With the increase in solar flare activity, we need a way to balance and neutralize the electromagnetic energy fields and free radicals produced from these energies. The best way to do this is right beneath your feet!

Walking barefoot conducts and naturally discharges the buildup of electrical stress, sending it into the earth to be transmuted back into pure energy. This energy also goes back into healing our planet.

Earthing is a form of balancing your energies and connecting with the earth. Earthing, or grounding, provides amazing calming, healing effects on the physical, mental, and emotional bodies.

When you are affected by electromagnetic energy, whether it's physical pain, anger, scattering, or confusion, connect with earth and the universe. Take off your shoes and walk or stand barefoot for a bit in your yard, on the beach, or anywhere in nature. Find a mineral spring. Soak up the nourishing earth minerals. If you can, take a mud bath or smear mud over your entire body. Let it dry and rinse it off. Eat grounding vegetables, especially those grown under the earth, like onions, garlic, yams, and carrots.

Does your home have a copper tub or copper pipes? If so, you will have the effects of earthing when you bathe or shower. Create a sacred bathing experience by bringing in your crystals and placing them in and around your bath. Taking a salt bath remineralizes your body to remove toxins. Make healthier and inexpensive bath and cleaning products from minerals that come from earth. Did you know you can make your own laundry detergent from natural borax? Drink some pine-needle tea. Use visualizations and meditations of the earth, or of a tree with its roots deep in the ground. Stroke and cuddle with your pet. They always walk barefoot and are naturally grounded.

Connecting with the earth allows you to soak up pulsing, healing energies, creating a better balance in your life. Also, it's a free energy source and available any time you desire to use it.

Stand in the Power of Your Divinity and Magnificence

కొ-ఠ Begin again, and trust yourself. For today, let go of the past, refine your thoughts, purify your spirit, and continue to work toward your goals. There is only room for positive thoughts and actions. You create the reality of your thoughts.

Who you are is not your 3-D physical body. That body you wear to go to work or to go to bed at night is only the temporary vehicle your soul or spirit took on when you were born into this life cycle. In the place before time, before you were born into physical, you were able to look at what lessons you wanted, which direction you wanted this lifetime to go in, and how you wanted to help. That is what you get to discover in this lifetime. This discovery process started when you were born into your physical body, but you forgot why you are here.

Sometimes you will have dreams that will nudge your awareness, but most of the time you will have no idea you created the reality you are living in at this moment. Creating a reality has very little to do with your past lives, although your past lives are part of your lessons. Now, today, you have a choice, and that choice is to say, "My past lives do not have to interfere with living a joyous life today." You do not have to worry, because you are yourself, and you have your personality.

You create the obstacles or any number of different things in your life. You are pure energy. Create the life of love and abundance you truly desire. You do not need to be in this life to be miserable. Imagine being the ugliest person in the whole wide world, or being handicapped. Let's say you are in a minority. Does that mean you are going to have a miserable, horrible life? You do not have to. You dealt that deck of cards before you came into physical; it is absolutely up to you what you want to do with that deck. It is not as if someone else gave it to you. You can choose how you want to live with the deck you have. It is endless.

You can choose constantly to learn, gain knowledge, and become more intuitive because life is ever-changing until the end of your life cycle. You can choose not to have knowledge, or to blame everyone for everything that is going on in your life. It does not really ever work, but you can choose this if you want to. Choosing to blame the government ... choosing to blame your parents ... choosing to blame a past life ... choosing to blame being born ... choosing to blame having bad luck with everything, does not necessarily mean what you blame is truly at fault. It only means that in the reality you created, this is true. Change this if you want to have the life you deserve, the experiences you want.

Blaming God for your misconception that he created it all and made you to be punished for everything does not work. You reap what you sow. Man has free will, so how can you blame God for anything? This is the easy way out. God is not going to zap you for blaming God. God does not care if you blame God or not. You live what you create.

Your spiritual journey more than likely began as a personal search, maybe just because you were curious, but probably because you were feeling unsatisfied at some level. You were looking for something to help explain why you are feeling or thinking about why things were happening in your life. Maybe you did not resonate or vibrate at the level you needed for truth, or were dissatisfied with the answers and solutions your religious organization gave you. Many of you began your own searches. Some may have read books or done research on the Internet. In searching, your energy opens, and you find others. When you ask for this information, ask for knowledge; the request will be answered. In being given the answer, your energy and the energy of others who want to share will be drawn together to be involved with you and your dream. Whether you meet those others at the grocery store, a spiritual retreat, a community meeting, or a class, that is how you will grow and connect to discover you have choices. As you meet others of a like mind, a connection is made that enables you to validate your reality of existence.

You are one creator. Does not the mass consciousness of what is going on have more at play in the world? Yes, but you have the biggest role in what is going on inside of you and what occurs immediately around you. While you are creating your reality and living that play of your life, all the other actors, all those other people who have their own lives, are doing the same thing. So if you are like-minded, you are going to connect with those souls at the same energetic level as you.

If you are one of those who blames the world and everyone around you for every problem you have, those same types of personalities and spirits will connect with you. Those who want to control the world are also energetically connected in mass consciousness.

Everything is a choice. Some things are more difficult, but they are all choices. When a thing is meant to be, it will happen no matter what. It depends on the life journey you chose.

Susan resisted being a trance channel. That was good for me and other light beings and it was good for Susan. She did not know what it was and did not have any desire to be a trance channel. Part of the cycle was to bring Rob in to play a very important role in Susan's life. Rob had the initial curiosity about what was happening and allowed Susan the freedom to explore.

Deep trance channeling is a very rare ability. Rob's role as the companion of Susan was critical; Rob creates balance. He is the person who helps to bring about alternate realities. He too spent many lifetimes as a wise shaman and believes absolutely in Susan's abilities. In the beginning Susan didn't believe. She didn't want to believe; it was not a part of her reality. It took a few years, with Rob encouraging her and incurring her anger, for Susan to go in, to explore, to discover. Primarily because of Rob's belief, Susan became more agreeable to deep-trance channeling.

This is when others and myself are able to do more of what we do, which is to give information. We watched as the opportunity unfolded for Susan to see the results of the information we had given her. We waited for her to experience the outcomes we foretold. We allowed her to do the exact opposite of what we suggested, and fall flat on her face. It was all okay.

From day one, Susan could have refused and said, "I am not doing this. You cannot make me do it. No way." And we would have waited until another time. At some level, Susan agreed, during this lifetime as well as in the soul place, that this is what she offered to humanity. Did it take numerous lifetimes and life experiences during those past lives to bring her to where she is today? Of course. Does this mean that Susan has to bring each of those lifetimes through into this reality? No, she does not.

(Rob: From Susan's perspective of not believing, everything had to be proven, so there was no blind faith. Susan didn't automatically trust this to be truth. She demanded 100 percent proof for a long time before she would admit that what she was doing was real. She needed demonstrated truth as Jesus taught. He spoke truth, then changed water to wine and raised the dead.)

࿇

Q: Is awareness a choice? I mean, when we choose to live a life here, do we choose how aware we are? Or maybe to some extent is it a choice? Does it also have to do with how much experience we have from the lives we have lived? The same as wisdom is technically learned.

DM: You have never been your body. Your soul, your mind, and the essence of who you are is connected to your body, but it is *not* nor ever has been your body. If this were not true, I, DreamMyst, would not have a voice to share with you.

The physical body is a limited vehicle. It gets older and damaged as the years go by. The soul essence of you is in no way limited except for your perceptions of the truth. Before you were born in the physical world, you chose this lifetime and the experiences of this lifetime. Then when you were born, your consciousness forgot the reason you came to earth. This is why when difficulties, hardship and, yes, tragedies happen, you gain experiences. You are responsible for your life and life experiences. This means coping, living through the experience or not, and loving.

Depending on how you handle any situation, it will bring wisdom to the degree you resolve it. Sometimes humans forget they are more than the body. You block your consciousness to remain focused on the experience for which you wrote the script. I call it doing your best to stay in the 3-D reality you and every other human are experiencing to some degree or another.

Awareness levels are different as well, and none are linear. When you fight what is beyond your physical senses, you do not move very far from it. The awareness from that level is slight. Humans form their fears, and that too limits awareness. Fear is what you do not want to look upon, and so that awareness is a choice.

When you open to your inner sensing, the awareness changes as well but at different levels. From this level, your perceptions beyond your physical awareness depend on all the life experiences you have ever lived. Awareness allows your consciousness to flow in all directions. It is not based on any concept of reality. It is beyond reality and is never used consciously.

Can you open to the ancient wisdom within you? Yes, but that would take looking at the chair in front of you and believing it is not solid. Your consciousness knows no limits. Know that the soul that is you is much more than the physical body and the environment you have chosen to live in now. Your *real* environment is not limited to time and space as you know them here.

Q: Is it possible that the economic collapse and the major earth changes can be avoided by raising the earth's vibration with spiritual prayer among the masses?

DM: Where there is an abundance of focused energy, anything can be raised. The energies can be transformed. They can become even better and bigger. So yes, prayer helps. Meditation for healing will help, too.

Why do you think children who are coming into this existence have these beautiful gifts to be developed? It's so that they can help their future as well. Everything has energy. There is always the possibility to alter energy to create whatever you need—to create something better, something healthy, something good. What you focus on expands. As you focus on hope, helping your environment, healing for your planet, and clean water to drink, then you are helping a better outcome, a solution. This understanding keeps you in that place of belief that everything is transformed into love and into health.

When you have hope, when you have belief, you will know the miracle of seeing transformation in front of your eyes. So yes, meditation helps greatly. Human beings need to remember to meditate. They need to meditate all the time, not just say, "Oh, today I think I am going to meditate on healing the Earth." They need to do it with consistency, with focus, and with passion. That is what creates changes. When enough people gather to focus on a desired goal, it will happen; yes.

One time, Susan and Rob with three other people and me, DreamMyst, performed an energetic healing ceremony for a physicist three hundred miles away. They were able to make an energetic pyramid above the physicist's head move for the healing of glaucoma in his right eye. When the healing was done, he did not have glaucoma anymore, and other things within his body were healed. He is still alive today. The prayer helped his body to do the natural healing he wanted and what his body needed to do.

Q: DreamMyst, my dog has glaucoma in the eye. Can an energy ceremony heal the glaucoma?

DM: Animals accept healing wonderfully well because they don't have any doubts that it can't be. Animals accept and absorb healing, and they will take as much as they need for that healing. Giving her the proper nutrition and the herbs her body needs will start the healing process. A healing ceremony will help clear the dog's eyesight so she can see. It takes longer if the disease is advanced, but if it's there, it can be removed. Animals love healing.

Q: In the near future, people who have never hunted animals will do so for survival. When Native Americans killed an animal, they gave a blessing. Would you please suggest a blessing for people to offer so they may show gratitude to the animal sacrifice?

DM: Thank the animal for giving its life to you so that you may live, and you have made that offering. You will be part of it in the spirit, which is the blood that has fallen from the animal. That becomes sacred.

Human beings have a physical birthday suit. So do animals. The animal spirit rises from its physical body and goes into the heavens so that it can be transformed into spirit. The physical body is a gift that they give to human beings so that humans may live. Bless the animal and say, "Thank you for living, for giving me life. Thank you for giving up your life so that I may eat I may live and survive. We thank you, animal. We thank you and bless you on your journey."

Q: For the first time, there will be humans who will be burying others either because they had to defend themselves or because they cared for loved ones who died. There may not be a priest or minister to say a prayer. Can you offer a few beautiful words to say when burying those who have passed into spirit?

DM: Gather in a circle and say a blessing of thankfulness for the person who has passed Say something wonderful about that person: what he did, the biggest impression he left on you. Why were you grateful to have him in your life? Share the stories he told. Share what it was about him that made him special to your heart. Saying these kinds of prayers helps those who have left their physical bodies go to that place in spirit, in heaven, in the universe. Enjoy singing their praises as they journey to their new home in a different but loving environment.

Sing the praises of a loved one and speak your praises joyfully, acknowledging who he was to you in this life and rejoicing in his place in your world. That is important. If it is someone you did not know, thank him as well because he played a part in this new world. He did exactly what he came to earth to do. Thank him for that effort. Create your own ceremony to make your heart feel better.

You don't have to have a license to be a minister, nor do you have to read the Bible to say prayers. You definitely don't have to be other than yourself to give a blessing. That is just as valuable as the wonderful prayers others speak.

Give what is of value, as long as it is heartfelt.. Someone who speaks about the person who is no longer in the physical sends powerful energy that travels far and allows a person who is now spirit to experience a beautiful transition into his new world. That is good.

Q: When people die in a small community, should the body be buried or wrapped and burned as they did in ancient times?

DM: A burial under the ground would be the best, especially if it's for a lot of people. The beautiful energies of the physical body have many minerals to feed more trees. Burning of physical bodies will smell, which will alert others. After the body is burned, the ash will blow and settle like dust in your home. It is better to bury the physical bodies the souls have left behind to feed Mother Earth.

Yes, death is sad for human beings. Yet if you create something worth saving, the physical passing will be easier. That beautiful physical body, which at one time contained a personality and a spirit, is now an empty shell that can provide nutrients for the trees and flowers and plants to grow. It gives to Mother Earth what she needs to thrive. Later you can look at the tree or plants and remember your loved one while they help you to stay alive, even in their death.

Love your family. Make amends with those you love. Always know that human life is short. Do not let your loved ones leave this physical earth without knowing how much you care. Looking into the future. You may want to consider setting goals. What can you accomplish between now and the fullness of the year that will come?

Q: In 1991, Argentina had an economic depression. Children were kidnapped, then traded back to their parents for valuables or food and water. Should parents be concerned about kidnapping during this economic depression in the United States?

DM: Yes, it's important to be aware of this possibility. Desperate people will do anything they can think of to feed themselves, to take care of their needs when they have not prepared. If half the people are prepared and the other half are not, there will be great chaos everywhere. Your government is not going to make a public announcement to inform people to prepare for living several years without electricity. The government is not going to tell Americans that their world is going to go in a very different direction. Even your media is not talking about these coming events in a way that is saying, "Wake up. Prepare. Get ready."

Q: It's tricky, isn't it? There is a humane desire to help people in need, yet their state of mind is scary, desperate, and dangerous.

DM: During the chaotic and desperate period, people will want to take everything. You must hide most of what you have. Look at other ways you can protect your house if you live in a city. Do what you need to do to protect your home, your environment, yourself, and your family.

Gifts from the Universe: Miracles

Have you been in a place of fear or despair and thought, "I need some sort of miracle to help me"? I know I have had a few throughout my lifetime. Unfortunately fear blocks the flow of getting what you really want, which is a great outcome for your dilemma.

DreamMyst taught me to use the energy of fear to bump up my energy, because when we are emotionally charged, it bumps up universal energy a gazillion times. This is because we are like a satellite with our thoughts and emotions broadcasting into the universe. To get what you want, you need to send the right signal. At this moment, what is your heart's desire? Focus on what you desire to have happen in this situation, but be sure you are crystal clear as to what you want your result to be.

Next, write it out. Visualize your miracle manifesting even better than you expect. Ask what else is possible. Own your desire and expect it to manifest.

Now, give it to the universe and allow the space for the universe to give back to you what you desire. Practice receiving your miracle by acting and thinking as if you already have your heart's desire. Imagine and say aloud how you feel about having exactly what you want.

Believe and receive the gifts from the universe. Is it as easy as DreamMyst says? Yes. If you believe with every breath and ounce of your being, you will create the outcome you desire.

When your miracle or gift from the universe arrives, will you be ready to receive it? Will you recognize it? One day while driving on the freeway, a flash of green blew across the windshield. Rob, who believes in signs from the universe, decided to investigate. Backing up the car, he stopped it and got out to discover what had flown by. Not more than a few steps away were two one-hundred-dollar bills lying together, flattened in the road, waiting for him to claim his miracle. If he had continued to drive without stopping, another wind would have blown this gift on to the next person who had asked for a miracle.

≈≈ Words give truth or hide truth. Great lessons will be learned from discerning truth. Use discernment in sharing what you learn. Share the parts you feel the person you are speaking with can accept. Information is a powerful source of knowledge. Even if the truth will upset people, it will save their lives. Think about it. How would you feel if you woke up one morning and your whole world had changed? If you were prepared, it would be easier for you, correct? Use discernment of who, when, and what to share.

Dig deep within your core of being. If you resonate to what is said, share this information with people so they can use their discernment, even if they look at you as if you are dreaming or crazy. Spread the word. The dream begins with you, and if you are dreaming, if you are living and breathing, if you want good things for your life, and if you want to live within this hope, then prepare. It all begins with you. You are the dream, the fruitful vision. Celebrate. Celebrate that you are in liberation toward the new earth that is emerging, the new way of being after the earth changes.

Yes indeed, the amount of prayers, good thoughts, and vibrational healing you give helps to protect your world. These good-thought energies help those from the astral and other dimensions to assist in the healing of the planet. The same energy that derives from good thought strengthens spirits, whether human spirits or multidimensional spirits who battle to save humans from themselves. This is a job of immense necessity.

From enlightened experience, humans, for the most part, seem bent on destroying everything in their path. "Not *me*," you might say. Yes, you! Every time you have a thought of hate and the desire to destroy this thing or that thing, poison spews out. This energy does not create healing. We know it is not what humankind desires. However, being human means you react from your instinctive, physical body, which is left behind when you transition into the spiritual world.

So how can each individual help save the earth and humankind? Envision sending the power of love. Use a pink quartz crystal as a focal point or find an image of the world. Hang a globe where you see it all the time. Picture this replica of Mother Earth bathed in a glow of pink, loving light to add more power in your healing prayers. Another tool to use is something small that fits in two open hands. Cradle it. Love it. Not a single heartfelt prayer is wasted. It cannot fail. You need this place to live. Remember, the earth will survive, but will humans?

Prepare to give, having enough not only for you and your loved ones, but for those who you want to help. They may be friends or family who are visiting. Have extra food and blankets. Have an extra toothbrush or toothpaste. You can give those things. You can go to thrift shops. You can buy on sale. You can buy material to create blankets so that if somebody needs a blanket, he can wrap up in it and stay warm or use it to hold those precious items. He can carry a baby on his shoulders with that blanket.

The act of charitable giving comes from your heart and comes from giving from that place of love. There will be those who will need that charitable giving, so to have it available is good. Know that you are the one who is choosing to give. Use discernment when choosing to whom to give. You do not want to give to a person who may cause you problems later, who might take more than you want to give. So use discernment in who you give a gift to help them on their journey. Maybe you will give to a mother and her children who are walking, trying to find some place to go. If they come to you, you will decide if you choose to help them.

The changes your earth and its people are experiencing are of the mind, the body and the spirit. Spirit is the driving force of the mind and the body. Get prepared at all levels. Allow endless possibilities! Attain your mind's desire by shifting your physical consciousness to your astral consciousness. As you prepare in the physical, prepare your mind and spirit for what is going to come. This will sustain you. To find peace and harmony, practice the arts of gratefulness, of adapting and thriving, and of accepting those things you do not have control over. Harmony is agreeing to be a part of something. Harmony is a choice. Communities are built from person to person by sharing a like belief or purpose to discern and prepare.

Wrap yourself in wisdom. Wrap yourself in knowledge. This is what is meant by the expression of love and light. The light of this energy protects you, but it does not change what is to be.

Create a circle of love by joining your hearts and minds with prayers and meditation.

"You are eternal beings. Expect miraculous transformations of mind, body, and spirit." DreamMyst

DreamMyst a heavenly being uses Susan's body and
consciousness to deliver her message to humanity.

You can see, hear and feel, how amazing and beautiful DreamMyst is. People say they feel DreamMyst's wonderful energy for hours after a demonstration. DreamMyst does not have an ounce of self-consciousness as she speaks with one or a hundred people.

In an environment of love and community, DreamMyst enjoys
her first dance at the Festival of Enlightenment. DreamMyst
also enjoys a bowl of chocolate ice cream, bright colors, and
her beautiful gems (crystals) which Rob willingly shares.

"Make a BIG noise. Take Actions to Create Change" DreamMyst
loved the energy and vibration of a rainbow of colors that
emanates from the music and humans having fun.

"Do Not Put Boundaries On The Gifts From the Universe!"
DreamMyst's big energy of love and encouragement
shines through time and space to a packed standing
room only demonstration of Trance Channeling.

"Words give truth or hide truth. Great lessons will be learned." DreamMyst speaks with emphasis her words of warning and assistance for all of us. You can almost hear her saying "Wake Up!" "DO something!"

Susan and Rob Norgren. Rob is a shaman, and the host of the Ask DreamMyst radio show, and the person who knows DreamMyst the best. Rob facilitates the process he devised to bring DreamMyst's message to all of us.

Susan and Rob bring DreamMyst's message to the New Life Expo
in New York 2010. DreamMyst chose the booth space, colors,
and decorations for the booth in addition to designing the large
signs and apparel worn by Susan and Rob for these events.

Susan Norgren is the bridge that allows DreamMyst to share her messages. *"Life is a dream YOU create into reality."* DreamMyst

❧ "Prepare" is DreamMyst's core message to humans. ❧

Insights about Ron Paul

❧ Enlightenment does not always mean nice things, and it does not mean you will always be joyous. Give up the illusion that the government of today stands for liberty and the American Way. See it as it really is, and let go of the way you wish it to be. Once you can *believe* in the possibility, the opportunity to change becomes a reality.

Ignored by the media and government corruption, it would take more than a grassroots movement for Ron Paul, the shining hope for your country, to become president.

Someone like Ron Paul will be the person who can help Americans when your government is abolished. His values of liberty for your country qualify him for the position of president.

When martial law is imposed, Ron Paul will be considered a terrorist by the US government. His belief in American freedoms established within the original American Constitution opposes the plan of the New World Order. Ron Paul will need to have very good protection because there will be those who will want to assassinate him. Texans will protect their own.

After the election, Ron Paul will quietly retire until it is safe for him to help Americans. He is not filled with ego; he has enough ego. He knows how to play the part he needs to play. He is one of the few patriots left at this point until others are discovered. His main motive is not taking away from the country, but giving back to it.

❧

As Ron Paul wrote in his book, *Liberty Defined: 50 Essential Issues that Affect Our Freedom*, "There is a third path here that I highly recommend, and that is the path of winning hearts and minds through education, first of the individual, and then of others through every way possible." [41]It may be that Rand Paul will assume his father's role, holding the same values as his father.

41   Paul, Ron. Liberty Defined: 50 Essential Issues that Affect Our Freedom. New York: Grand Central Publishing, 2012.

Benjamin Franklin Speaks via Trance Mediumship

During Susan Norgren's weekly show, *Ask DreamMyst*, the show's host asked to speak to the spirit of Benjamin Franklin. This would only be possible if Mr. Franklin's soul had not yet reincarnated and his spirit was willing. Mr. Franklin offered insight and information about our government and America. Here are the inspiring words as spoken by Benjamin Franklin.

Ben Franklin and His Role in Our Nation

No other individual was more involved in the birth of our nation than Ben Franklin was. He wrote sections of the US Constitution and the Declaration of Independence. He is the only person who signed all four of the documents that assisted in creating the United States.

- » Declaration of Independence (1776)

- » Treaty of Alliance, Amity, and Commerce with France (1778)

- » Treaty of Peace among England, France, and the United States (1782)

- » United States Constitution (1787)

Benjamin Franklin Interview—November 5, 2011

Q: Hello, Mr. Franklin. Please share with us some personal information about yourself.

Ben Franklin: I am B. Franklin, printer. This is who I am. Most of my life I would have been considered part of the working class, and I was proud. Let me tell you a short story. I sailed to England to get printing supplies for what I thought was to be my print shop. The governor was to send me the money for this business, but he did not. I was stuck without a way back. On one side, it was a great experience, and I made do the best I could under the circumstances. Later a friend sent me the money, and I came back to America.

When I was back home, I worked in someone else's shop, typesetting and writing articles. Later I found my future partner, and we went into business together. I know what it is like to be a struggling American. I know what it is like to have a job and work for someone else. I know how it feels to be beaten. My first employment was with relatives, and if I did not do what they said, I was beaten.

I relate to what others have gone through after me. As a young man struggling, I experienced frustrations, but the frustrations led me to solutions. Some would consider me very fortunate. My mind was seldom quiet and worked overtime so often, I rarely ever got a quiet moment. I always had to find out what would happen if I created a certain thing. Americans need to learn how to think critically and to seek resolutions.

I filled my day contemplating life and science, the universe, and how all works together. A regret of mine is I was not able to save my body to bring forward into the future. If they wanted to put me in a cask of good wine, that would have been satisfactory as well (*chuckle*). Interesting is this skill of communication I am doing now. I am honored.

Q: Wonderful, Mr. Franklin, I feel honored to speak with you. Here is the next question. Americans have started a protest all over the country that is called "Occupy Wall Street." They are protesting corporate greed and dishonesty. Is the current American sentiment similar to when you were alive during the American Revolution?

Ben Franklin: Very similar, on many different levels. Americans desire to get out from under the enslavement of the government and of Wall Street, as you call it. In my day, we wanted to get out from under England. I used my influence as a politician, writer, and diplomat to encourage an exchange of ideas. Recognize what you want. To ascertain the outcome of the best actions for all Americans takes planning and coordinated action.

When I was invited to contribute to the creation of the Declaration of Independence and the Constitution, we devised scenarios. We sifted and sorted. Some of what I proposed was never used, such as the "We are One" motto for the new currency. Then there was my recommendation for the turkey to stand as the national bird. Eventually, all fell into place. We knew what we wanted and went after it. You have many choices but do not know what to protest.

Where there is effort, there is action and a reaction. The reaction is to motivate others to join your cause. This is what you want. Use the passion even if it comes through desperation. Take the passion and mold it. There does come a time when an old society no longer works. Dissolve it to produce something worthwhile and worthy to put your name to. Then it is you who are the founding fathers to make the change for a new world, a new America.

What you read in the newspaper saddens me. I ran a printing press and wrote articles most my life. Your newspapers do not speak the truth. They distract your attention rather than writing and speaking truth

There is nothing within the Constitution or Declaration of Independence that is not plain and clear. Yes, you can change the words to make them more current, but you do not want to change what is within the words. I would leave it precisely the same; leave in those items of usefulness. Like freedom and justice for all. It works, and it will continue to work for many generations.

Do not allow your government to take away what is yours in the eyes of God and by right of being you. The Constitution was set up for everyone. Not for the rich to plunder, and definitely not for corrupt politicians to alter to their advantage. It was set up for every person.

Your nation is corrupt. Begin again. Dissolve the government. Disband. Bring back. Change. Renew. Resurrect. The organization is faulty. Elected officials had the honor to serve their country and have abused the privilege because of greed and the desire to control. Remove those people and bring in others who are less greedy. Politicians are a different breed of people. They are salesmen, and give you a dream as they briskly fill their pockets. That is why they are politicians.

There is not an ounce of honesty in your government. That is not to say we were perfect or that we did not do the same. Politicians and those who run the world, your government, are going to have agendas. They are going to have their own needs to satisfy. They are going to dip into the pot occasionally. This happened in my time. It will happen again in the new society. However, keep it to where you, the people of America, have control.

Get someone who wants to create a new America. It is not free now. You do not have freedom. There is no freedom in America. I have gone to many countries, especially France and England, assisting and observing as they created colonies. Your system is good. What we set up is good. Those hired to do their jobs are not.

Today you will lose your freedom and America, the country we helped to build. America is being sold to other countries, piece by piece to the highest bidder. You are your name; you are the word you give. Stand tall. Take action. Create a new America, a better America.

Q: What goal would you suggest that the protestors of Occupy Wall Street set for themselves as their first priority?

Ben Franklin: Your banks will crash, and you will go into an immediate fall. You will not come out of it for years. It is important at this time to keep the banks and Wall Street running. The money in Wall Street goes to a few corrupt individuals. This has happened in earlier presidents' days, even during George Washington's term. With the exception of a few, your House and Senate members are corrupt. This is why I was not friends with very many politicians. There were a few I liked. We were of a like mind to create something great, and we did. That is what America needs to look at now. Look at the rights of the people. Look at what's been taken away and what is important to bring back.

Q: Mr. Franklin, can you offer the names of one or two politicians you enjoyed?

Ben Franklin: Thomas Jefferson was definitely a politician. He wasn't always honest, but he had integrity. John Adams was another one, but we were not close in later years.

Q: Mr. Franklin, Ron Paul is an American who is running for president of the United States. How does his energy feel to you? Ron Paul is low in the popularity polls. Do you have advice for Ron Paul to help him become more popular and embraced by Americans?

Ben Franklin: He is not filled with ego; he has enough ego. He knows how to play the part he needs to play. If I had met him, I would have shaken his hand and invited him to join us. He is one of the few patriots left at this point until others are discovered. His main motive is not taking away from the country, but giving back to it. You need someone like him to help lead.

Unfortunately the system of government you have is so extremely corrupt that they won't ever allow Ron Paul to pull out from behind. The only way this will happen is if enough masses of people, Americans, get together. All of them must vote for him and make sure that those votes cannot be cheated.

Q: Mr. Franklin, many years ago the government developed a system called welfare. If you were alive today, would you agree or disagree with the welfare program?

Ben Franklin: I think it should be modified. It is important to give back to communities, just as it is important to have a monetary cash system. Yes, it is important to give back, to help others, but not bankrupt the whole. I created volunteer fire departments and libraries and gifted money to numerous funds. Those funds were used for good works. Many Americans do not give back to help their country, to help others who live in America. Yes, I believe everyone needs to receive through his efforts. I believe in education.

Q: Mr. Franklin, what actions can Americans take to get back their freedoms? Are you suggesting we stop paying taxes?

Ben Franklin: If you do not pay taxes, if everyone joins you and none of you pay taxes, then you will become free men and women and learn the laws under which you live. You can stand by your legal right of not paying taxes. Your government politicians will not like it. The rest of the world will not care very much for it; after all, they would not get very much either. However, the fact remains paying income taxes was introduced as a short-term measure, not for the long term. This was the beginning of the erosion of your freedoms and of your wealth. Fair taxation is necessary to maintain a government.

I do not know if you realize this, but during the American Revolution, George had incredible amounts of debt and hyperinflation. He joked that a wagon full of money would not be enough to buy a loaf of bread. This is why I believe silver and gold are so important. They would protect your country from being exactly where it is today.

Q: Mr. Franklin, our government denies access to anyone who requests to see the gold at Fort Knox. During a government committee hearing in August 2011, employees with the Treasury were questioned about the existence or nonexistence of America's gold in Fort Knox. One employee answered that there is no physical gold. There are only gold certificates. Is it your understanding that there is no physical gold in Fort Knox?

Ben Franklin: That is because the country allowed the gold and silver to be bought by other countries. Not good … There is plenty of gold and silver sitting in numerous banks across the ocean. America's gold sits there, and not in your treasury, not in your banks. Other countries acquired it when your country sold it.

Q: Mr. Franklin, when we start to recover and rebuild our country, should we bring back the income tax?

Ben Franklin: To some degree or another, there will always be taxes. It will be up to the people to decide if taxes are necessary and how much. I think not. I think the money any Americans want to make should be theirs to do with as they choose. This is the reason they are working.

Q: Thank you for sharing your opinion. If there is an income tax after rebuilding the country, is it your opinion that each American should pay the same amount of tax or that those with greater income pay more taxes?

Ben Franklin: It would depend upon the amount of money you make. If they were, in fact, to reinstate income taxes, I would hope Americans will have learned from this experience. Even Thomas Jefferson did not want money tied up out of the United States. He did not want the country's bank to be in England. He wanted your bank here with all of you. Now your money, your gold, your silver, is all over the world. Others own it.

Q: Mr. Franklin, as the protests continue in the United States, it is believed the government will direct the National Guard to enforce what is called martial law. Martial law is when military rule is used to maintain order during times such as protests. Do you have any words of guidance for the military as to whether they should support the government or the people?

Ben Franklin: The military will quickly realize who they should support, and it won't be the government. It will not be the president, either. Will there be martial law? Probably in this environment, yes. As the English put restrictions on us, your government will put restrictions on you. The difference is that in my time, it was a different country putting restrictions on colonies. It was not our own country. It was not Americans hurting Americans.

Q: We arc told the US government is creating false reasons to collaborate with Israel so it may go to war against Iran. DreamMyst has also said that in the year 2013, the government will bring back the draft, a process that forces Americans to fight in wars.

Ben Franklin: You would think Americans would be happy to fight for what they believe in; otherwise, maybe they should be drafted.

Q: When the government is going to war for power and money, should Americans die for those causes?

Ben Franklin: I agree, freedom is worth fighting for, but Americans have not taken action for their freedom.

Q: Some young men will decide not to fight for power and greed and chose to go to Canada to avoid the draft. This may be viewed as un-American. What is your opinion?

Ben Franklin: They have the right to choose, especially in this environment of greed and corruption. As you said, why fight because you are told that you have to? Listen to what your government is telling you. Use critical thinking to discern the truth. Critical thinking will allow Americans to make good choices before an event happens. Critical thinking allowed me to make scientific discoveries. Scientific thinking allowed me to move beyond restrictions of the religious church, to realize there was much more than what my religion taught. Critical thinking allowed me to do the accomplishments I enjoyed. Critical thinking provided solutions to situations.

Q: Mr. Franklin, would you please offer a brief, inspirational speech to the thousands of Americans who are protesting greed and corruption and want their freedom back?

Ben Franklin: Let freedom ring. Let freedom ring loudly. Be that ringing voice. Be the words and the actions that show integrity, but also show you will not tolerate or accept the behavior shown to you right now. Join or die. Be willing to defend your right to freedom with your life.

Find your focus. What do you want to accomplish? Take the time to look at the issues. Set your priorities—first things first. Live your life in such a way that you can be proud of who you are and what you stand for.

What we set up could not have been too bad because it has lasted all these years. Go back to what is written in the Constitution, the Declaration of Independence, and the Bill of Rights. Those are your freedoms and your rights.

You are here to call out your name and stand for freedom. Your actions state, "I stand for the American way. I stand for peace, liberty and the pursuit of happiness." Stand tall and take action. The momentum will follow.

What has begun does not go away. You take it to the next level. Whether you defend yourself or defend your family, there is always going to be someone who can be hurt. Do not worry if you're going to get hurt physically. Those are wounds of valor to carry with you proudly because you stood up for what you believed. You carried the day, and you will carry the day when freedom is yours once more. Stand up and allow your name to stand for integrity. Speak your name proudly. Your actions show how much you care.

Q: Mr. Franklin, that was powerful. Thank you very much.

About Susan Norgren

As a Deep-Trance Channel, Susan speaks for Enlightened Beings. The Beings speak in their own voice, gestures, and mannerisms. As a psychic/medium, Susan's spunky approach warms the crowd and touches the soul. She has been practicing metaphysical arts for more than 30 years and has the experience to understand and communicate on both the physical plane and in the higher realms.

Susan is at home in the bus, Sedona Synergy, with her husband, Rob Norgren who is a Spiritual Healer. Their love of adventure drives them to sights unknown . . . *or are they?*

Susan

DreamMyst

Comments from DreamMyst's Friends and Ask DreamMyst Show Listeners

I have been listening to DreamMyst's show for a year now and enjoyed every minute of it! When DreamMyst said gold & silver prices were going to go down, they went down. Also she warns us about earth changes and how it affects our weather. DreamMyst talks about our economy and how it is headed down hill and how food prices go up, which they have. It pretty nice that such a beautiful Universal Light Being is watching over our Earth and sending messages through Susan. *Shelley Spaulding*

"DreamMyst listens to the question and answers closely and directly for your enlightenment. I'm sure if you ask the question as daringly as you possibly can, DreamMyst will surely surprise you with as deep and profound an answer that will prompt you for more thinking and questioning than you initially thought. I can't wait to get the book because I'm sure there's a lot I'm missing already about DreamMyst's wisdom." *Jose Mascarenhas*

"I had the pleasure of meeting Susan (& Dreamyst) The reading I had from Dreamsyt was amazingly accurate and helped me realize my own psychic potential and see clearly through a period of confusion. Love and light" *Richie S Moore*

DreamMyst says, prepare, prepare, prepare and that can be done to a certain extent, but when you sit back and soak up all her information, it's a reality that is coming and I don't think you can ever be prepared emotionally for something as intense as what our Government is doing to our country. It's frightening to think all they have to do is pass a bill and all our rights go out the window. The more I watch the news, the more I know that what DreamMyst says is true and the less I believe what the media is telling us. DreamMyst has this way of giving you that deep breath to take and it allows you to look at what she is saying in a different way. *Dave Lee*

I had the most amazing exciting session with DreamMyst. I received total clarity regarding a new business. She was excellent on marketing tips and suggested things I hadn't thought of. I asked about the health of someone close to me, she said she's ok and suggested various things they can do that will help. I can't recommend highly enough if you are wanting clarity in your life, to ask DreamMyst. *Joanie Morgan*

DreamMyst recently said that my business would expand greatly, especially in March and April. I am a real estate investor, I buy homes that won't sell, and I sell homes to people who can't get a loan. At the beginning of the year, I had no homes, no students, and not much business. In less than 3 weeks, I had three students, and by the beginning of February, I had FIVE houses to sell! By the beginning of March, they were all sold! With the information, DreamMyst provided, I *KNEW* I had to step up my marketing efforts, and it has really paid off! Everything is moving with grace and ease, falling into place, with incredible synchronicities! Thanks DreamMyst, Susan and Rob! *Stacey M. Powers*

"I had the pleasure and priviledge to do a session with Dreamyst during the Festival of Enlightenment. They ARE LOVE, which they shared freely with all of us. Love you guys" *Barbara Hofmeister*

DreamMyst speaks from a much fuller perspective, with palpable love and nurturing pouring through. The reading spoke to me on multiple levels, touching and moving me beyond my mind, BUT did give details that were specific to me, to my healing, my journey, and to my daily life and work. I highly recommend this unique experience to anyone who wants to connect on broad, multidimensional levels to expand your awareness and receive the great love and wisdom available through these entities. *Kimberley Simon*

I was intrigued by the trance channeling. DreamMyst seems like somebody I could just give a big hug!! I enjoyed listening. *Erik Wilson*

You are truly a very gifted channel Susan, and you can trust that DreamMyst loves and protects you. I can hear and feel it when they speak about you. You are so fortunate. It's a rare gift. *Anne/ Allaure*

DreamMyst is so awesome at highlighting the information that is important for you. And, just like she talks on the shows, she talks to you about your own life. A lot of what she says indicate the future of your life and as you're moving through it. It's just super fun. I can say for myself that DreamMyst has told me some things about myself, and then I kind of check awareness around me and bounce it off other things, but it's a nice kind of stable direction and it always feeds back to what she has told me. *Alexandra Teklak*

"I have experienced DreamMyst's wonderful, fantastic, amazing energy!! It was one of the most amazing things for me. Dream's energy is totally different than anything I have felt before. It is like being able to sense/feel a pure energy that has never been polluted by anything negative. Does that make sense? The only other time I have experienced something similar to Dream's energy was the energy of my animal totems in their realm." *WhiteOak Thomas*

Our Recommended Web Sites and Resources

Our Websites:

Purest Herbs on the Planet: www.sedona2.amazonherb.net

DreamMyst's Web site: www.dreammyst.com

Susan's Web site: www.susanpsychicmedium.com

Rob Norgren's Web site: www.shamanicshifts.com

Ron Paul's Farewell Address http://www.campaignforliberty.org/

Colloidal Silver

Generator: http://www.colloidalsilversecrets.com;

http://colloidalsilversecrets.blogspot.com/2011/06/colloidal-silver-and-e-coli.html

Books:

Country Wisdom & Know How By The Editors of Storey Publishing's Country Wisdom Boards

Meltdown: A Free-Market Look at Why the Stock Market Collapsed, the Economy Tanked, and Government Bailouts Will Make Things Worse—Tom Woods

The Rothschilds, Financial Rulers Of Nations—John Reeves

Secrets Of The Federal Reserve—Eustace Mullins

Red Fog Over America—William Guy Carr

The Rothschilds—Frederic Morton

The Hidden Tyranny—Benjamin Freedman

The Last Days In America—Bob Fraley

Who Owns the TV Networks—Eustace Mullins

The Elite Serial Killers of Lincoln, JFK, RFK & MLK—Robert Gaylon Ross

The Elite Don't Dare Let Us Tell the People—Robert Gaylon Ross

Websites

EB-5 visahttp://en.wikipedia.org/wiki/EB-5_visa

Special economic zonehttp://en.wikipedia.org/wiki/Special_Economic_Zone

Idaho Project/60 http://www.project60.idaho.gov/foster.html

China stakes claim to S. Texas oil, gas http://www.mysanantonio.com/business/local/article/China-stakes-claim-to-S-Texas-oil-gas-858329.php

Chinese investors renew interest in purchasing Marina District http://www.toledoblade.com/local/2011/05/26/Chinese-investors-renew-interest-in-purchasing-Marina-District.html

Solar Flares:

NOAA http://www.swpc.noaa.gov/drap/index.html

ACLU American Civil Liberties Union http://www.aclu.org/blog/national-security/senate-rejects-amendment-banning-indefinite-detention

Government:

http://www.congressmerge.com/onlinedb/

Corresponding with the White House http://www.whitehouse.gov/contact

Congress Merge: Online Congressional Directory

Library of Congress http://thomas.loc.gov/home/LegislativeData.php?n=PublicLaws

18 USC § 2385 - Advocating overthrow of Governmenthttp://www.law.cornell.edu/uscode/text/18/2385

How to Impeach a President http://www.ehow.com/how_2093097_impeach-president.html

U.S. Senate Committee on the Judiciary http://www.judiciary.senate.gov/about/subcommittees/privacytechnology.cfm

Government Printing Office http://www.gpo.gov/

Fourth Amendment to the United States Constitution http://en.wikipedia.org/wiki/Fourth_Amendment_to_the_United_States_Constitution

Convention to propose amendments to the United States Constitution http://en.wikipedia.org/wiki/Convention_to_propose_amendments_to_the_United_States_Constitution

Continental Congress http://en.wikipedia.org/wiki/Continental_Congress

Constitutional Convention (United States) http://en.wikipedia.org/wiki/Philadelphia_Convention

Article Five of the United States Constitution http://en.wikipedia.org/wiki/Article_Five_of_the_United_States_Constitution

State ratifying conventions http://en.wikipedia.org/wiki/State_ratifying_conventions

Executive Orders

White House Official Site http://www.whitehouse.gov/briefing-room/presidential-actions/executive-orders

Executive Order 13547 --Stewardship of the Ocean, Our Coasts, and the Great Lakes http://www.whitehouse.gov/the-press-office/executive-order-stewardship-ocean-our-coasts-and-great-lakes

Executive Order -- Assignment of National Security and Emergency Preparedness Communications Functions http://www.whitehouse.gov/the-press-office/2012/07/06/executive-order-assignment-national-security-and-emergency-preparedness-

Executive Order 12472--Assignment of national security and emergency preparedness telecommunications functions http://www.fas.org/irp/offdocs/eo/eo-12472.htm

FBI

Facial Recognition and Identification Initiatives PDF: vorder_bruegge-Facial-Recognition-and-Identification-Initiatives.pdf

Gun Control

Obama Administration Expands ATF's Power to Seize Property

https://www.federalregister.gov/articles/2012/08/27/2012-20923/authorization-to-seize-property-involved-in-drug-offenses-for-administrative-forfeiture-2012r-9p\

Authorization To Seize Property Involved in Drug Offenses for Administrative Forfeiture (2012R-9P) www.federalregister.gov

Military Check Points

Military Checkpoints on the streets of America http://johnconner1984.wordpress.com/2012/02/04/military-checkpoints-on-the-streets-of-america/

Agenda 21 EXPLAINED, full version http://www.youtube.com/watch?v=9GykzQWlXJshttp://www.examiner.com/article/new-rules-make-it-easier-for-atf-to-seize-guns-without-due-process

Drones

Police employ Predator drone spy planes on home front http://articles.latimes.com/2011/dec/10/nation/la-na-drone-arrest-20111211

Obama To Sign Bill Authorizing 30,000 SPY Drones To Fly Over AMERICA http://www.youtube.com/watch?v=WyBJScMDeU8

FEMA:

PDF Internment and Resettlement Operations http://info.publicintelligence.net/USArmy-InternmentResettlement.pdf

PDF COMMANDANT INSTRUCTION M3010.14 Subj: Civil Disturbances Support Plan, Coast Guard (COGARD GARDEN PLOT) http://www.uscg.mil/directives/cim/3000-3999/CIM_3010_14.pdf

Civilian Inmate Labor Program PDF http://armypubs.army.mil/epubs/pdf/r210_35.pdf

War Relocation Camps

Papers show Census role in WWII camps http://www.usatoday.com/news/nation/2007-03-30-census-role_N.htm

U.S. government's illegal concentration camps:

Japanese American internment http://en.wikipedia.org/wiki/Japanese_American_internment

Eugenics:

Eugenics http://www.merriam-webster.com/dictionary/eugenics

Origins of Eugenics http://www.hsl.virginia.edu/historical/eugenics/2-origins.cfm

The History of Eugenics in the United States https://people.creighton.edu/~idc24708/Genes/Eugenics/History%20of%20Eugenics.htm

Bill Gates Eugenics TED video http://www.youtube.com/watch?v=JaF-fq2Zn7I

Stocks:

Re-Evaluate Your Stocks and Mutual Funds http://dailyreckoning.com/

How to Survive Total Economic Collapse: http://www.ehow.com/how_2130484_survive-totaleconomic-collapse.html

Banks

Safe Deposit Box Laws http://www.ehow.com/list_6936210_safe-depositbox-laws.html#ixzz1GVvylpGJ

Open Your Own Bank (Protect from the Collapse of the Dollar):

How to Start a Bank http://www.ehow.com/how_2062432_start-bank.html

How Banks Work http://money.howstuffworks.com/personal-finance/banking/bank5.htm

Bank Ownership Benefits http://www.mybankinglicense.com/bank-ownership-benefits/

Legally Open A Bank Account In Non-U.S. Currency To Protect From The Collapse Of The Dollar: https://www.everbank.com/

How To Open Bank Accounts In Foreign Countries: http://www.ehow.com/how_6646322_open-bank-accountsforeign-countries.html#ixzz1GDUajJNe

CPSIA information can be obtained at www.ICGtesting.com
Printed in the USA
LVOW05s1207101013

356209LV00003B/5/P